THE
HEALING POWER
OF
PYRAMIDS

EXPLORING SCALAR ENERGIES FOR HEALTH,
HEALING & SPIRITUAL AWAKENING

JOSEPH ANDREW MARCELLO

With an introduction & biographical chapter by

DR. G. PATRICK FLANAGAN

Front and back cover art by Russell G. Chong

Copyright © 2016 by Joseph Andrew Marcello

All rights reserved. No portion of this book, except review, may be reproduced, stored in a retrieval system, or transmitted in any form or by any means—electronic, mechanical, photocopying, recording or otherwise—without the written permission of the author.

Printed in the United States of America

DEDICATION

In memory of Nick Edwards—'The Pyramid Man'-- architect of Sacred Geometries, whose life was given in pursuit of creating structures through which human beings might realign themselves with the power of their Source.

And to the Seekers of the Ages—all those who have been willing to find and follow the Truth, no matter where it took them—and those who now explore this offering—may the light break surely and swiftly, and a New Dawn arise.

Inscription above the doorway at the Temple of Delphi:

"MAN KNOW THYSELF AND YOU WILL KNOW THE GODS AND THEIR ENERGIES."

*

SECRET OF THE PYRAMID

"The pyramid is the secret essence of Knowledge, in which you will discover the Great Truth, the right proportions and the rule of moderation. The pyramid stands proud, filled with silence and meaning. Stand at the top of the pyramid, and in the center you will find the Whole."

Abraham Abulafia, 13th century mystic and scholar

NOTE

While the information in this book contains abundant scientific and medical research, as well as non-medical empirical data, it is presented neither to diagnose nor prescribe for any condition or illness, but rather by way of sharing information.

TABLE OF CONTENTS

Foreword— A Tribute to Nick Edwards--Dr. G. Patrick Flanagan	1
Introduction—Pyramids and Human Destiny—Joseph Marcello	5

I—POWER OF PYRAMIDS—THINGS TO COME — 11

Pyramidology for the 21St Century	13
Contemporary Explorers	14

II—THE COMPELLING CONTEMPORARY RESEARCH

Pyramid Detoxification and Heightened Immunity	18
Pyramid Anti-Viral Effect	19
Pyramid Normalization of Infantile Pathologies	20
Pyramid Regeneration of Human Behavior	21
Pyramid Radiation of Massive Ionic Fields	21
Pyramid Regeneration of the Environment	22
Pyramid Enhancement of Agricultural Yields	22
Pyramids—Scientific, Yet Beyond Science	24
Funny...	26

III—THE POWER OF PRESENCE

Frequency—The Hidden Dimension	29
Victims or Creators?	31

The Porous Human	33
Sacred Geometry: The Art of Space, Form & Frequency	34
The Sanctification of Space	35
Space: The 4th Dimension	37

IV — THE POWER OF FOCUS

Recollection	39
Harnessing the Life Force	40
Living with Pyramid Energy — Charging Your Day	42

V — PYRAMIDS AS HEALING TOOLS
— ASTONISHING RECOVERIES

Thomas Thompson — Pyramid & Cone Healer	44
Recharging the Human System with Pyramid Power	45
A Surgery Avoided	46
A Difficult Case Resolved	47
Recreating the Body's Energetic Template	47
Amazing Help for the Learning Disabled	50
Healing for our Animal Companions	51
Pyramid Energy for a Stricken Pet	54
Inside Pyramid Energy Healing: The Flanagan Research	56

VI -- THE INNER DYNAMICS OF PYRAMID ENERGY

Torsion Fields	60
Ancient Pyramid Technology for the Golden Age	60
Pyramids as "Torsion Siphons"	61

Enhancing the Mind with Pyramid Power	62
The Pyramid Research of Jaroslaw Mironski:	64
Sacred Geometry & Cosmic Sound Transmission	64
The 'Song of the Pyramid'	65
Prana (Life Force)	68
The Protective Field	69
Pyramid Power and Performance	70
Home Pyramid Models	71
Pyramid Aura Photography	75
Experiences of Pyramid Experimenters	76
Significant Benefits for Pyramid Users	78
Healthful Sleep	79
Pyramid-Facilitated Therapy	81
Pyramid Energy & Relationships	82
Access to Wisdom	83
New Ideas	83
Spiritual Fruits	84
Intuition	85
Growth/Self-Awareness	85
Control of the Mind	87
Working with Pyramids	88
Oscilloscope and Lie Detector Experiments	89
Kirlian Photography	89
Meridian Testing	91
Monitored Pyramid Research	92
Neutralizing Negative Environmental Influences	93

VII — PYRAMID REFLECTIONS

Insights into the Inner Meaning of the Pyramid	95
Moving Beyond the Box	96
The Shape of Life	98
Youthful Explorations	99
The World Within	99
Mass Hallucination — or Shared Reality?	100
The Continuing Mystery	101
The Challenges of Increased Life-Force	102
Pyramid Meditation	103
The Benign Nature of Energy	104
Learning to Trust The Wisdom of 'The Force'	104
Energy Forms — Powerful Catalysts	105
The Parameters of Pyramid Power	106
What is a Pyramid?	107

VIII — PYRAMIDS FOR WELL-BEING

Pyramids as Energy Antennas	109
Pyramid as Frequency Resonators & Field Generators	110
The Subtle Dynamics of Pyramids	110
Research & Feedback: Pyramid Energy For Animals, Sleep, Nutrition & Rejuvenation	111
Pyramid Water — A Powerful Elixir	112
Water in our Organism	113
How Pyramid Water Influences our Organism	114
How to Make Pyramid Water	114
Pyramid Energy for Pets	115

The Pyramid Insights of Nick Edwards	115
Pyramid-powered Supplements	116
Pyramid-enhanced Nutrition	116
Pyramids & Razor Blades—Fact or Fiction?	118
Pyramid-enhanced Spirits	120
Pyramid Alignment	120
Pyramid Numerology	121
Pyramid Prosperity	121
Magnifying Dollars	122
The Pyramid Crystal Treatment Dish for Crystals	124
The Safety of Pyramid Energy	124
Pyramids for Pain Reduction	124
Pyramids as Solar Energy Shields	126
Concentrating the Charge: The Power of Multiple Pyramid Configurations	127
Rediscovering the Power of Verticality: The Nubian Pyramid	129
Nick Edwards on the Nubian Pyramid Design	130

IX—REFLECTIONS OF DR. PATRICK FLANAGAN

Pyramids & Prodigies	133
Pyramid Power—The Beginning	134
. . . And a Little Child Shall Lead Them	136
Scientific Exploits & Military Interventions	138
Breaking Free	141
Strange & Serendipitous Experiences: The Samurai Kid	142
A Golden Opportunity	144
A Mysterious Messenger	145
The Power of Vibration	147

Pyramid Power at the 2-dimensional Level	149
The Russian Connection	150
New Reflections on an Old Friend	151
Pyramids & The Kirlian Phenomenon	153
Energy & Brain Wave Enhancement Through Pyramid Power	154
Pyramid-powered Aquifers	156
Torsion—Expression of Energy Through Spiral Flow	156

X—APPENDICES

Appendix A—The Golden Mean	158
Appendix B—The Russian/Ukranian Pyramid Research	163
Appendix C—The Bosnian Pyramid of the Sun	166
Appendix D—Recent Research on the Bosnian Pyramid	168
Appendix E—The Human Energy System	183
Appendix F—Pyramids' Effect Upon Chakras	186
Appendix G—Indian Pyramid Vastu	191
Appendix H—Melted Pyramids in Egypt?—Russel G. Chong	212
Appendix I—In Search of Underwater Pyramids—Nick Edwards	226
Appendix J—A Night Inside the Great Pyramid—Paul Brunton	229
Appendix K—Russian & Ukranian Research—David Wilcock	262
Appendix L—Torsion: A 'Fifth Force'—Brendan D. Murphy	279
Appendix M—The Russian & Ukranian Studies (Original Texts)	280
Appendix N—Some Frequently Asked Questions—Bill Cox	306
Appendix O—Influence of Alignment of the Pyramid	299
Appendix P—How to Build Your Own Pyramids	312
Suggested Reading	314
About the Authors	315

FOREWORD

A Tribute to Nick Edwards—'The Pyramid Man'
by Dr. G. Patrick Flanagan
(Author *Pyramid Power, Beyond Pyramid Power* & *Pyramid Power II—The Scientific Evidence*)

Nick Edwards was an amazing man—and a personal friend.

I met Nick in 1973 after I self-published my book: *Pyramid Power* through DeVorss and company. After writing it, I tried to get it published but no one was interested; I then borrowed $5000 and self-published it. Over the next few years, over one and a half million copies were sold, and within a few years, people were building pyramids all over the world.

Then Nick Edwards came along, with his awesome titanium tube pyramids. While Nick was already aware of me and my stuff, I first heard of him when a dentist told me that Nick's pyramids improved the acceptance of dental implants in his patients.

I had been building my own pyramids—but they weren't very good; they used wooden dowels with molded plastic sheets over them—and were more like pyramid tents. Prior to using Nick's pyramids, the dentist had been having a 40 percent rejection rate on his implants, but by treating them under Nick's pyramids, the rejection rate declined.

I had to see this dentist and his pyramids, and went over to his lab to behold a wide array of Nick's slender-tubed pyramids being used to treat a variety of implants.

When I asked him where he had gotten his pyramids he said "Nick Edwards—he makes them, and I buy them from him." I said to myself, 'Okay, I've got to meet Nick Edwards.' He gave me Nick's phone number, and I called him up.

He was clearly making the best pyramids. And though, when we met at first there was a little bit of a challenge—because we were basically in competition with each other—he was selling pyramids and I was selling pyramids—we eventually became buddies, and were really good friends for a while, until I moved away from LA. I had a Lincoln Mark IV—and he was driving a Cadillac Seville—and we'd go and kind of race each other all over town.

I moved from Glendale, California to Marina del Rey and he was in Burbank at the time. He never sold my products and I never sold his. I had a business partner named Duke Langrey, and we had a company together called Pyramid Products. Duke and I had a parting of the ways; Duke had intended for his son to take over the business—but his son was like a little rich boy who wasn't tuned in to it, and Duke wound up giving the business to Nick, unbeknownst to me, something Nick only told me recently.

We hadn't been in contact since 1978 until we met again at Chichen Itza; the reunion was awesome—it was wonderful—by then we were communicating. I had bought a Tesla coil about a year and a half earlier—I drove with him to the Health Consciousness Expo where we had a booth together and did a little lecture spot.

Nick was a humble, beautiful, spiritual man whose insight you had to pull out of him—but once you started pulling it out you realized how amazing he was. And my experience has been that you can't get through life without a sense of humor.

Nick and I had a lot of fun over the years.

Nick Edwards was very much like me. He was a maverick and has the intuitive ability to "tune in" to subtle energies.

My friend Deepak Chopra says that I have access to the Akashic Record library where the knowledge of all Creation is stored.

The "knowing" does not come easily. In my own case, I often work for years on a project learning what does not work. Then, when I give up in frustration, entire technologies, circuits and formulas are downloaded into my consciousness in a flash— almost like someone feels sorry for me and gives me the answer.

I believe Nick Edwards had the same kind of Akashic library card. He was a humble man and a hard worker who had his own unique access to the "records".

Nick's insights into the pyramid as a lens are unique. The Golden Ratio or Fibonacci series of numbers is a key to Universal Harmony and the secrets of life. All lenses are mathematically designed to focus energy. We have optical lenses, microwave lenses. Lenses can have any shape, depending on the energy being focused.

The entire universe is constructed of precise mathematical constants and ratios. The same numbers that form the dimensions of the pyramids are found in the geometries of billions of galaxies and in every aspect of living form down to the structure of DNA and further into the quantum soup.

Ancient pyramids and sacred temples found all over the world incorporate these mathematical ratios.

I am sure that this book will remain a treasure to all who read it.

Gillis Patrick Flanagan
November 23rd 2012
Sedona, Arizona

PREFACE

PYRAMIDS AND HUMAN DESTINY

> "Know ye not that ye are the temple of God, and that the Spirit of God dwelleth in you?"
>
> 1 Corinthians 3:16

It has been some two thousand years now, and still Paul's radical wake-up call revealing the true dwelling-place of the divine has yet to fulfill itself in the experience of the human species—*homo sapiens*—which, perhaps somewhat ironically, means 'wise man.'

Whatever could have gone wrong? Why have we had such a mixed track record in fulfilling our higher destiny—of fulfilling our divine birthright? While philosophers, psychologists and sociologists have been pondering the problem since the days of Genesis, cogent answers remain scarce.

Contemporary philosopher Eckhart Tolle observed that if the history of the human race were that of a single human individual, it would have to be considered the record of a genocidal maniac—with hundreds of millions dying at the hands of their fellows' hands through the centuries.

On the brighter side, we have the radiant legacy of beauty bequeathed us through the milennia by the Mozarts, Monets and Michelangelos of the planet, and the self-sacrifice of the Christs, Gandhis and Kings.

Can these alternately hellish and heavenly really be fruits of the same species? Seemingly so—but the question remains—what is the all-important secret that makes the critical difference as to whether we unpredictable humans will choose to descend to the depths of hell or ascend to the shores of heaven?

Why have mankind's spiritual reservoirs remained so tragically impoverished? The solution may be far simpler than most have imagined; it is concealed, I think, in this seemingly unremarkable moment from the New Testament:

> And when he had finished speaking he said, "Launch out into deep water and let down your net for a catch."

One can't gather fish—at least not an abundant harvest of fish—without a net; a net is—so to speak—a receiving apparatus—a structure designed to attract and ensnare fish—a 'receptor site' for what the fisherman seeks. Likewise, it may be raining torrents but little water will be retained without receptacles—or 'receivers.' Both primitive, hand-woven nets or modern micro-wave antennas are, in effect, nothing but open invitations to the universe for infilling.

On a biological level, our bodies will not greatly benefit from the presence of vitamins, minerals and micronutrients in our bloodstream—no matter how many of these we may purchase and consume—if our tissues lack open receptor sites for them.

A receptor site is simply a location on a cell's surface where certain molecules, such as enzymes, neurotransmitters, or viruses, attach themselves in order to interact with the cellular components.

Without these receptor sites or receiving stations there is no interaction, and therefore no transformation, no benefit within a system lacking them.

There is a poignant Zen story about four men gathered about a campfire in the evening, all illuminated by bright moonlight; one is blind, one is playing his lute, one is sleeping, and one is gazing at the moon. Bear in mind that, in Zen tradition, the moon is employed as a symbol of spiritual reality.

The man gazing at the moon is in direct relationship with reality—his eyes are open to its radiant beauty and his heart is full; the man playing the lute has confined himself to the beautiful but still limited world of his music and experiences only that and nothing else; the sleeping man has abandoned himself to unconsciousness and sees only the contents of his own dreams; and the blind man lacks all apparent 'receptor sites' to see the light at all.

Yet the moon of Truth is shining upon all of them equally and without favoritism—clear and bright.

By virtue of our ability to choose what we focus upon, and due to our narrow—often fixated—field of view, we often render ourselves blind to all else that lies outside our viewfinder—and for us, that which we ignore literally ceases to exist.

And so we see—and receive—nothing; our receptor sites, our receivers—are shut down. We have not issued the universe a proper invitation, a recognizable receptor site, for its vast and varied gifts and energies. We have not opened our spiritual arms to take in its cosmic 'hug', and so we remain empty-handed—not to mention brokenhearted.

The universe is always giving—both from within, as life, breath and consciousness—and from without, as light, energy and substance; but are we in receiving-mode or in shut-down mode?

Human consciousness is such that most of us are often in partial or total shutdown mode, with, perhaps, if we are lucky, a glimpse of universal essence leaking in here or there, now and then, through relatively brief, narrow openings in our field of awareness.

A telling cautionary tale from the New Testament:

> *He called out to them, 'Friends, haven't you any fish?'*
> *'No,' they answered.*
> *He said, 'Throw your net on the right side of the boat and you will find some." When they did, they were unable to haul the net in because of the large number of fish.'*
> (John 21:6)

In this parable, the 'right' side becomes a metaphor for the correct way, the technically effective approach. The water was always present, and the fish were always present; but the nets, also, needed to be present at the same place and time.

And, lo, their nets were suddenly full.

Pyramids are hard-wired versions of Simon's suddenly fertile fishing nets: they are 3-dimensional receptor sites, reaching out to gather universal energies and carry them, via conduction and convergence, into time and space in such a way that we in the 3-dimensional world may experience and take advantage of them wherever and whenever we so choose.

Like the all-luminous moon of Truth pyramid power is always receiving—and therefore always giving; it plays no favorites; it cares nothing for believers above unbelievers, or Christians over Jews, whites before blacks or Americans in favor of Ukranians: it shines on all—the just and the unjust alike—the atheist as well as the theist—upon everyone and everything which may have the good fortune to come under its life-enhancing influence.

Aside from the latest cutting-edge contemporary discoveries on pyramid energy, *The Healing Power of Pyramids* contains abundant personal insights on the part of pyramidologists such as Patrick Flanagan and Jaroslaw Mironski, as well as many Russian, Ukranian and European and American researchers. There are also chapters on practical health-giving pyramid protocols, personal pyramid healing testimonies, and pyramid-oriented meditations and spiritual practices. As if all this weren't enough, *The Healing Power of Pyramids* offers 14 fact-filled appendices on subjects as diverse as contemporary archeological quests to explore the unexplained burn patterns on the Egyptian pyramids, the energy dynamics of torsion fields, and the complete chapter by mystic-author Paul Brunton on his incredible night spent alone in the Great Pyramid—alone worth the price of admission.

Even allowing for those sections or ideas which seem to challenge the reader beyond his or her capacity to believe, it will be many moons before the mysterious world of pyramidology sees as intriguing, scientific and enlightening a book as *The Healing Power of Pyramids*.

All that remains is to sit back, open oneself to the possibility that there exists an energy just beyond the horizon of our understanding—a Something which seemingly emerges out of seeming nothing—just as we ourselves do.

And then, just perhaps—provided we cast them—our 'nets shall be full.'

May the ocean of Life bring you many fish!

Joseph Marcello
May 8, 2016

I

BEYOND THE KNOWN—A PREVIEW

The Healing Power of Pyramids is a hands-on, practical guide to enhancing our lives with pyramid energy; it is not a book of pyramid theory or history. For those interested in these aspects, we highly recommend Dr. John DeSalvo's *The Complete Pyramid Sourcebook*—an exhaustively comprehensive documentation of the author's research encompassing every procurable volume written on the subject over the course of some five centuries, including many rare early accounts of journeys to and through the Great Pyramid.

We can think of no more compelling way to begin this book than to share the most recent research about pyramids and pyramid energies. If even only half of what that research were shared it would still qualify as revelational, including research that has confirmed that Golden Section Pyramids neutralize geopathic zones, possess powerful anti-stress effects and slow aging by enhancing the immune system, increase the vitality of cells, tissues and organs and reduce the negative influence of the environment on humans and nature.

The strange fact is that, in our own era, the first century of the new millennium, some 5,000 years after the first pyramid prototypes first appeared on the planet, pyramid power is a verifiable scientific reality; pyramids actually do 'work' and produce palpable and measurable effects upon people and organic structures. Used with understanding, they possess the potential to benefit human lives in countless ways—ways well outside the parameters of mere wishful thinking or any supposed placebo effect—and benefits that occur only when pyramids are presen, whether or not we believe in their powers.

Contemporary pyramid research owes an incalculable debt of gratitude to Dr. Alexander Golod, who almost single-handedly brought about a renaissance in pyramid science through his construction of over 50 geographically strategic pyramids throughout Russia and the Ukraine, where teams of physicians and clinicians extensively documented their stunning powers in a variety of venues.

Summarized below is an impressive shortlist of recent, reproducible, scientifically documented pyramid phenomena; if, after reading these accounts, the reality of pyramid power still seems in question, it might suggest a disinclination to accept the facts as documented.

Pyramid researcher David Wilcock shares: "Pyramid technology is indeed far more advanced than we ever realized, and has the power to completely transform our planet—as well as our own lives. The only thing holding us back was that our own science had not yet progressed to the point where we could identity and understand such a high technology … I realized that pyramids were indeed the most stunningly advanced technology ever built on Earth.

"Thankfully, multiple teams of accredited, mainstream Russian scientists did the work for us. Their results suggest that pyramid technology and its offshoots could save the world—and substantially improve our physical, mental and spiritual health along the way. In addition, these results tear the roof off everything we thought we knew about our own bodies and about science in general. The more you learn about it the more wonderful the implications become."

Wilcock has also rightly observed that all things harmful to life are to a greater or lesser extent neutralized or rendered less harmful through exposure to pyramid energies. Among other remarkable potentials for use of pyramid power are earthquake control, effected through the fragmentation of major quake tremors into minor ones. There is also evidence that pyramid power induces the emergence of springs and streams from within the earth; pyramids have also been shown to repair gaps in the earth's ozone layer. Perhaps best of all, no one has ever been able to discover any even marginally negative side effects of exposure to pyramid power. (See Wilcock's article, Appendix J, for a multitude of remarkable research findings on pyramids' ability to enhance life processes.)

PYRAMIDOLOGY IN THE 21st CENTURY

While it may sound too good to be true, if the magnificent pyramid construction initiative of Alexander Golod were to be emulated by major governments throughout the world, the proliferation of these free-energy conducting structures might potentially be capable of restoring the earth—and its human family—to ecological and personal balance and wholeness.

Author Russ Michael has initiated a movement to do just that through his site devoted to disseminating planetary and personal healing through pyramid energy: http://GoldenKeyLibrary.info.

In the following pages, in addition to a treasure trove of startling new scientific findings, the reader will treated to many intriguing empirical accounts by people who have ventured to experiment with pyramids—from small scale models to entire homes constructed along pyramidal designs.

CONTEMPORARY EXPLORERS

Readers will also learn of the pioneering work and elegant creations of contemporary pyramid craftsman Nick Edwards— 'The Pyramid Man'—and of those of his longtime friend and colleague, Dr. Patrick Flanagan, author of the best-selling *Pyramid Power* and *Beyond Pyramid Power*—books that first opened the eyes of the contemporary world to the phenomenon of pyramid power.

Indeed, an entire chapter is devoted to the unique life and insights of Dr. Flanagan, whose own work and inventions have been the subject of long fascination on the part of the scientific and spiritual communities.

While therapeutic pyramids may be created without great difficulty at home, creations such as those Nick Edwards and others offer immediate and effective ways to implement personal exploration into working with pyramid energy. Although professionally produced products may be more elegant and aesthetic, simple construction skills can produce pyramids with virtually many of the same benefits.

The Healing Power of Pyramids taps into the research and discoveries of many individuals across the globe.

In later chapters of the book the reader will find actual techniques, meditations, and protocols for using pyramids of various sizes for different purposes, and for energy and life enhancement.

All this and much more awaits discovery in *The Healing Power of Pyramids* —with a decided emphasis upon practical personal benefits over scholarship.

A sizable archive of scholarly writings already exists on pyramids, many of them full of arcane theories purporting to fathom how and by whom they were created. Some predicate visitations by intergalactic entities harboring lofty agendas for earth and human evolution; others attempt to explain them as an outgrowth of the mystery traditions of earth's ancient civilizations, such as the Mayan and the Egyptian cultures.

But to wait for the many quasi-scientific and magical theories to sort themselves out would be to squander the great opportunity available to us now; whether highly advanced interstellar beings seeded the earth with its pyramids or they are the work of prescient earthlings is ultimately not the most critical issue at hand.

Life is short—and speculation largely fruitless, and an ounce of personal experience is worth more than a ton of theories. We can make our own empirical trial to discover for ourselves whether or not there is anything to the world's continuing fascination with mystery of pyramids.

If we find no benefit, we can safely drop the magic and mystery and move on to more rewarding endeavors; but if, in spite of our doubts, we find benefit, we can choose to embrace them as life-enhancing tools. Based upon my own experience and that of a great many others, laymen and scientists alike, they do reward personal experimentation with palpable results.

While the focus of *The Healing Power of Pyramids* is primarily upon healing and wellness, the reader will find a rich archive of solid scientific information; and, for those who enjoy theoretical speculation, lengthy and detailed historical overviews are included in several appendices.

In spite of the fact that they are anecdotal and do not technically qualify as 'hard science,' we have included many accounts of life-enhancements, healings and transformational experiences occurring as a result of individuals' experiments with pyramids, cones and similar energies.

These will hopefully inspire the reader to make his or her own personal pyramid trials.

Granted, some of the anecdotes and accounts may be challenging to accept; yet the odds of so many otherwise intelligent, rigorous scientists coming confirming the reality of pyramid power are perilously slim. Whichever way one seeks to explain it, a genuine phenomenon whose effects are measurable is at work.

The research contributors for this book offer some intriguing and compelling answers to the strange, continuing phenomenon of just how something can seem to emerge out of nothing—and how a very palpable field of force—a "flame in the middle" (pyr (flame) amid (at the center) can be conjured through the alchemy of form and space.

The Healing Power of Pyramids is a factually—as well as anecdotally—compelling book on the power underlying an ancient mystery—one that the impatient seekers of the 21st century can implement and explore without further delay.

The Russian-Ukranian studies that follow are purposefully presented in a strictly clinical manner, in order that their scientific rigor be as unassailable as possible.

But a final word of encouragement to the reader: suspend any doubts at least until a fair trial has been made—there might, after all, *be* a pot of gold at the apex of that pyramid!

II

PYRAMID POWER:

THE COMPELLING CONTEMPORARY RESEARCH

The following research was performed under the auspices of the Institute of Physics in Kiev, Ukraine, a part of the National Academy of Sciences of Ukraine, one of the leading scientific centers in the former USSR and the premier military research association, the laboratory of Dr. N. B. Egorova, of the Mechnikov Research and Development Institute at the Russian Academy of Medical Sciences.

1.) PYRAMID DETOXIFICATION & HEIGHTENED IMMUNITY

Research Focus: At the laboratory of Dr. N. B. Egorova, of the Mechnikov Research and Development Institute at the Russian Academy of Medical Sciences, the impact of a pyramid field on the reactions of living organisms to purposely introduced toxins was studied.

Research Method: the study was conducted on a model strain of mice known as the exciter S.typhimurium. strain 415. White underbred mice weighing 12 to 14 grams were kept in the pyramid in various numbers and for varying time periods. After several days, the mice were infected with four increasing doses of S.tiphimurium, starting with 10 and increasing to 104 microbial cells. The control was supplied with mice from the same strain, and was contaminated with the same doses of culture, but without exposure to the pyramid-field.

Research findings: the survival rate of mice who received exposure to the pyramid-field considerably exceeded those in the control group. At smaller doses of contamination, 60% of the mice exposed to the pyramid survived, whereas in the control group only 7% survived. At larger doses of contamination, 30 % of the mice exposed to the pyramid-field survived whereas just 3 % of those in the control group survived.

Conclusion: Exposure of mice to the pyramid-field essentially promotes the heightening of their resistance to consequent contamination of S.tiphimurium. Therefore, it is possible to speak about a powerful immunomodulating influence of the pyramid on nonspecific reactivity of the organism of the animals. An analogous pattern was observed with the mice introduced to different carcinogens. Mice in an experimental batch drank water that was held in the pyramid. Control animals drank non-pyamid water. The odds of the appearance of growths in control animals was greater than for animals drinking pyramid-treated water.

2) PYRAMID ANTIVIRAL EFFECT

Research Focus: Professor S. M. Klimenko and medical doctor, Dr. D. N. Nosik, of the Ivanovskii Research and Development Institute of Virology at the Russian Academy of Medical Sciences, studied the pyramid field's effects on the antiviral activity of immunoglobulin. The object of the investigation was venoglobulin—a human polyvalence immunoglobulin prepared for intravenous administration in lyophilized (fat-bound) form. The study was conducted on a culture of diploid cells of fibroblasts from the test subject. They utilized the encephalomyocarditis virus (EMC) in mice for the determination of antiviral activity of the treated immunoglobulin.

Research Method: The antiviral activity of the drug was determined by its capacity to protect cells of the person from the cytopathic (cell-destroying) impact of the virus. Pursuant to the operating instructions, venoglobulin was diluted in distilled water up to the concentration 50 mg/ml. In this study, the drug was tested in two concentrations: 50 and 0.5 microg/ml. Then, aliquots (a portion of the total amount of solution of venoglobulin from both concentrations were housed in the pyramid. Venoglobulin was deposited into cell-like cultures 24 hours prior to their contamination by the virus.

Conclusion: It was found that venoglobulin in concentration 50 microg/ml considerably inhibited the breeding the virus, approximately 300%. The antiviral effect was still maintained at further dilution of venoglobulin up to the concentrations 0.005 and 0.00005 microg/ml, with consequent exposures in the pyramid. Antiviral activity of venoglobulin practically ceased to develop by these concentrations.

3) NORMALZATION OF INFANTILE PATHOLOGIES

Research Focus: Professor A. G. Antonov's team from the Russian Research and Development Institute of Pediatrics, Obstetrics and Gynecology investigated the influence of 40%-s solution of glucose intravenously and distilled water orally on 20 premature babies with grave medical problems which would have normally resulted in death within a few days.

Research Method: The infants were each fed a few milliliters of tap water that had been stored in the healing pyramid energy field. (Technical details: they then compared the indices of the instantaneous state (IIS), which mirror the state of the sympatho-adrenal system of the patient. The data on 20 patients were analyzed.

Conclusion: in all cases of applying of 40%-s solution of glucose in amount 1 ml the IIS essentially increased practically up to normal values even for the patients with very low initial values of IIS, close to zero point. The results were the same after applying 1 ml of water, which had been exposed to the pyramid.)

4) REGENERATION OF HUMAN BEHAVIOR

Research Focus: to determine the effect of pyramid-treated objects on the subsequent behavior of a population of 5,000 prison inmates.

Research Method: crystalline substances were stored in one of the fiberglass pyramids built under the direction of Dr. Alexander Golod, and later distributed through the prisons.

Conclusions: the incidence of criminal behavior in the prisons virtually disappeared within a few months. Dr. Golod's conclusion: the decrease in incidence of criminal behavior obviously suggests a corresponding increase in feelings of peacefulness and goodwill among the inmates within the facilities involved in this research.

5) PYRAMID RADIATION OF MASSIVE IONIC FIELDS

With the help of a series of radars working in the centimetre range and placed at 60 km, 32 km and 30 km from the Pyramid, scientists conducted radiolocation of the area of vertical axis of the Pyramid. During this research, the existence of an ionic column with a height of 2000 meters and width of 500 meters along the vertical axis of the pyramid was established. This allegedly ionic column was constantly changing its height from 800 meters to 2000 meters. The reflecting ability of this formation is comparable to reflecting ability of a plane.

6) PYRAMID REGENERATION OF ENVIRONMENT

A Golden Section pyramid harmonizes space within its radius of influence. New streams appeared in the area of the 22-meter pyramid on the Seliger Lake, a stork set up a nest, and nearby fields became covered with previously extinct species of flowers.

7) PYRAMID ENHANCEMENT OF AGRICULTURE

Before planting crops, seeds were placed inside the Pyramid for 1-5 days. Tens of thousands of hectares were seeded with over 20 crops.

Conclusions: In each case there was a 20% to 100% (improvement in) crop productivity; the crops were disease-free and not afflicted by droughts. The quantity of toxic substances in plants decreased. Similar results were obtained when closed contours of stones previously exposed to the Pyramid energy were placed around the crop fields. 500 small stones with total weight of 20 kg were placed around a 10 hectare field (1 hectare = 10,000 square metres.)

OVERVIEW OF RESULTS

In short, research, experiments and tests in medical laboratories and science centers have confirmed that, among other effects, Golden Section Pyramids: neutralize geopathic zones, have powerful anti-stress effects, slow aging processes by enhancing the immune system, increase the vitality of cellular tissue, slow the development of negative processes in living organisms, and reduce the negative influence of the environment on humans and nature.

(This concludes the summary of research findings.)

* * *

Were these research findings to have appeared in any single issue of the Journal of the American Medical Association (JAMA) or the Lancet—its British equivalent, the entire world of contemporary medicine would have been on its feet. There would likely have been claims of fraud or quackery or worse, because the across-the-board improvements in immunity, health and biological function would, by any conventional criteria, appear to be too outstanding, even for any single pathology— much less multiple pathologies; and no doubt the pharmaceutical complex would be less than thrilled by the discovery of a healing protocol that might compromise their future sales.

Likewise, on the holistic side of the equation, if any reiki or qigong healer were to have been documented as reliably reversing everything from lethal levels of toxic bacteria to criminal behavior, the world would have begun flocking to that person or place literally en masse.

Yet, the research is rock-solid and real—and best of all—readily available to professionals and non-professionals alike for the taking.

PYRAMIDS—SCIENTIFIC YET BEYOND SCIENCE

So much for the world of hard science; in the less easily quantified realm of spirituality, we find the admittedly anecdotal, but firsthand, testimonies of pyramid-home dwellers in *Pyramids and the Second Reality*, the third volume of pioneering pyramid research by Bill Schul and Ed Petit:

"I would say that the biggest change that comes over you, living in a pyramid house, is the spiritual change" ... "Almost everyone who enters our home feels as though it is a spiritual place."... "The thing that you really notice is that you have more energy"..."Your rate of healing is so much faster than ordinarily" ... "I've noticed that she is much happier as a person" ... "All your senses are enhanced" ... "Your thoughts are brought to one with your physical body..."

Debbie Noble, living in a pyramid home near Coyle, Oklahoma, reported: "I would say that the biggest change that overcomes you living in a pyramid is the spiritual change. My whole life has been spiritually oriented, but it seems to me that you notice everything has become more purified; you notice how life is and you notice the energy of life. You understand what life is and that is very overwhelming. Also, people who come to our house feel spiritually affected. Almost everyone who comes here feels as though it is a spiritual place, a very spiritual place. When you pray, your prayers are answered; you receive a response to your prayers. You can feel an immediate one-to-one feeling of contact with, you know, the Heavenly Being. You feel as though your home is really protected and that everything you do is guided. It feels as though your whole purpose in life was known before you were born and that everything you have done is leading up to that purpose and it is being fulfilled."

"When you do come in contact with those who are sick, you might get something like a cold. But the thing that you really notice is that it heals remarkably faster. Your rate of healing is so much faster than ordinarily. You really notice that you have more energy. You feel younger, you feel so young."

What more—one wonders—could we possibly be waiting for? The time for pyramids has come: pyramids as healing modules, environmental resources, spiritual tools, nutritional and potentiators for everything from foods to water to supplements— all coming to us as a free energy system.

Let the wise proceed accordingly!

FUNNY ...

When I was working on this book, Nick Edwards gently nudged me from time to time to "make it funny," because, for him, humor provided the spice of life. I did my best to indulge him, for he was someone who got a kick out of making mischief and having fun whenever he could. But given the mysterious and, at times, even mystical nature of the subject matter, I feel that I may have fallen short of fulfilling his request.

There is, however, something—if not quite 'funny'—then at least extremely ironic—about humanity's difficulty in contemplating the validity of pyramid power.

Here we are—some seven-odd billion of us—reliably rotating upon a blue-green planet revolving about a central sun amidst a cosmic web of other circling celestial orbs and their orbits, having not the faintest idea how we ever came to be her, from where our life springs or where the unthinkable expanse of the universe ends. Fortunately, we are prevented by some infinitely benign interplay of forces from being sucked into the sun's molten core and being instantly incinerated—or of being unhinged from our trajectory by random gravitational anomalies and hurtling off into the abyss of interstellar space—and oblivion. But these mysteries aside, what we do know is that the overwhelming majority of us enjoy, day in and day out, the illumination of just enough sunlight, just enough warmth, just enough cloud cover, just enough oxygen-rich atmosphere to support a working, living, thriving earth with all its myriad landscapes, species, glories, wonders ... enabling those 7 billion lives to fulfill their unique destinies.

Like Sleeping Beauty, we have fallen under a spell that blinds us to the mind-boggling miracle—the wild impossibility of existing at all, and even more—of existing in an ecstatically beautiful, astonishingly balanced cosmos that seems to truly be a 'world without end.'

And instead we go on pretending that this surreal process is all merely business as usual—routine and commonplace reality. In this way we at least avoid being overwhelmed by the fathomless mystery in which we subsist; we prefer to forget that we are suspended—with no visible support—in the abyss of space, hurtling through eternity, dancing the 'Born-Against-All-Odds, One Chance in a Lifetime' tango.

If anything is 'funny,' this is—our absurd ability to become unconscious to the awesomeness of being alive, and pretending there's really nothing special going on here, when in fact, what's going on here is, beyond doubt, the most mind-bending miracle that one could possibly imagine.

Once we awaken from this state of sleep-walking—and look upon existence as if for the first time, we can never again fall victim to the illusion that our lives are inconsequential—or in any way 'ordinary.'

Pleasant or painful, up or down, sweet or shocking—there is every reason to believe that Creation itself is the living form—the body—of what, once upon a time, people called 'God'—the Living Source; to ignore this reality is to set the stage for a shallow, shrink-wrapped life—a very boring journey—and a painfully narrow view of What's Actually Out There.

If anything is 'funny,' this is… so funny that it borders upon being tragic.

There's an intimate connection between this sense of living wonder and such explorers as Patrick Flanagan, Nick Edwards and Alexander Golod—and the strange journeys they make: it is almost as if, in order to make those journeys and explorations—one needs, consciously or unconsciously, to first possess such a magical vision—whether it be to create a Sistine Chapel, compose a 'Claire de Lune' or plumb the age-old mystery of the pyramids.

It is because of such vision that ordinary' people become empowered to do extraordinary things—to push beyond the realities into which they've been born, cut through all obstacles and explore, create, transcend and revolutionize their world. This is the fabled Pearl of Great Price.

Which is much more than funny—it's outright inspiring.

Pyramids aside, the mere fact that a human being spends his or her life in revelation of such mysteries is a sure sign that they feel the calling of a source beyond the regions of the known.

To those who have been attracted to unravelling its age-old secrets, the perennial question posed by the pyramid is, "Here I stand—an ongoing mystery throughout the ages—yet also a present and contemporary reality, with an impact that cannot be scientifically denied; I exist in time and space, yet I am a portal for That Which is Beyond Time and Space. My purpose here is to show you that earthly existence is not merely a random accident of molecular chain-reactions, but a precious gift from an infinitely mysterious Source.

Which is much more than inspiring—it is awe-inspiring.

III

THE POWER OF PRESENCE

Sri Yukteswar, guru to Paramhansa Yogananda, often admonished his disciples, "Environment is stronger than willpower."

Coming from an enlightened soul, this is an arresting statement; it can only mean that, contrary to our assurance that we are autonomous beings endowed with the power of choice, we are shaped and influenced to a far greater extent than we would like to believe by the environments and atmospheres within which we live out our lives.

From birth to death, our worlds are ceaselessly shaped and choreographed by the sounds, scents, colors and moods of our environmental matrices; city or seashore, slum or palace, bar or chapel, we are all constantly processing, absorbing and internalizing the frequencies and flavors that envelop us—long before it ever begins to dawn on us that we are being so deeply conditioned and formatted.

By the time—and if ever--we come to perceive this elusive truth we may find that there is precious little choice left to be or do anything other than what our life-long programming—or, for traditionalists, karma--has ordained.

If we're fortunate, we're blessed with conditions and companions that uplift and expand us—body, mind and spirit: we're cherished, encouraged and supported in our coming of age. Alternately, we may find ourselves struggling against the undertow of nameless forces which seem to frustrate our every attempt at fulfillment and happiness, plunging us—again and again—into conflict, confusion and despair.

Often, we find ourselves simultaneously negotiating the crosscurrents of both dynamics: we're half awake and half asleep, trying our best—as the song goes—to "accentuate the positive and eliminate the negative," yet continuing to be challenged on all sides.

What, then, are environments made of? While one could conjure a list of thousands of aspects, distilled down to the bare essence, it could be said that all environments—indeed, all manifestations of any kind—are an interplay of 1) space—or formlessness, 2) substance—or form—and frequency—or vibrational atmosphere.

A parallel equation might be: $E=S+Fm+Fr$—environment equals space plus form plus frequency.

The room one occupies, the air one is inhaling, the sounds and colors striking one's ears and eyes, the thoughts one's brain generates and the feelings flowing forth from the heart are all configurations of space, form and frequency; together they constitute one's present internal environment or living space.

But ever since humanity abandoned its roots in the natural world and opted for the comforts of civilization and the temptations of technology—the spaces, forms and frequencies it has created for itself have largely ruptured its connection to its natural biological and spiritual endowments.

What has largely rescued the human race from such self-inflicted impoverishment and helped restore it to its birthright are its cultural sacraments—the arts—the transcendent music, visionary painting, enlightened writings and the re-emergence of the Mysteries—the sacred practices and architectures of the ages.

With conscious spiritual intent or not, the artists, scientists and spiritual seekers of our world have provided the incalculably vital function of keeping alive humanity's connection with nature, beauty, and the sacred—or 'spiritual'—dimensions of life, dimensions from which it unknowingly would otherwise have completely been disconnected.

The greatest creators in every medium have gifted us with sacred forms—poetry, art, music—that have rescued us from what might have otherwise been a soulless and mechanical existence. Indeed, there are, even now, parts of our world which have been almost completely co-opted by the military-industrial complex and the nuclear industry, not to mention the sterility of any mall or urban sprawl.

VICTIMS OR CREATORS?

Yet, against Sri Yukteswar's insistence that environment trumps will power, there is an astonishing verse out of Omar Khayyam's *The Rubaiyat* that shocks us with the assertion that, in the end, we create our own internal reality.

> "I sent my soul through the invisible,
> some letter of that afterlife to spell;
> and by and by my soul returned to me,
> and answered, "I myself am Heav'n and Hell"

The poet seems to be admonishing his readers that, in the end, it is our own inner world of thought and feeling that ultimately determines our spiritual destiny.

It is a sobering to realize that this inner essence becomes one's inseparable traveling companion, whether demon or angel, accuser or redeemer, adversary or beloved.

The question arises—how can we be both the creators and the victims of our life-experience? Mustn't it be one or the other? The paradoxical answer—yes and no. Short of divine intervention, no baby—human or animal—will long endure a loveless, ceaselessly hostile environment, much less months, never mind years—of inhuman treatment—without crippling wounds, and very possibly a premature departure.

While we are aware of such souls as Helen Keller, who managed to surmount seemingly hopeless hardships and to ultimately triumph—even to the extent of becoming way-showers, we do not see the many others who lost their way and succumbed to the darkness.

There needs to be some deep initial Yes!' in the life of a soul in order that it desires to be--and continue being—here at all—some shred of light, love or goodness that graces it with a sense of brighter possibilities that lie beyond its present painful frame of experience—even if those possibilities may take decades to fulfill themselves.

Without this all-critical 'chance at life,' the soul has no opportunity to grow into its inner potential; it needs, at the outset of its journey, at least a marginally life-giving environment, and a life-condition that allows it to move beyond the level of sheer survival. Lacking this first 'gulp of air,' no sentient young being would ever find the will to go on, and would almost certainly give up the good fight.

THE POROUS HUMAN

Why then are we so terribly vulnerable to our surroundings, our worlds? Is it simply human frailty? A poor defense system? An inability to get one's act together? Or is it perhaps because we are built with ingeniously bi-directional nervous systems—ingeniously designed not only to sense what is going on within but also to monitor what is transpiring without? And fortunate we are that this is the case; consider how impossible life would be if we were constructed such that we were only able to contact and perceive what is occurring internally—a solipsistic or self-imprisoned mode of living that would ultimately become hellish; or else to were able to experience only what is transpiring outside ourselves—and so be constantly isolated from our own beings and at the mercy of external conditions.

It seems that we have very little choice in the matter due to the way we're neurologically designed. Our openness to world-reality is the actual cause of this apparent vulnerability—and the reason Sri Yukteswar perceived so clearly that environment trumps will-power.

The unspoken admonition encoded in his sage observation was: 'Therefore take great care and choose your environments wisely.' Or, going even further—possibly, 'Create your own ideal environments, forms and frequencies."

SACRED GEOMETRY: THE ART OF SPACE, FORM AND FREQUENCY

Fortunately, there have always been impassioned seekers throughout the centuries who have somehow sensed or been gifted with conscious awareness of these realities, and who have explored ways of reclaiming humanity's rightful heritage—inner peace and well-being—from the distorted and chaotic forms and frequencies generated by the post-industrial world.

Some, like Yogananda, were skillful navigators of the inner dimension—seeking to lead souls back to their origin through spiritual disciplines, and creating powerfully uplifting environments in which seekers could do so.

Others, like the master artists, have created sacred forms—whether musical, artistic, architectural or literary—which act as psychospiritual catalysts, leading humanity—as the Brihadaranyaka Upanishad intones—from the unreal to the Real, from darkness to light and from death to immortality; thanks to these path-makers, innumerable seekers have been able to experience inner breakthroughs and revelations.

Even though traditional religions have attempted to address humanity's need for balance, they have largely failed to fulfill their promise, merely substituting narrow belief-systems for genuine wisdom, with the result that many seekers have been led even further into illusion and disappointment.

Creators of sacred 3-dimensional forms understand that reality is a dance of space, form and frequency, and that these are within our power to create and control. By the skillful re-structuring of space through the creation of resonant forms we can bring about the desired frequency—or vibrational rate—

within that form and space—which then actively becomes our environment.

THE SANCTIFICATION OF SPACE

From this dimension emerge the practitioners of the 'art of environment,' Feng Shui, and the architects of Sacred Geometry across the globe, seekers who discovered ways to recreate and restore the energetic balance originally bequeathed us by the natural world, and to allow the human spirit to access its greatest potential. This is the common thread that binds them to each other, and to the healing power of pyramids.

Lest one imagine such wisdoms as Feng Shui or energy-sensitive architecture lie purely in the eye of the beholder, one has only to consider a lavish living space with a generous picture window, which, when the shade is drawn up, is discovered to be facing a brick wall a few mere feet away.

Without even having to actually experience this anomaly, we can feel its wrongness—both visually and energetically. It would be the denial of the very essence of what a window is—or should be, which is a view trajectory, a vision out into the world—spanning the trajectory from near to far, as one's gaze extends into the distance. A window is a portal beyond the confines of one's limited dwelling space, a sight-channel that pierces through our personal enclosure. A window with an unobstructed view imparts a feeling of uplift because it allows our life-energy to flow unimpeded—to resonate through the greater world, allowing our awareness to effortlessly expand out into that space.

SPACE AS SPIRIT

Conversely, all dysfunctional 3-dimensional forms and architectures cause a contraction in our energy field or aura; we find the life-force that naturally wants to emerge and expand rebounding back in upon itself and imploding inside us.

The situation is much the same with houses, apartments and work spaces; much of this world lives and moves within the confines of little cubicles—boxes—of various sizes—small, flat-ceilinged, minimally-windowed—or even windowless--cells which have the effect of interrupting—and often, virtually eliminating—the spirallic vortices of the natural world, leaving their occupants uninspired and palpably enervated.

From a steady diet of such anti-dynamic, lifeless spaces, what, in other environments, might have been vital, creative human beings become fatigued, faltering effigies who lack even a frame of reference by which to perceive which essential element is so critically lacking in their environments.

Our instinct for an expansive energy experience gives birth to the spontaneous joy we see in schoolchildren let out for recess. They may not know the how or why of their bliss; but even so, their nervous systems intuitively sense their abiding hunger for the energies of earth, air, scent, sound and movement.

A true human being is far more than a functional brain—or 'talking head'—he or she is a globally sentient organism that resonates life through every plant-like cell of his or her being, whether or not such sentience is conscious or not.

As both the world of nature and the world of art reveal, it is not always necessary to scientifically comprehend a thing before we can experience—and benefit from—its essence; whether it be the deep peace engendered by a pilgrimage to the ocean or the great exhilaration felt upon hearing a Mozart allegro, we are spontaneously and instantaneously nourished by these fruits far beyond our ability to explain them.

And so it is with pyramids and other sacred forms; while free of any religious or philosophical referents, and even now inscrutable to many scientists and intellectuals—both of whom discount even the faintest possibility that force could ever be harnessed and generated by form—we may begin now to avail ourselves of their potential.

SPACE: THE 4TH DIMENSION

It may seem strange to contemplate the fact that form can actually re-format the energies in play within a space, and that, once reformatted, such a space is able to transduce or transceive energies not previously present, yet such is the case.

From a purely materialistic point of view this claim seems almost absurd; how could anything circumscribing or contained with a space conceivably alter the inherent characteristics of that space in any essential way? Yet this is exactly what has been found to occur—impacting the physical, psychic and spiritual levels of those within that space in new and beneficial ways.

Sacred Geometry is the name given to the art of re-choreographing the energetic matrix in which we live through the creation of resonant forms. Belief-systems, theories and abstract principles play no direct part in the process, because the phenomenon is not a matter of faith, but rather of natural—if as yet undiscover—processes, provable by anyone willing to experiment.

IV

THE POWER OF FOCUS

As a boy, on a sunny day I would wander outside in search of adventure. When the mid-summer was high, the sunlight spilling through the trees, over the lawns, gardens and sidewalks, I would yank a magnifying glass out of my back pocket, look about for a dry leaf, and kneel down, concentrating on converging the sun's rays into a single, laser-like beam, then wait.

It would be only a matter of seconds before the dry surface of the leaf would begin to brown, blacken, smolder, then finally blister open as the white-hot rays of solar energy seared through its surface.

I could not have explained the science of the phenomenon at the time, but I intuitively understood that I was accessing solar energy and, through prismatic convergence, concentrating it into a more potent—even destructive—form.

Similarly, we can take an iron bar whose molecules are randomly aligned and disorganized and try to attract another metal object with it, but nothing much will happen. Yet, if we apply a powerful electromagnet to this same bar, its molecules will come into a coherent alignment—or polarization—and we will find that we can now attract and even lift heavy metallic objects with the same previously 'non-attractive' bar.

There is a curious paradox concealed in these childhood experiments. While it was the same sunlight before and after the intervention of the magnifying glass, and the same metal bar before and after the molecular alignment process, in each case something has fundamentally changed.

That something—when sufficiently concentrated—undergoes an essential enhancement that results in a shift in critical mass or observable effect.

That critical threshold might best be understood by the phenomena of water's changing states; with the application of enough heat, water is no longer water, but steam, or—moving lower on the frequency scale—ice. As its vibratory state changes, there is a radical alteration innate qualities and capacities.

With a change of state come an entirely new set of potentials.

HARNESSING THE LIFE-FORCE

Likewise, through receptive, resonant structures, the ambient energy of the universe can be attracted, focused and condensed—and used for the benefit of living organisms.

These conductive matrices, quite apart from their structural aesethics, function as sacred energy forms and the surface of the planet is studded with them, from Egypt to the Andes, from Stonehenge to the Ukraine. Some are widely known while others remain privy to only a few. Some are meccas to which millions make yearly pilgrimages, such as Lourdes in France and the Taj Mahal in India—and others, such as a power-suffused chapel created by Ronald Beesely, a gifted healer in rural England, well off the radar screen.

But in each and every case there is no mistaking the palpable—almost magical—transformation that almost instantly overcomes those coming into the charged atmospheres of such environments.

There is a hush—a silencing of the human world and the often chaotic energies which issue from it—an almost tangible peace; one can feel the very fabric of pure existence, like a deep, soothing cocoon that completely enfolds one. In such spaces, we find we can easily let go of thought and all its myriad offspring— care, worry and doubt —and instead indulge the God-given luxury of simply being.

Some of these atmospheric settings are the result of the pure vibrations left resonating in the wake of those who dwelled within them, and who lived exemplary lives of prayer, meditation and healing. The town of Assisi, Italy, the home the universally beloved St. Francis to this day, a deeply moving experience for many who journey there, overcome with its profound spiritual vibrancy.

Those who have extended subtle vision have described perceiving an immense, radiant energy vortex towering high above Assisi, which continues to flourish as a living testimony to the life and mission of Francesco Forgione.

Contrastingly, other naturally created high-vibrational environments such as mountains and seashores also possess powerful energetic resonance.

But whether the result of human or natural creation, these sacred spaces and power places impact us due to a continuous concentration and outpouring of and high-frequency energies.

Wherever energy fields are generated and sustained, a dynamic intelligence comes into being—a vortex of consciousness which has an organizing and ordering effect upon its immediate and extended environment and upon all those who are present within it.

LIVING WITH PYRAMID ENERGY— CHARGING YOUR DAY

It is early morning: I lie in bed, not quite ready to arise, as my awareness spans the bridge from sleep into waking. As I've done countless times before, I draw a nearby pyramid over my torso. Within a matter of seconds a subtle stimulation kindles my core, flowing through the spinal channel—the brain, throat, heart, solar plexus, pelvis and sacrum—all of which seem to fill and expand. It is a familiar yet curiously surprising experience, almost magical despite its reliable consistency through the years.

Like a silently streaming liquid, that energy galvanizes my metabolism into activity—the vital organs within the torso and the brain in particular, intensively kick-starting circulation and peristalsis.

Fully awake now, psychically and physically, I wander barefoot over the grass in my robe, embracing a tree or two, and return to meditate in a pyramid in the loft, a cockatiel contentedly nestled upon each shoulder.

Here again I feel the pyramid energy vortex converging within my upper chest, neck and head, cushioning my body within its protective embrace.

I see no angels, visions or omens; I experience no prophesies, delusions of grandeur or arcane revelations—I only feel a benign, current-like flow surrounding and infilling me.

I am not lifted instantly into transcendence, out-of-body journeys, nor endowed with miraculous powers. But if I am agitated, I find myself increasingly serene, and if weary, decidedly more restful.

Obviously, one's presence with the pyramid does not replace the need for personal spiritual initiative and practice—but in courting its presence we find the going that much easier.

Suspended above my computer workplace and my piano seat—the two places that account for the lion's share of my workday (I am a composer and a writer) is a structure known as the 9-Pyramid Grid—a potent convergence system that is a gridwork of nine contiguous down-pointing pyramids housed beneath a single, much larger upward-pointing pyramid umbrella; positioned along a convex arc, the separate energies of the nine smaller units converge into a powerful beam suffusing the region below.

If not extremely preoccupied, I feel a consistent stream of energy playing through my upper body.

This is not instant enlightenment, nor a cosmic cure-all—but rather an energetic cascade which is clearly the result of the energies of the transformation of space produced by the nine torqued down-facing pyramids and synthesized by the field of the overarching pyramid, further resonated by a strategically placed plexiglass mirror reflector, which Nick Edwards is convinced further magnifies the overall effect.

A similar phenomenon exists in the ancient pyramids of Giza, which house chambers whose purpose appears to be to act as water-containers, reflecting, when full, the dynamics of the pyramid above.

V

PYRAMIDS AS HEALING TOOLS—
ASTONISHING RECOVERIES

The following remarkable testimonies are excerpted from the second of two chapters on pyramid healing in *The Psychic Power of Pyramids* by Bill Schul and Ed Petit:

THOMAS THOMPSON, PYRAMID & CONE HEALER

"A discussion of pyramids and healing would not be complete without telling about Thomas Thompson of Vancouver, Canada, a remarkable man who for fifty years has dedicated himself to the healing and helping of others. His ability to heal has brought him a long line of followers. In his half-century of healing he has tried many methods but is quick to point out that "it is usually the seeker and the administrator getting together that actually produces the results. Understanding of the approach and the acceptance of methods of healing are important to receive a definite healing, whether it is from a doctor, the physicians, the minister or any of the different methods of healing that are currently offered," he said, and adds, "In actuality, the patients themselves are the final proof. Too often, the seeker does not realize that there is a power which can bring about the desired results."

"Thompson has used both pyramids and cones for many years in his healing work. In some instances he found that the cones worked better than the pyramids. We asked him to relate some of his healing experiences with both pyramids and cones.

He was kind enough to allow us to use the following experiences in this chapter on healing. The cases are more interesting when told in his words. The first case has to do with a type of iron-lung apparatus with pyramids placed on top of the box:

"The box was shaped like an iron lung with the head sticking out. Three pyramids were placed on top of the lid. Everyone using this box reported that all tension seemed to drain out of them in two or three minutes. They became so relaxed that invariably they would doze off to sleep. I usually woke them in twenty minutes to half an hour.

RECHARGING THE HUMAN SYSTEM WITH PYRAMID POWER

"One old gentleman used to come down every Saturday morning. He managed one of the hotels downtown and would be very hypertensive with all the things which happened in the hotel. He would stay there for an hour and come out young and vibrant again, ready for another week's work. He was only eighty-three years of age.

"Many used the box and found relief from a variety of symptoms that they couldn't seem to get rid of in any other way. The pyramids seemed to give them a new life and energy. Their minds seemed to clear of many difficulties. The healings with the pyramids and the cones took on a more definite effect when they were built to correspond with the need of the person requesting help. I incorporated the feeling of the individual into the cone or pyramid.

"Between the cones and the pyramids, the cones were the more flexible of the two to work with. I have found that the cone and the pyramid, used in many different ways, i.e., placed on the head, or the feet, or the abdomen, or wherever the person is experiencing pain, soon relieves the pain.

A SURGERY AVOIDED

"A friend of mine who had helped me demonstrate the cones many times tried to get his wife to try one for her bleeding hemorrhoids. She had suffered with them for years. They had become so bad that the doctor had prescribed surgery. My friend took a cone home but his wife tossed it in a corner because she thought it was dangerous and would have nothing to do with it. She could not throw it out because her husband would become angry. She was cleaning one day and sat down to rest. She had a funny sensation around the hemorrhoids, but when she got up to check out what was going on, the itching stopped, so she sat down again to drink her tea. When she sat down again, it started all over. Strangely, every time she got up the itching stopped and when she sat down it started again. Bewildered, she looked around and found that the cone had gotten under her chair. The next day she deliberately sat on the chair with the cone under it.

"She had an appointment with her doctor to decide whether it would be one or two weeks before the appointed surgery. The examination revealed that the hemorrhoids had shrunk and there was no need for surgery at that time. She was told to come back in a week to be checked. Every morning for that week, she sat on the chair with the cone under it. When she went to the doctor again, she knew what he was going to say because she felt so different. She felt like her whole body had changed. The doctor confirmed her feelings. She would not be having the operation.

A DIFFICULT CASE RESOLVED

"Another victory for the pyramid was a lady who had suffered for years with a problem of an abnormal tongue. Her taste, speech, and food consumption were affected, in addition to which she suffered from an extremely sore throat and her tongue was swollen and a very dark brown. She was afraid that she might be wasting on the davenport. The pyramid was placed so the point was directly over her throat.

"She was to use the pyramid for half an hour a day and phone me when there was any change. In two days, she called and the soreness had disappeared and the color was starting to change from the root of the tongue, the tip still being dark brown. She was instructed to keep up the treatments. The next day she called and asked me to come to see her. When I arrived, she stuck out her tongue at me. She was so excited. The tongue had resumed its normal size and color and she could eat food again. As an added bonus, her eyesight had improved.

RECREATING THE BODY'S ENERGETIC TEMPLATE

"The cone and pyramid took a definite part in the restoration and confidence of a young lady who was the owner of a beauty parlor in downtown Vancouver. She explained that her beauty parlor meant so much to her as she had invested $25,000 and three years of hard work. She told me of a peculiar accident that she had had a week previous.

"She had forgotten something in her house and had jumped out of her car, forgetting to put on the brake. In front of her house were two large pillars of cement which held up the walkway. She tried pushing against the car to stop it but a slight incline got the best of her and she was driven against the pillars. Her arm was smashed against the column of cement, the bone, wrist to the elbow was shattered. Someone rushed her to the doctor, but she was told that it was going to be about a year before she would be able to use the arm and hand. He put on a very heavy cast, saying that it was necessary that the cast go up to the shoulder to hold the elbow in a definite place. But he said that the difficulty was that the bone in the elbow was so shattered that they might have to take the cast off and operate to take out the little splinters of bone. He told her this so that she would not expect a quick recovery.

"She began to realize what had happened and viewed her three years of hard work going down the drain. She sensed that the beauty parlor girls would go into business for themselves and she would be ruined. A mutual friend had told her to come and see me, that I could help her.

"After a lengthy conversation, I persuaded her that I would do my best. But, I wouldn't guarantee her recovery until she could specify a definite date by which she would work toward being well. She indicated six weeks to six months as the time she had in mind. Six weeks being her preference, but six months seeming the most realistic. She was extremely concerned that I be totally honest about the length of time my treatment would cover and that I not give her any time limits that could not be met.

"I told her that in six weeks she would be back to the beauty parlor. That in itself seemed to give her hope instead of that downcast feeling she entered my office with. She said that she would go along with this time schedule. At this I told her that there were two things that she had to do: (1) Use the pyramid and (2) use the cone. I added that if she used these as I told her, she would be surprised at what would happen. She asked, 'Aren't you going to pray, aren't you going to do something else besides just using those?' I told her, 'No, you'll have to do your own praying.' I was just offering the pyramids and cones.

"A week later she returned, the pain had gone the first night. There was no more pain in her elbow or her hand. The second week she phoned to say that she was beginning to feel life in the hand and by the third week the doctor wanted to change the cast as the swelling had gone down so much.

"The break down the arm seemed to knit, the splinters seemed to disappear, and the elbow was free. By the fourth week she was washing hair in the beauty parlor and during the fifth week she was once again setting hair. At six weeks, her shoulder, hand, elbow, wrist—everything—was in order and she was operating the beauty parlor again. After that she placed pyramids on the shelf above where her customers sat while waiting. She found that this was relaxing to them while they were waiting.

AMAZING HELP FOR THE LEARNING DISABLED

"I was called one morning by a very athletic young man who asked me if I could do anything for retarded children. He told me that he had thirty children from the ages of nine to sixteen. They were all retarded and he thought it would take two years before anything could be accomplished with them. He had heard about the cones and had wondered if it would be possible for the group to be helped collectively. I suggested to him that I come to his place to see just exactly in what way I might help. I brought thirty cones with me and suggested a large pyramid be put in the center of the room.

"The day I went down I was touched by the condition of the children. He told me that they were in his charge for two years. He had a contract that each one of them would be completely well in his findings or well enough to go home. He had a waiting list of 175 others, but he couldn't possibly take more than thirty with his present situation. As I went over the entire place with him, I saw that each room had the possibility for placement of a cone. He warned me not to make the cones easily taken down because some of his patients had a habit of destroying anything that was movable. So, I sealed down some cones and left the rest loose, suggesting that there might be times when he could put the cones over the feet or over the abdomen. To my surprise, within thirty days he contacted me and suggested that I come down as soon as possible.

"When I arrived, he said, 'Mr. Thompson, I don't know whether or not I should keep those cones.' I asked what had happened. He informed me that there had been so much improvement in that month that many of the parents wanted to take their children home immediately.

"The cones seemed to have made such a vast improvement that I wondered what would have happened if he had kept them. But he had lost so much control of the situation that he asked me to remove the cones.

HEALING FOR OUR ANIMAL COMPANIONS

"I have witnessed the effects of a pyramid on animals, especially horses. I have a friend who trains race horses, raises them, and boards sick horses. He asked if I thought the pyramids would be of benefit to the horses. I suggested that a pyramid be placed in each stall above the feeding pail. He had been trained to use the pendulum and this alone showed quite a difference after just one night. He found that he did not need to keep the sick horses more than two or three days whereas before it sometimes took weeks. While watching a horse work out one day, he told me that the horse had had trouble breathing. It could only work a short time before it was blowing. Now, as far I could see, it was normal.

"Pyramids appear to have been beneficial to our pets, particularly a large German shepherd. Whereas we have had experimental pyramids around for several years, he was not allowed inside them as experiments were always in process. But when we built the large outside pyramid, he was allowed to spend some time inside. This he was eager to do and did so at every opportunity. For more than a year he had been partially crippled with arthritis, but we started noticing an amazing difference in his mobility after allowing him in the pyramid. Now, for the first time in many months, he played catch, wanted to be chased, and so on. A number of people have written to us about experiences with their pets and healing, allegedly as a result of exposing them to pyramid space:

"'Our dog Sham has always seemed to have asthma or a breathing problem, especially if she gets excited. We remembered tonight that this hasn't happened since she has been in the pyramid with our daughter.'"

A PET BREATHES FREE AGAIN

"Asthma was also mentioned by Florence McClure when we interviewed her; 'My little Boston terrier has asthma and every day she would have attacks and was unable to get her breath. She hasn't had asthma trouble since she has been getting in the pyramid with me. And I have a toy poodle that has had chronic sore throats since she had her tonsils out. Since her exposure to the pyramids she has had no more throat problems; it's entirely cleared up.'

" 'Our cocker spaniel is ten years old and has had bad rheumatism for several years. We built her a new doghouse in the shape of a pyramid. She is now starting to show some improvement.'

" 'Our dog sleeps in the garage beside the pyramid and has grown the best looking and heaviest coat of hair that we have ever seen on her. She seems to be extremely healthy now and feels better than any time we can recall.'

"Several people have mentioned that they have obtained beneficial results by treating foil inside a pyramid and then placing it under their dog's bedding. One person put the treated foil in his bird cage and reported that his bird had stopped dropping feathers and was beginning to sing again.

Healing of animals as well as humans was mentioned by Dr. Olga Worrall in the talk mentioned earlier; 'Over the years I have discovered that this healing force is not only effective in healing humans, but also dogs, cats, horses, birds, chickens, and even plants responded to this mysterious energy.'

"If the use of pyramids is beneficial to animals, as it appears to be, that should be welcome news to all animal lovers, ourselves included. But what was of particular interest to us in these reports was the evidence that we are dealing with something more than psychosomatic-type illnesses. If humans reported healing benefits and these successes could not be duplicated with animals, we would tend to suspect that the pyramid was nothing more than an effective placebo. This does not appear to be the case.

"We (Schul & Petit) have received many other reports that have not been mentioned simply because they warrant further investigation. Some of these have had to do with various serious illnesses such as cancer, tuberculosis, diabetes, and heart ailments. Due to the seriousness of these illnesses and the fact that we do not have documented information, they have not been discussed for fear of offering some people what might prove to be false hopes.

"In the two chapters on healing we have related our own experiences and those of others, and we have endeavored to offer some explanations along the way. There is nothing sacred about our explanations … we are quite sure that at best they are only partial. But we have tried to supply scientific data where possible in the hopes that it would provide a framework for greater exploration."

(End of Schul/Petit healing excerpts)

HEALING FOR A STRICKEN PET

As a lover and a breeder of cockatiels, who are my constant companions when I write and composer, nibbling my ear or sleeping on my lap—I am as distressed when they are suffering just as any devoted pet owner—because, like all beloved animal companions, they have become dear friends.

About 6 months prior to this writing, Misty, a bird I'd raised from the nest, suddenly began experiencing fits of weakness and episodes of partial paralysis after his flights, with labored, shallow breathing, to the extent that, upon several occasions, I was sure he was in the process of dying. This was followed by weeks and months of debility, weak grip, wobbly balance and inability to maintain his grip on his perch.

I immediately went into action to bring him into a healing mode, sequestering him for long periods of time—every night and goodly portions of the day—in a small carrying cage under which I placed two 4 x 6 x 1—inch ceramic magnets, taking care to expose him to the negative field—a field which, in this case, extends more than 8 inches and penetrates all solids, including living bodies, and which is widely known to be anti-inflammatory and pathogen-killing.

I covered the inside floor-space of the cage with two large Tachyon energy discs, whose effectiveness I had empirically experienced on many prior occasions, and which I knew to be genuinely helpful. And finally, I covered the cage each night with a well-made cardboard pyramid with a 12-inch base.

While Misty clearly disliked his new and confining quarters, and vociferously complained about his being separated from his beautiful, beloved yellow mate Aggie, I kept this regimen up many—but not all—nights thereafter.

His was not an overnight recovery, and there were several subsequent episodes of fits and paralysis, during which I would hold him and generate energy—as well as much love—into his trembling body, which leaned passively against my palms, willing and watching for him to recover his breath and his energy.

At many points, we observed him struggling stay on his perch, or painfully trying to climb up the ladder to his feed tray—never mind fly—a truly heart-wrenching sight.

But as the weeks and months passed, I noticed that when I would take the once-ornery but recently unresisting Misty into my hands, he began to put up a much feistier struggle than before, suggesting more energy was stirring within him.

Each day he struggled and scrambled with greater force, until—with the growing absence of episodes of weakness—it was clear he had entered the land of the living again; he was his old, cantankerous self, stubborn and taking no nonsense.

In those intervening months I had grown lax about locking Misty's cage door because he was in no condition to go anywhere, but increasingly he had taken it upon himself to slip the unlocked door up and escape, taking furious, free-ranging flights about the room—flights, I hasten to add, followed by no ill aftereffects.

INSIDE PYRAMID ENERGY HEALING: THE FLANAGAN RESEARCH

In his *Pyramid Power II—The Scientific Evidence*, a now rare companion volume to *Pyramid Power*, Patrick Flanagan collated the most up-to-date hard research in pyramid power. While sophisticated in style, it rewards scrutiny.

In it, he states,

> There appear to be two separate but related effects which contribute to the total 'effect' of structure configurational energy relationships. There is the property of the structure to act as a wave guide to capture, focus and transduce cosmic energy of the electromagnetic spectrum (energy originating from outside the earth system). A structure such as a pyramid chamber acts as a resonator to collect energy and focus this energy. An example of a structure which 'captures' energy is the crystalline antenna of a crystal radio. This crystal captures the radio frequency electromagnetic energy, amplifies it, and transduces it to electrical signals which power the speaker. The second effect is the use of a shape which has highly reflective inside material so that almost all energy generated inside is kept inside and is not lost to the environment. Energy is thus added to that of

the internal system by recycling of the energy given off by the system.

In both cases one sees an increase in energy for any system which is placed with the pyramid structure. The question then becomes, does the existence of the added energy reinforce or cancel the energy processes naturally occurring within the pyramid structure? Effects of this added energy influx to various systems by use of reflective pyramid structures has been documented in hopes of answering this question, and hopefully to note the general characteristics of systems whose energy processes are positively reinforced and those which are canceled. Note that in general the flow of energy through a system tends to organize the system. This may be interpreted as saying that in general the negentropy (tendency toward order) of a system is increased or that entropy (tendency toward disorder) of a system is decreased. The question then is rephrased in these entropic terms.

One of several theories shared is that pyramidal structures act as reflectors,". . .and as such will refocus energy fields emitted by items (or persons) placed inside the structure back into (those) items (or persons) so that the energy could be re-used."

The other pyramid energy theory involves the action of the pyramid as a 'tuned' waveguide or cavity resonator. In this theory, random energy fluctuations of cosmic origin (outside the earth) are assembled by the pyramid structure into a coherent standing wave of energy whose wavelength is determined by the geometry and physical dimensions of the structure. This externally concentrated energy field would then have an effect on substances treated inside.

The Czechoslovakian engineer Karel Drbal has indeed demonstrated that the pyramid shape acts as a high efficiency elecromagnetic resonator. He further proved that the shape could focus enough energy to create powerful physical effects on both organic substances and inorganic crystals such as that found in high quality razor blades.

Our own research at the Innergy Laboratories in Tucson, Arizona has shown that the pyramid structure acts as a high efficiency cavity resonator for both acoustic and electromagnetic energies.

There are dozens of claims for pyramid effects that are not supported by any type of valid research. Unfortunately it is hard to separate fact from fiction when it comes to pyramid claims. Most pyramid researchers are not trained in the scientific method, and therefore do not know how to set up proper research protocols.

In the mid-1970's, Mankind Research Foundation, with the financial aid of Ms. Frances vos Sacher, hired a dozen independent scientists and testing laboratories to conduct a controlled study on the alleged pyramid effect. The scientists chosen for the job were among the best in their respective fields. These men have impeccable credentials, and have all published in numerous journals of science.

The research protocols for the various projects were carefully designed to ensure that the testing was done according to well established scientific methodology."

A few among Flanagan's many findings:

1. The growth rate of bacteria is markedly decreased (from 50%-25%)—throat bacteria probability of chance results at 0.05 (half of a percent) and yeast bacteria growth probability of chance results of approximately 0.10 (one percent).

2. Sleeping within a pyramid structure tends to create an energized state upon awakening.

3. The growth rate of black-eyed peas and lima beans is increased at a probability level of chance results of 0.06 and 0.26 respectively.

4. Raw hamburger meat is relatively preserved at a probability level of chance results of 0.001.

Dr. Patrick Flanagan has personally shared the interesting insight that the pyramid torsion field effect can be further enhanced by exposure to an active air current, such as positioning a simple fan so that it blows through the structure.

VI

TORSION FIELDS: THE INNER DYNAMICS OF PYRAMID ENERGY

Dr. Patrick Flanagan is now convinced that the underlying matrix for the delivery of pyramid energy is comprised of torsion fields—standing spiral wave-forms. A full-length article on the subject by Brendan D. Murphy, excerpted below, can be found in the appendices at the end of this book, as well as online, at: http://blog.world-mysteries.com/science/ancient-pyramid-technology-for-the-golden-age/

ANCIENT PYRAMID TECHNOLOGY FOR THE GOLDEN AGE

by Brendan D. Murphy

Torsion fields are generated by spin or angular momentum; any object or particle that spins produces torsion waves and possesses its own unique torsion field. This is neither a magnetic phenomenon, nor an electrical one, though torsion has been referred to as "pseudo-magnetism" by at least one researcher. Since torsion fields influence spin states, one object's torsion field can be changed by the influence or application of an external torsion field. "As a result of such an influence, the new configuration of the torsion field will be fixed as a metastable state (as a polarized state) and will remain intact even after the source of the external torsion field is moved to another area of space. Thus, torsion fields of certain spatial configuration can be 'recorded' on *any*...object." (emphasis added)

The realization of the unique properties of torsion fields immediately suggests compelling links to various psi or parapsychological phenomena: the "charging" of an object with intent in voodoo; the informational recording of events in "inert matter" so that the record can later be "read" by a "psychometrist"; spoon bending and other psychokinetic phenomena; telepathy and more. While we lack the space for even a small survey of such literature here, the theme of primary interest for us is the link that has been established between torsion fields, the physical morphology (form-nature) of building structures (pyramids in particular), and consciousness.

PYRAMIDS AS "TORSION SIPHONS"

Russian and Ukranian research into pyramids has yielded some very interesting results regarding torsion waves. The Russians found that the pyramid shape naturally harnesses torsion waves emanating from the earth, as if amplifying them. It has been experimentally established that objects that feature the Golden Section, which expresses Phi (1.618) or phi (0.618), can be described as passive torsion generators. In point of fact, objects featuring the phi ratio of 0 to 0.618 made the best passive torsion generators in the research carried out at the Physics Institute of the Ukraine Academy of Sciences and at Chernovitsky University by the Akimov group. The logical inference to make, then, is that torsion waves are indeed phi spirals. This spiraling force in the vacuum/aether (a virtual aether, or hyperdimensional domain—not the lumeniferous aether of the late 19th century) can enhance not only biological functions, but psycho-spiritual operations as well, as we see in a moment.

ENHANCING THE MIND WITH PYRAMID POWER

Various researchers consider torsion waves as being synonymous or identical with consciousness itself—an idea I elaborate on at length in TGI 1. Since torsion waves are a fundamental and ubiquitous feature of the cosmos we can therefore see how consciousness is also; consciousness has a real and detectable force which can act on the environment both locally and remotely. Suddenly the notion of something like psychokinesis is not so 'paranormal." For author Sol Luckman (creator of the Regenetics Method), terms like prana, chi, and orgone are just different names for "the light-based aspect of...torsion energy." Thus, harnessing more torsion also means harnessing more light, and possibly facilitating "enlightenment."

In Russian jails, pyramid power reduced criminal behavior in a total population of about 5,000 prison inmates. By storing crystalline substances in one of the fibreglass pyramids built under the direction of Dr. Alexander Golod, and later distributing those objects through the jails, the incidence of criminal behavior within the jails virtually disappeared within a few months. The decrease in incidence of criminal behavior obviously suggests a corresponding increase in feelings of peacefulness and goodwill among the inmates within the facilities involved in this research. (Perhaps we should have a Golden Section pyramid built near the Pentagon?)

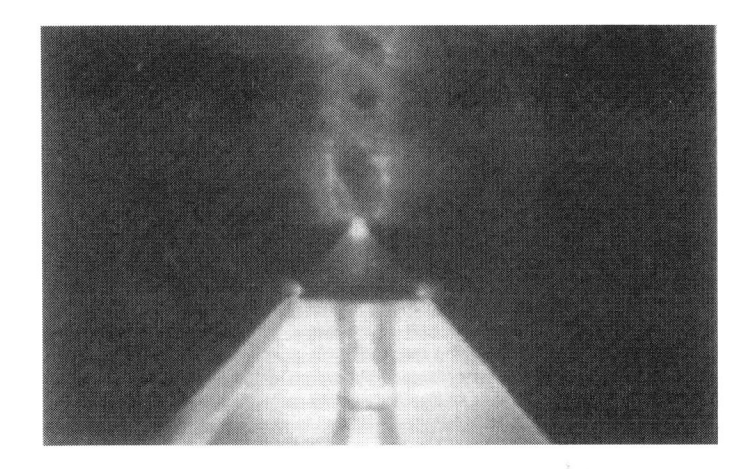

THE PYRAMID RESEARCH OF JAROSLAW MIRONSKI

(Reproduced, in the English, by permission of Jaroslaw Mironski)

Shri Yantra, literally means 'sacred tool'—or in contemporary language—'structure,' 'device,' 'matrix,' or 'form by or through which a process may fulfill itself. It is one of the oldest complex geometries of mankind, dating back some 12,000 years. It symbolizes the essence of God and the dynamics of creation in triangles representing the male and female energies.

Patrick Flanagan has discovered that the action of Shri Yantras on the etheric level is similar to that of the great pyramid of Cheops. He is convinced that, through meditation on the Yantra diagram we can experience and explore our subtle energy and spiritual essence.

In the following section, Jaroslaw Mironski, a contemporary Polish pyramid researcher and architect, shares highly provocative and inspiring ideas about pyramids and pyramidology that seem worthy of consideration and exploration.

SACRED GEOMETRY & COSMIC SOUND TRANSMISSION

Mironski believes that the proportions of intersecting pyramids create a fractal electric field, a design perfectly attuned to the vibrations of the heart and to the source of the universe, allowing one's energy field to open and expand.

His empirical experience with intersecting pyramid energies has convinced him that the presence of such energy fields enhances our freedom from false emotions such as fear and guilt, can repair DNA, awaken intuition, and a sense of connection with—rather than separation from—others, thereby improving interpersonal relationships. For him, holy geometry is virtually a gospel—a matrix which is the root cause of everything that was, is and will be, revealing the essential unity of all things, and fulfilling the underlying relationship between the structure of space, music, mathematics geometric forms and the processes of life.

THE SONG OF THE PYRAMID

The ancient Egyptians claimed that holy geometry is nothing but frozen music, the graphic or architectural equivalent of sound and harmony of the cosmos.

The Pythagoreans taught that the cosmos produces sounds in perfect harmony, sounds which are the most exquisite music, inaudible to us both because of their sublimity and the imperfections of our hearing. French physicist Joel Steinheimer stated that a properly selected sound is able to transform our cellular system, and even the information contained in our DNA. The human aura is an integral part of the vibrating universe, and is filled with vibrations that penetrate deeply into its molecular structure.

From this basis of knowledge emerged music therapy, 'vibrational massage,' and the sound-world and richness of Indian mantras. Each mantra has a corresponding graphic form, or so-called Yantra—a visual pattern incorporating Sacred Geometry.

Legendary Hopi shamans knew this phenomenon to the extent that they could chant words in such a way that the sand immediately formed geometric patterns. (Indeed, sand poured upon a drum head will take on symmetrical patterns when the drum is struck).

Today the science of cymatics can reveal all this to us. As the frequencies re-pattern the notes on the screen we see a true 'tonoscopic' evolution of simple designs into increasingly beautiful and more complex mandalas.

The discoverer of cymatics, Dr. Hans Jenny, proved this by displaying the mantra OM on the tonoscope, or 'sound screen.' As the "Oooooooou" began to appear in circles, a series of triangles in the middle and with the articulation of the "M" appeared in a clear outline of the classic Shri Yantra. This finding tallies well with former NASA physicist and healer Barbara Brennan's clear observation that the chakras or energy vortexes of those who chant specific syllables and frequencies will have the immediate effect of enlivening depleted bio-energies and causing the force-lines or 'petals' of those chakras to become buoyant and healthy again. Sound is energy.

In this way, it was discovered that the geometry of the Yantra is the "frozen music" of the mantra 'Om' (Aum). We begin to understand why meditation with or within the (3-dimensional) Yantra (of the pyramid) gives the same or similar results as hours of chanting the mantra Om. In addition to its extremely subtle inherent energies, the pyramid affects us as a spatial Yantra—that is, a self-actualizing sacred form.

Joel Steinheimer observed again that the note A (436 Herz) comes into resonance within the chamber of the royal pyramids of Giza. In our own era, however, there has been an increase of vibrations on our planet, causing the standardized A to now be 440 Herz. All the evidence points to the fact that our brains now react at a much higher frequency than in the past. Therefore, Mironski believes we need increasingly complex pyramids.

"Pyramids meet humanity's needs for the New Era. By interacting with pyramids we can penetrate the mystery of the universe, access inner wisdom and naturally activate the Merkaba—or 'Vehicle of Ascension'—by which all our innate potentialities are fulfilled without any special effort on our part. This opens us to the transcendent possibilities of the Spirit." (Mironski)

Mironski explains his theory that the appearance of three-dimensional pyramidal forms featuring a downward-facing—or 'female' triangle intersecting an upward -facing—or 'male'— triangle implies that in humanity's task in this era will be to activate the feminine or intuitive faculties and balance them with the already developed masculine forces—intelligence, entrepreneurship, growth and technological initiative.

With this symbol comes the Jewish "Star of David"—also the eternal emblem of the Anahata chakra, through which we derive a sense of emotional security, relationships with people, goodness, intuition, empathy and love.

Following, we quote, with permission, extensive excerpts from the writing and research of Jaroslaw Mironski. While not always in the most flawless of English, the text clearly conveys the passion of an explorer who harbors no doubts about the power of pyramids and of their potential to endow almost every area of human life with benefit.

And despite obvious technical differences between counterposed and regular pyramids, many of Mironski's overall findings, as quoted below, largely hold true for all skillfully constructed pyramids—the classical Cheops, but particularly those conforming to the Nubian—or more vertical—design.

"When we interact with the complementary love energies of the male and female, it is possible to create something that the world has never before seen: new currents in art or philosophy, and truly great works, of which the greatest is in a new human being.

"The Ideal functioning of the Anahata center therefore results in the discovery of God-the-Creator within ourselves. It is only when we love in this way that we bring Heaven to Earth, and do no harm to anyone here in creating own paradise."

PRANA (LIFE FORCE)

"Pyramids attract a stream of particles of prana (vital energy) from the environment, sometimes seen with the naked eye as a fine, white mist or golden light.

"Smog, electrosmog, noise, pesticides, pollution, radioactive substances, poisons in water and food, and stress tend to consume or destroy prana, and to deplete our energy reserves. Personal power is consumed in the effort to counteract this degeneration and leaving us with lowered reserves of life-force with which to fulfill our goals and desires, and to fulfill our humanity.

"Pyramids as an invaluable aid in our troubled times. Once within these structures we feel as if they have taken a refreshing shower after a tiring journey in the heat and dust. We experience these results only when we are in the field of a functioning pyramid. Pyramid energy cannot overdose us! Just as one cannot pour more fuel into a tank than it can accommodate, so also, we can't become more than full.

THE PROTECTIVE FIELD

"Planet Earth is surrounded by a 'cocoon' to protect life from deadly cosmic radiation, and this also screens out our perception of finer energies. This permits us to experience only a three-dimensional perception of reality. We 'stew in our own juice,' so to speak, and, without appropriate antennas or receivers, we are unable to perceive other frequencies. Up until the present, only particularly sensitized individuals have been able to penetrate through this heavy, earthly vibration in order to experience such cosmic dynamics.

"We are currently undergoing a great transformation of the Earth wherein we all become more sensitized. Wherever we resist the mystical ability to awaken within ourselves, and where rigid beliefs resist the natural changes, there will be slower evolution and more suffering.

"The pyramid pulls this cosmic energy into our functional range of perception. The interior (of the pyramid) blends these cosmic energies with accumulated earth energies. This 'blend' of external energies and prana conjoined creates what we call the Yantra Energy Pyramid (2 counterposed pyramids).

"With its powerful, cosmic light, this energy is 'digestible' — or absorbable — by living beings and does not cause the turbulence or agitation that many people feel as a result of the energetic transition to the Aquarian Age.

"For example, on February 8, 2012 news went around the world that the solar system ran into an interstellar energy cloud. At the same time it was observed that over the many pyramids in the world a clear pole of luminous energy could be seen with the naked eye. Researchers at the time speculated that perhaps the pyramid acts as a kind of safety valve for such high energy encounters.

"For us, it was nothing new! The fact that each pyramid is used to stabilize the magnetic field of our planet, was written about almost a century before. Wherever pyramid energy issues forth becomes, in a short time, a special place of power, full of cosmic pulsations. It manifests as a bioactive field which protects us from all kinds of external stresses (electrosmog, noise or frequencies associated with harmful radiation, etc.), strengthening the processes of physical purification (detoxification) and making it easy to excrete it all that harmful. Our body and soul begin to truly 'breathe' — or function freely.

"Therefore, anyone who installs energy pyramids, creates benefits not only for himself, but also for his immediate environment and the planet as a whole.

PYRAMID POWER AND PERFORMANCE

"The power experienced from the pyramids increases from the time of their assembly and comes to full strength after about

4-6 weeks. During this time, a powerful stream of pyramid energy creates a more vital aura that becomes wider and more strongly saturated through time. Its size and intensity depends on the size and the pyramid, as well as the degree of contamination by the surrounding earth and terrain. The presence of a sphere inside the energy pyramid gives it a much larger radius and further strengthens its intensity.

"In addition, these structures complement each other, creating a network of luminous energy. Their influence increases in proportion to their number.

"Most people easily feel this incredible energy. In order to do so, simply move your left hand to the side of the pyramid to feel the impression of a gentle breeze, not unlike the extremely pleasant coolness as a refreshing breeze during a hot day. When, by gently inserting a hand into the pyramid space, we can sense a clear difference in the climate of the pyramid, we feel within its interior a 'different humidity', another nature of pressure.

HOME PYRAMIDS MODELS

"These units almost literally change the atmosphere of the rooms they are in. In the apartments in which they are positioned, they function as 'cleansers,' encouraging reflection, meditation, prayer, dreams, constructive plans and projects.

"I must stress that pyramids work outside, and that one does not have to enter them. In this sense, the energy of the outdoor models is comparable to the action of a waterfall. While it is a great pleasure to breathe the air right next to a waterfall, suffused with sunlight and moisture, and we might feel we would like to remain there, or at least relax there, we can only bear a strong stream of direct water for so long.

"Inside the pyramid, sensitive people feel a pleasant vibrational energy or flow of "power" through the body as if they were in the presence of a gifted healer. A common phenomenon is a sense of the disappearance of gravity, or even the disappearance of one's body. It is then that we begin to understand that we are spiritual beings.

"Typical also tend to be colorful visions and other metaphysical experiences; there are often creative ideas, uprising of memories from the past or even from past lives. Some people spontaneously perceive errors they have been making or receive answers to important questions. There are sometimes also cases of spontaneous enlightenment.

"To recharge ourselves with a greater amount of energy, we should come to the pyramid facing east and lay hands on the axis in such a way that they do not touch each other. It is necessary to relax at the knees (as if they were the shock absorbers of a car), as strained leg muscles block both energy flow and subtle feelings.

"During this 'energy bath' we can focus on observations of signals coming from the body and the soul, but it is best to give attention at this time to one's dreams and goals. If we are sufficiently strong and in harmony with the Great Plan, a benign, universal current carries them into manifestation.

"A 15 to 30 minute 'energy dip' in the pyramid will fill us with energy that stays with us, diminishing gradually, for a period of up to several weeks.

"People who clearly feel the pulsing of the pyramid as being hot are usually heavily toxic (common in the industrial world) and are simply undergoing a process of purification. At first glance, they may experience severe sweats and a variety of unpleasant symptoms, including unconsciousness. This means that they need some time before they attain their natural condition and begin to feel the return of the universal prana or 'cosmic breath.'

"Those who are overwhelmed by pyramid (energy, and who experience) a sensation of piercing cold (and lack of energy), are usually under the influence of disembodied beings or other energy-stressors.

"Under the influence of the pyramids, people feel a strong charge and strengthen their inner vitality. The pyramid works on all living organisms. There are garden or outdoor models for various species of birds and mammals, who will even come despite the presence of domestic animals! Throughout the year we are continuously accompanied by birdsong and see many other bird species, of whose existence of which we had no preconceived notions.

"Many creatures make frequent stops to be in our beautiful pyramid specimens—pigeons flock here, neighborhood cats, families of hedgehogs, and even foxes. Small children as well as animals are attracted to them, and one does not do not need to say or do anything to convince them—they instinctively want to be near these structures, and at times of crisis will come inside them. Living beings instinctively feel that they can use this energy to regenerate. My dogs and cats are also very eager to recharge themselves in this way, especially when something is wrong with them, or before roaming outdoors.

"A similar sensitivity to the pyramid reveals itself throughout the whole of nature. My garden grows into an amazement of unusual, almost tropical luxuriance. Plants grow like crazy, and some bloom 2-3 times during the season.

"For example, shortly after bringing home for the winter a new pyramid model autumn flowers bloomed all at once, datura and Christmas cactus—i revealed their beauty at the same time ... Even Yucca palm—which is virtually impossible (to grow) in the home—bloomed, and in our climate! - Every night we were literally drowning in the intoxicating scent of these exotic flowers.

"The power of Nature, which allows us to grow and mature flowers, is as intrinsically benign to us humans as it is to the plant world. Its presence supports our will and power, strengthens the personality, raises awareness of the integrity of the inner self. It also evokes the power of love and warm feelings toward each other, the world and people.

"People living or working in the energy field have a higher and more rarefied vibration, and a much more subtle aura, which can be seen and felt. I perceive pyramid-users as being "rarer," "lighter" and more ethereal. They become, in a very real sense, more human beings—more friendly and willing to focus upon their inner unity.

"This makes it possible, when the pyramids are aligned, to have harmonious relationships. Where there are significant differences of opinion, people much more quickly (tend to) reach agreement. All 'emotional charge' is removed before it becomes armed conflict.

"The strong charge of life energy also has a beneficial effect on the quality and taste of our meals, and on the energy of the tap water (though I would not advise experimenting with Polish "tap water"). Simply place the container of water into the interior and the difference will be felt after a few minutes. I checked also the changes that were taking place in an ordinary table wine, which has stood for some time in the pyramid. Wine tasters lose their (usual) orientation. Food can also be placed in the newly pyramid field in order to partially neutralize its harmful contents. small pyramid can be taken on every trip. (One) can not imagine accommodation in any dwelling, even the most luxurious hotel, without this wonderful energy.

PYRAMID AURA PHOTOGRAPHY

EXPERIMENTAL RESULTS

"My aura was photographed after traveling over 1,000 miles by car to Vienna (photo left), an arduous journey in the middle of a hot summer. Virtually all of my aura appears to be the color of ketchup and indeed, there can be seen traces of dark red, illustrating the aftereffects of experiencing motorway aggression. There is a large amount of bright red, but it shows activity (without nervousness), and orange and yellow creatively — indicating the presence of a joyful attitude. The green section shows the beginning of the process of purification and regeneration. - and is the result of many years of working with pyramids.

"Another photo, taken after a few minutes of meditation in the garden pyramid reveals the aura unexpectedly broadened and transformed into the color to a pale lilac, indicating the dynamic of a great mystic, a visionary, a telepath ... one who, more than anyone else, sees and knows. (The enclosing dark background right above the head is not an aura, but the lack of it, and is the effect of holding a pyramid—rather than the electrode—in the left hand.) According to research specialists, it is a result absolutely impossible to achieve in such a short time!—presenting a state of mind similar to that of a child safely cuddled in her mother's arms. In civilized adults this is only possible after many years of practice in an environment such as a Tibetan monastery.

"With an aura of bright red, while you can act in every sphere, it is more difficult to access inner wisdom. Through the work with the energy of the pyramids at any time we are able to put aside emotions tormenting us, to come into full contact with our higher self, and, after some time—return to our real jobs and normal activity full of energy. The Spirit becomes present in our actions and enables us, without wandering, to achieve our goals.

THE EXPERIENCES OF PYRAMID EXPERIMENTERS

"(The) outstanding dowser Kirlian Kurlus discovered that almost everyone who uses the garden model pyramid has a biofield output radiating colors similar to those of the halo of saints. The Bovis scale increases from a normal level of 6.5 thousand units to approximately 80 - 100 thousand! It requires just a few minutes of relaxation for a completely exhausted person to restore the desire to resume movement. Thus reinforced, the body rapidly identifies and removes toxins, cleanses and regenerates itself.

"Pyramids attract cosmic energy, thus activating the much more subtle forces of spirit. They help to protect us not only against negative earth energies, but also against radiation, and even electrosmog and the effects unhealthful food, as a strong body will immediately expel any toxins.

"Our daily struggle with stress, noise, electrosmog and radiation is a constant one. When we are tense, excessively vigilant, and all our energy is co-opted in order to neutralize negative influences, we have no energy remaining with which to feel the subtle vibrations of love and reverence.

"The presence of pyramids raises our vibration and changes the structure of the energy body, creating a grid of large, permeable openings or apertures. As a result, pyramids cause us to become more 'rarefied' and transparent; thus any impediments or obstructions pass through us like water through a mesh screen and they are not able to harm us. Without spending our energy reserves, we regain our original spiritual strength and joy.

"Until now, a person searching for contact with his inner self or with God had to isolate himself in a monastery most of his life.

Probing deep spiritually was only possible in the process of silent meditation, far from the bustle of everyday of life.

Active, working people are usually far removed from the realization that God exists within themselves. That is why we have such a crisis in spiritual awareness in our world, severely felt in politics, business and the financial spheres.

"Within the space of the pyramid, we are able to move between states of consciousness as easily as if we were walking from one room into another. "At any (given) time we are able to push away self-debilitating emotions and achieve full contact with our higher self. Then, filled with energy, we may return to our daily tasks and activities. Not unlike the energy paradigm of Aikido, which teaches that the best way to replenish one's force is not merely to rest, but to re-establish the natural flow of out-flowing and incoming 'ki' or life energy, pyramids are by no means passive environments, but rather dynamic catalysts which encourage our systems to restore this intake and expulsion of energy.

"Our own experiments prove that every pyramid user can be a spiritual mystic as well as a man of action. Thanks to this capacity, the spirit becomes present in all of our activities and we can achieve our goals without getting lost in the outer levels of life.

SIGNIFICANT BENEFITS FOR PYRAMID USERS

"The first law of nature is the desire for one's own happiness."

Jeremy Bantham

"As the pyramid's subtle force flows into us it implements the great plan of spiritual purification. It is a wonderful "medicine" for our modern loss of orientation, our overall frustration and collapse of values. Gently we are 'enforced' to come into alignment with the underlying laws and principles of nature that are part of the Grand Design of Life.

"Pyramids help clear the mind and to bring us into the Void (or Silence), where everything takes on a new beginning. This leads to the delineation of new, far more interesting life paths and alternatives. Encouraged to focus on the inner creative power, we can work together - the forces of the spirit—to create a better world.

"The pyramid fills us with vital energy, optimism and a boundless sense of security. In the presence of this vibration every person has a chance to experience how great is the gift of life.

HEALTHFUL SLEEP

"Through being charged with pranic energy, we miraculously experience much better sleep and vitality for our recreational life. Any disturbances of sleep, in most cases, disappear quickly. Depending on individual needs and stresses, (the need for) sleep either gradually or dramatically diminishes or else increases, but, in either case, always becomes deeper and strongly regenerative.

"In the first days or weeks after the procuring of the pyramid, people who are greatly depleted or toxic fall into a kind of healing "coma." This is a sign that they have been in great need of regeneration. It is highly beneficial to give oneself up to this need. Pyramid energy raises our vibration, and this is much more easily achieved with a dormant (quiescent) mind. In any case, one has to get accustomed to this new energy. After a period of time, everything usually comes into balance.

"People who are healthy and active, if they begin meditating, experience reduced need for sleep, thereby gaining many extra hours and experiencing a new way of life. They feel regenerated and motivated to seek new paths and solutions. Their new supply of strength and great enthusiasm seeks new ways of expressing themselves.

"When this energy is not directed into constructive work or recreation, this new wakefulness can become burdensome. Generally, the power flowing from the pyramids 'dislikes' stagnation and seems to always push the pyramid-user forward, into the search for new paths and activities, leading to eventual fulfillment.

"A small pyramid, set in the bedroom—particularly away from sources of radiation, such as computers—exercises a positive influence on the content of dreams. Many people have observed that dreams have become colorful, expressive, feature films, logical, sometimes warning and extremely helpful in the struggle with daily troubles.

"The most astonishing phenomenon here is the extension of REM sleep, which must be associated with a sudden, increased production of melatonin. Everything indicates that the presence of pyramids has a positive effect on the brain! (We are) waiting for progressive scholars who wish to study this phenomenon with scientific methods. Frequent—even fantastic—dreams (as well as unusual visions and daydreams) are themselves an invaluable aid in raising awareness and problem-solving. In the realm of dreams, the intellect does not block the channel to awareness, through which much critical information emerges. And the ascending energy is conducive to establishing a deeper contact with one's soul (or superconscious).

PYRAMID-FACILITATED THERAPY

" . . .pyramid energy provides an extremely strong impact on the solar plexus—our centre. It strengthens the vegetative nervous system and changes our perception of reality. It 'speaks to' anyone who has problems with a sense of security, or who suffers from depression and who has trouble sensing the meaning of life. It allows us to open the gateways to deep peace, confidence and strength, and allows us to deal with problems on this level much more easily.

"Finally It enables us to adopt other therapeutic methods, make new decisions and find the strength to carry them out.

"In many cases, pyramid-users find themselves releasing addictions to excess smoking or eating, overwork or even to the wrong partner. Many automatically become aware of emotions which may be blocking their progress, as well as spiritual wounds that require healing. For this reason, any hypnotic regression therapies undertaken under the aegis of these pyramids are shorter and much more efficient.

"In any case, the depths of the unconscious become more transparent and more issues are spontaneously solved! With skillful methods of clearing, one can rid oneself of even the most intense of past traumas. (The pyramid design) has proven itself many times as a basic interior design within which courses in yoga and group meditations, workshops, esoteric and motivational training are conducted. And because it adds vitality, it can also be an invaluable aid for massage therapists or physiotherapists.

PYRAMID ENERGY & RELATIONSHIPS

"The presence of pyramids strengthens the heart lotus, which discreetly prompts the opening of the channel of love. In this way we can get out of each others' way and develop a boundless sense of emotional security and foster the correct attitude to one's self, one's partner, one's friends and other people. We awaken to the deep LOVE and - through a deep understanding - to reach out even to the (perceived) enemy. As we begin to see what we have in common, we experience a chance to rise to the level at which our differences, opinions and views are less important.

"A sense of common unity comes to us, (even while) taking into account the uniqueness of each. The language of love is an international language - a universal one. It creates a positive base for communication and mental understanding between people. This leads to the removal of prejudices in the international arena. With a little good will, a world of old conflicts can be removed and we can achieve a lot together. It is extremely desirable to install the pyramids in conference rooms, especially where people from different cultural arenas meet.

ACCESS TO WISDOM

"Energy pyramids encourage reflection, meditation and exploration within oneself—where the answers to all the important questions lie. Using (the pyramid) during sleep, meditation, or in moments of relaxation, releases the energy from which we draw knowledge. For this very wisdom, yogis practice and meditate for decades in solitary confinement, and spend years of chanting the mantra Om.

"Pyramid-users do not need to do this. At these moments of creative reverie, pyramids replace (even) the best meditation techniques. In many cases, there is a spontaneous spiritual enlightenment the same as that which is achieved after years of monastic meditation. Knowledge and understanding are then deepened by leaps and bounds. The crowning achievement of MIND is dedicated to this great knowledge of the laws that govern our destiny and happiness, the opening to the cosmos, new ideas and new technologies.

NEW IDEAS

"People are constantly looking for new ways and solutions. This energy in fact opens us to inspiration, creativity and awakens the desire to make changes or improvements - in one's self, in the home, business and the environment. Many followers suddenly solve problems or answers to important questions (if they ask!). Previous inventions are always based on the same eternal principles and are merely modified, much as the principle of 'making fire' in a cave. Whether it Is a steam engine or an 'improved' internal combustion engine - they function on one and the same principle. Now we learn to overcome time and space, go where no one has gone ... We are lifted up to unknown heights, and, to use a technical analogy—approach the condition of a 'spacecraft'. We see then, that we can be radically different - to think, to feel, to receive a reality, create, build and operate.

SPIRITUAL FRUITS

"A huge number of users observe mental stabilization, developed while achieving ever-present inner PEACE. It allows us to assess each situation with a cool detachment. One of the most wonderful benefits is liberation from fear and a surge towards true freedom. It always makes me happy when another pyramid user reports back to me about peace, or a newly acquired skill, or a growing tolerance for others.

"In many cases, (pyramids can) overcome the so-called observed phenomenon of being a 'gene slave' (a victim of one's genetics). The history of human genetics is nothing but an endless list of mutual conquests. Constantly fighting for spheres of influence, they either subordinate or are subordinated by each other.

"It is not our desire to discuss here whether or not we are the result of genetic manipulation by aliens, (or whether) this (may have been) the plan of the Creator. In either case, the presence in our bodies of 'genetic enslavement' or limitation hinders our true development and our full process of cognition.

"If we are truly going to establish ourselves in a higher dimension, we need to overcome the limitations and fears which control our actions (and reactions). My wife—by overcoming gross obesity—is proof that genes do not (need to) affect us, or at least that we may overcome their influence when we focus on recreating our lives. Scientists have also been able to prove that we are able to overcome genetic predispositions (see video on Youtube, "Bruce Lipton—The New Biology—Where Mind and Matter Meet"). So all is ultimately in our hands.

INTUITION

"Every user of pyramids has observed that, from month to month, there is a great increase in intuitive feelings! This gradually renews contact with the higher 'I' lost in childhood as a result of unthinking obedience to the adult world ... and this again opens (the door) to the inner voice! This 'Inner whisperer' is an infallible advisor If you listen carefully, through which we are capable of perceiving the true intentions of others, no matter what their hidden motives may be. Nobody is able to tell us what to believe, what to buy, how to live our life; Then, without getting mired in details, we are able to discriminate as to what is good for us and what is destructive, and one's being is the best expert. This gives us freedom from the need for intermediaries to God, health and knowledge. This generates a sense of confidence, security and strength.

GROWTH/SELF-AWARENESS

"Connection with our interior allows us to become much more aware of one's self and the role we wish to play in this life.

We discover that we are the only presence in the world, unique and exceptional. We recognize our own value and pyramidal 'awakening' reminds us of the enormity of internal capacity. We would like now to express our greatness and we are ready for great things.

"We enter upon our true path; we do what we love and we live for that to which we are called. This is best evidenced by various writers who found a new source of creative power, able to reveal the fullness of their talent. Much like artists - the abundance of constantly flowing energy from the pyramid inspires every person to fulfill him or herself through the art to which he was appointed—the abundant energy that has opened the gates of the wealth of the universe, gaining access to the true abundance.

"For this reason, many entrepreneurs have also attributed to the pyramid an almost magical influence on the fulfilling of interest, often declaring the experience of an expanded sphere of influence, with multiplied profits and unexpected, new, interesting, even brilliant solutions. Often unusual ideas come in dreams or just suddenly come into one's head. There is nothing surprising in this, as in the case of business people, we can speak with a high concentration of thought, focused toward a specific purpose. Pyramids reinforce our thought forms, making our thoughts into intense, effective prayer. This always leads to accomplishment. Over time, we begin to understand that life—the process of existence and creation—is to fulfill plans, achieve goals—is truly a joy; we rejoice in every moment and all the attractions each situation offers us in our earthly life!

CONTROL OF THE MIND

"Our deepest dreams can come true, if in a methodical way we create around ourselves thought forms full of happiness and prosperity. American researcher Patrick Flanagan proved that placing a replica of (a) Cheops (pyramid) upon a person's head, when the eyes are closed, causes the brain to produce alpha waves. These waves appear as we move into higher states of consciousness.

"Human consciousness possesses the power of creation. Pyramids lead us to higher levels of awareness (theta, and even delta — the goal of yogic practice). Pyramids enhance all these, and even a fleeting thought or feeling. One could easily say that the field of the pyramid sustains — or nourishes — thought forms, which, in their realization or manifestation, magnetically attract the right people and events, transforming our longings into reality!

"(In pyramids) we are dealing with an incredibly powerful source of cosmic energy. Through becoming superconscious, everything becomes possible for us. Anyone who practices positive thinking or dreaming constructively and creating new plans, observes results!

"Naturally, it should be emphasized that a man still determines his own fate. A pyramid is only a tool that provides illumination at an astronomical rate, and so is able to convince its users of its internal power. The rest depends on our focus on our goals! Implementation of our innermost desires (should be) very important to us, because (if we are) frustrated and discouraged with reference to the future we can experience only sorrow and pain (and this would) never bode well. By contrast, people (who are) satisfied and happy are able to leave their children a world worth living in. Our task is to create a good life on Earth!

"The prospect of realizing (making real) our dreams awakens our original sense of happiness and joy in being alive. This means progress in all areas of our life. It becomes easier for us to rise to the next level of development, and it is easier to feel love, it's easier to heal body and soul, it's easier to understand our reality and our own being, full of spiritual power. We just need to make sure that our ways of living and thinking do not hurt anyone, and that we use this energy in accordance with high ethical sense—not manipulating people (otherwise known as black magic), which is a sin, and which eventually always rebounds upon its perpetrator.

"As the pyramids resonate our intent at a cosmic—or heightened—rate, they play a dynamic role in the development of consciousness. We are called to control our thoughts, emotions, and above all, our intent, and to find positive ways of solving all problems. As a result of embodying the correct spiritual attitude we become honest with ourselves and others, open-minded and full of energy.

WORKING WITH PYRAMIDS

"When (working with) pyramids, simply meditate, think, feel and in one flash of enlightenment (or in a slow process), everything becomes clear. The first step to this end is (creating) the correct proper setting of the pyramid, and then simply to observe yourself and the ensuing new unfoldments. If all is well, enjoy! The pyramid just reinforces positive plans and feelings. The more you create in the 'now', the better you will prosper and the earlier you will achieve fulfillment.

"You will see the lightning-quick realization of your constructive plans. Slowly you will begin to see an ongoing process of change within yourself. Then your intuition will develop into a constant. You will become a true man or woman for whom it will be difficult to cheat, lie or deceive. You will always find an appropriate reply to every clearly posed question. You will discover and learn how to properly use laws that govern you and have the opportunity to be simply happy.

"If you install the pyramid and something bad starts to occur, enjoy that as well! You will simply appropriately confront the effect of any irregularities or anomalies in your thinking and feeling. Then you will come into a special clarity of mind and find you have the ability to make adjustments. Preferably in the process of creating the 'New,' pyramid energy now strengthens everything you create.

OSCILLOSCOPE AND LIE DETECTOR EXPERIMENTS

"When a test subject comes into contact with the pyramid, a characteristic zigzag curve appears on the screen, It proves the existence of an energetic field which influences us strongly.

"To explain whether this action is positive or not, skin resistance tests have also been carried out. This is a factor used in crime detection which lets us know whether a person is tense and stressed or relaxed and in good condition. In results from repeated experiments, the skin resistance decreased many times from 50 to 25 kOhm (in 10–20 minutes).

"This proves that the pyramid energy leads to harmonization and the reduction of stress within a few minutes. Unquestionably this is a positive influence for our mind and body. The state of mind achieved is similar to that of a safe child, cuddled in its mothers arms. It is usually very difficult for adults from civilized societies to achieve this!

KIRLIAN PHOTOGRAPHY

"This is one of the oldest and the best known methods of taking pictures of the human aura energy. (See p. 95)

"Kirlian photography made before and after contact with the pyramid shows an unquestionable improvement in the human aura. In places where the flow of energy on the hands and feet is weak and insufficient, in just a few minutes of contact with the pyramids, all the interferences disappear and we can see expanded more powerful rays. Some felt charged with new energy and the effect usually lasts for a few hours.

"The field of this power protects us from all kinds of negative influences from the environment, such as electro–smog, harmful radiation and even from radioactivity. It makes the detoxification process stronger and facilitates the release of harmful elements from the body. Kirlian photography proves that the pyramids increase the flow of energy in the acupuncture meridians.

MERIDIAN TESTING

"Further testing, using the Russian equipment called Prognos, has brought an explanation of wonderful healings which have occurred frequently in the presence of the pyramids. It is a highly valued measuring apparatus, constructed by the Russian scientist W. Poljakow, to test the human condition in outer space. In January 2007, we had the opportunity to run tests by ourselves

"Using the Prognos: Doctor Jewgenij Sokolow from Mgnitogorsk, a Russian doctor and shaman — lent it to us. For this we are most grateful. According to Poljakows' practice and the theory of Prof. Zagrjadski, the energy in all acupuncture meridians should be kept at a balanced level. In places where there is too much energy, inflammation may develop, and in places where there is too little, there may be numbness (paresis) or even atrophy in organ functioning.

"Results: We tested a person who came to us in a state of physical and mental exhaustion. The first measurement upon arrival confirmed this (dark blue curve on the diagram). We made the second measurement after a 10-minute stay in the pyramid. The yellow curve appeared and showed a strong reaction of the body exposed to this energy. An hour later, the third curve (red) showed great, very balanced energetic readings on all the 24 meridian points. This state was maintained for the next few days. We could say that this patient was cured. Our tests have fully confirmed the results of a German company from Worms, Germany, obtained in 1999. They proved that pyramids stimulate the body in a specific way, giving it a physiological stability. This fully affects our health, our immune system, our condition and how much we are able to enjoy life.

MONITORED PYRAMID RESEARCH

"When the person being tested comes into contact with the pyramid, a characteristic zigzag curve appears on the screen as seen on the left. This proves the existence of an energetic field which influences us strongly. To explain whether this action is positive or not, skin resistance tests are also carried out. It is a factor used in crime detection and it lets us know whether a person is tense and stressed or relaxed and in good condition.

"In results from repeated experiments, the skin resistance decreased many times from 50 to 25 kOhm (in 10–20 minutes). This proves that the double pyramid energy leads to harmonization and the reduction of stress within a few minutes. Unquestionably this is a positive influence for our mind and body. The reduced skin resistance suggests greater likelihood of there being a dynamic energy flow as well as a lessened tendency toward inflammation.

"Below, two Kirlian photographs made before and after contact with the pyramid shows an unquestionable improvement in the human aura. In places where the flow of energy on the hands and feet is weak and insufficient, in just a few minutes of contact with the pyramids, all the interferences disappear and we can see expanded more powerful rays. Some felt charged with new energy and the effect usually lasts for a few hours

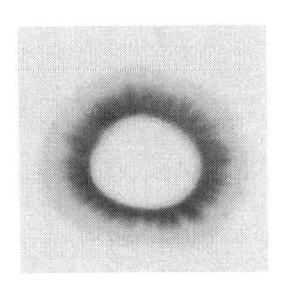

NEUTRALIZING NEGATIVE ENVIRONMENTAL INFLUENCES

"The pyramid's usefulness does not come its ability to neutralize harmful environmental influences, but rather from making the human energetic body stronger. It makes a person strong enough to combat these harmful influences. Our everyday struggle with stress, noise, pollution, electrosmog, radiation and toxins in our food can be compared to a never–ending fight. We are tense and we direct our energy in our fight against degeneration. That is why we lack the strength to feel the subtle vibrations of love and wonder. Our vibration rises in the presence of the pyramids and the energetic body construction changes from a dense net that everything hits, to a net with big, permeable holes. As a result of this, all kinds of negativity flow through us, like water through a sieve, and are not able to harm us. Without using up our energy reserves, we regain our fundamental spiritual strength and joy for life." (This concludes the excerpted passages of Jaroslaw Mironski).

There seems little doubt that Jaroslaw Mironski is a passionate researcher of pyramid energies with an impressive amount of empirical experience. It should nevertheless be borne in mind that, for reasons explained above, Mironski's preferred form or format is the Yantra pyramid configuration, which is to say, nested upward and downward pointing pyramids.

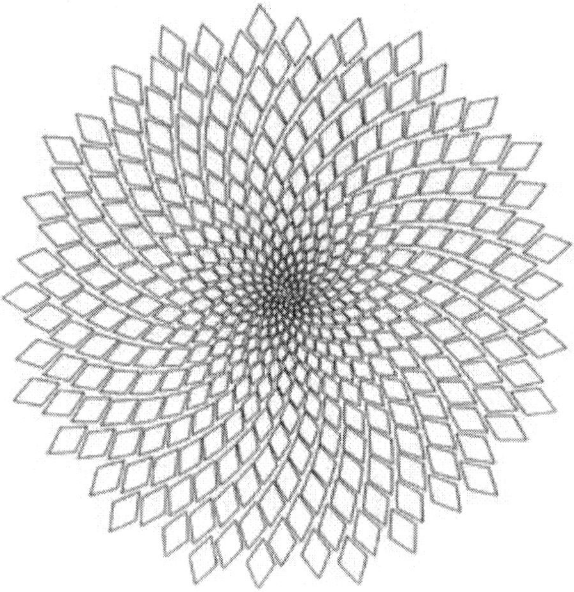

VII

REFLECTIONS ON THE PYRAMID

INSIGHTS INTO THE INNER MEANING OF THE PYRAMID

Over the past 35 years I have had occasion to reflect at length upon the inner meaning of the pyramid, convinced that there had to be one, because, from a practical point of view, there seemed no reason whatever that such a simple series of converging lines or dimensional relationships should produce the phenomena they do—yet, time after time, it was undeniable that they did.

As a non-scientist, I could not hope to bring any profound technical expertise to my quest—so my answer had necessarily to be intuitive rather than linear—yet at the same time congruent with scientific principles.

For many years the search led only to greater mystery, and I had to remain content with my empirical certainty that, for reasons unknown, pyramids did produce dynamic effects. I eventually realized that I had been pursuing the answer from a far too rational point of view; in spite of knowing so little, in my own way, I had been trying to play amateur scientist—expected to uncover a kind of modus operandus that would make linear sense

Then, in time, and growing confidence in my intuition, I began to sense an inchoate certainty about the pyramid's elusive meaning.

I began to apply that same intuitive process to my outer life that I had been already applying to the two worlds of my inner life—music and meditation.

When a composer worthy of the name sets out to create a new piece of music, the very last thing he wants—or should want—is to come at it rationally. Logic and linear thinking need to be left behind, or else he will find himself breaking no real new ground or rising to no new heights, but only turning over the well-worked earth of what has already been.

Paradoxically—it could be said that to the degree an artist knows at the outset where he is going, has he or she has ceased to be a true artist. Authentic artistic creation is nothing if not a trajectory into the Unknown—and to enter this realm one has to pass beyond all one's internal maps.

Thus, one of the first and most critical inner skills when one is truly seeking to create or explore is self-abandonment: to bail out of the cockpit of the self and move beyond the mind/brain database. While most natural artists do this unconsciously whenever they create,, many mystics have made such 'unselfing' seem like the labor of Hercules, often going to great extremes in order to achieve it.

But in the end, effort turns out to be the enemy of the spontaneity so essential to both artistic creation as well as scientific discovery, and experience reveals that a deep passion is the best way to achieve the desired state.

MOVING BEYOND THE BOX

It is liberating, during the creative process, to feel one's human boundaries give way and to let one's surface self reel out like a kite on a windblown day, dwindling in the distance as one's essence expands and takes the wheel. This experience is not only painless—it is actually a great and welcome relief, as the realms of music and art are so entrancing, and letting go of lesser things is quite effortless and automatic.

Gradually, with a little practice and trust, one learns to retain a marginal connection with outer reality while sustaining an intimate awareness of the creative dimension. From the outside, others may be quite certain the artist or scientist is the same person they're convinced they know so well, but they remain woefully unaware of just how radically a human being's inner reality parts company with the outer.

Now that the small self is no longer in control, one's viewfinder expands exponentially and one sees with new eyes, hears with new ears, and speaks and sings with a new voice. The truth spontaneously reveals itself.

Contemplating the elemental of forms of the pyramid from an intuitive point of view, it became clear that it is nothing else but a three-dimensional expression of Universal Truth.

While this may sound suspiciously lofty, it also happens to be true: the pyramidal form actually models and resonates the process by which all creation manifests, from the most infinitesimal subatomic particle to the incalculably vast cosmos; and that is—that all existence, all the myriad beings and things in this world are nothing but myriad, vortexing projections of a Oneness or Singularity—the Unified Field; from that One emerges what seem to be the many. From seeming nothingness—comes everything; from what the eye and the mind conclude is 'emptiness'—extends the fathomless fullness of an infinite universe, replete with countless galaxies and infrastructural worlds.

At the pyramid's apex, all projecting lines converge into a single, dimensionless point—which represents the Omega-point, Zero-point or Source-point of all Being before the creation of the worlds; the primal point without breadth, depth or dimensionality from which all spatial relationships originate. From this 'pointless point' the infrastructural vectors of Creation extend, tendril-like, literally creating Space, and generating a dynamic polarity of simultaneous attraction and repulsion, sustaining the physical universe and giving birth to the sub-forces of magnetism, gravity.

In the pyramid, then, Creation is revealing to us its secret template of just how Existence works—how manifestation happens. Tracing its lines inward brings us to convergence and unity—a singular, solitary source-point; tracing the exploding vectors outward leads into expanding webs of complexity and increasing orders of magnitude extending, without end, through galaxies, cosmoses, infinity itself.

THE SHAPE OF LIFE

In a logical universe, structure would seem to have little to do with energy—or contour with consciousness. After all, common sense tells us that a container is far different than its contents.

It would appear at first glance that form and essence are far removed from one another and that form is form and essence, essence—each quite distinct. But what if these, like Einstein's reversibility of form and energy, merely two phases of one phenomenon?' Then it would seem that all potentials become possible.

YOUTHFUL EXPLORATIONS

Taking myself as a case in point, some thirty-odd years ago, when, upon reading *The Secret Power of Pyramids* by Schul & Petit, I sensed the earnestness with which these two highly dedicated researchers shared their insights and experience, I allowed for the possibility that there might be some as yet unknown connection between form and energy, and resolved to put the 'form/energy' equation to a personal trial.

Taking note of their instructions, I constructed a series of smaller and larger pyramids, carefully cut four symmetrical segments from firm mat board purchased at the local art outlet, and fastened them tightly together with strong masking tape. Placing one over my head and leveling it, I sat, poised in 'Beginner's Mind,' expecting nothing—and everything.

THE WORLD WITHIN

It didn't take much more than a minute or so before the atmosphere under that first mat board prototype became enlivened with subtle forces. My attention was naturally drawn within, the reflexive attachment to the outer world attenuated by this new inner dimension. I was quite content to 'just be'.

I was quite comfortable, willing to drift in this realm between outer reality and inner reverie—as the Zen man put it, 'neither seeking nor not-seeking'—but rather, purely existing.

The unbeliever might protest, "How could a cardboard hat possibly do that? If you experienced peace and serenity, it must have been a placebo effect."

While seemingly a reasonable objection, it avoids the question of how this never-before-experienced wave of warmth and relaxation flowing over my head, shoulders and hands could possibly happen—for the inside story is that I have made no effort whatever to focus, concentrate or otherwise produce any special condition.

MASS HALLUCINATION—OR SHARED REALITY?

Having re-experienced this phenomenon—without exaggeration—thousands of times, I am certain that imagination and wishful thinking have little if any part in it.

The experiments went on—sitting, lying, standing—with pyramids small and large, and the results continued to be curiously consistent—so much so that I eventually found myself investing in a large, copper-tubing frame pyramids, in which one could sit or lie.

Sometimes the energy would be mild and diffuse, other times intense and concentrated; sometimes peaceful and pleasurable, then again, quite forceful and challenging. But, whatever its mode and intensity, it became increasingly clear that the phenomena daily transpiring within my body virtually never occurred outside the context of the pyramids.

In many ways my internal experiences reminded me of some of the experiences meditaters have described—vibratory phenomena, flows of warmth, increased mental or psychic acuity, spontaneous movements of energy through the torso and limbs, to name a few.

Fortunately, the sensations and experiences were so palpable and undeniable that their incontestability freed me from the possibility that they could ever be remotely considered imaginary phenomena, products of my own wishful thinking. No—these were palpable, organic realities, with no uncertainty that might tempt one to doubt one's empirical experiences whatever.

Better still, they were experiences resonated and well described in the narratives of numerous others—many of whom had no esoteric or energy-oriented backgrounds.

It seemed, then, that I was on solid phenomenological ground, even though I had no definitive knowledge of just what kind of ground that was. The admirable trilogy of works by Schul & Petit, including *The Psychic Power of Pyramids* and *Pyramids and the Second Reality*, were excellent way-showers, offering plausible theoretical frameworks for possible explanations underlying the phenomena produced by pyramids.

THE CONTINUING MYSTERY

Some 35 years after the fact, even when my attention is preoccupied with writing or composing—I still subliminally sense the energy coming from the pyramid structures in my workspace.

While these structures do not provide the ultimate panacea to life and its sufferings, they do offer supportive resources in our ongoing quest for peace and wholeness, without which we would that much the less in their absence. Readily available and easy to fabricate, they offer a framework of reliable energetic support in an increasingly stressful world—and at low or virtually no cost to speak of.

THE CHALLENGES OF INCREASED LIFE-FORCE

It may seem paradoxical to hear that the effect of pyramids is not always experienced as entirely pleasant. In this regard, it is not unlike fasting: once the body has a chance to unload its toxins and stresses it readily does so, and those toxins exit the tissues and organs and enter the bloodstream for eventual elimination. And while this catharsis is in process, we are personally treated to a condensed 'replay' of many of the symptoms and discomforts of those original insults to our system.

At times, I have placed myself under the pyramids to find the intensity of their energy almost overtaxing, creating even more discomfort; circulation and metabolism can increase noticeably, with the corresponding need to drink, to eliminate or simply to rest.

While the pyramids' heightened energy flow is not always guaranteed to be a pleasurable experience, it is almost always a beneficial one; If there are obstructions, blockages, vulnerabilities, it highlights them—as energy spontaneously seeks to flow into and fill in the gaps of one's field. If the emotional body is impeded by energetic knots, it may feel like an interior Roto-Rooter is working through the blockages. Similarly, if the mental body has become crystallized, we may feel strangely vulnerable as these accretions once again become solvent in the presence of the pyramid field.

After such energetic challenges, however, there is often a resolution or an improvement in functioning; hundreds of ordinary people have made identical claims, from users of small pyramids to those who went so far as to have entire pyramid houses constructed and gone on to live in them.

PYRAMID MEDITATION

This report from Patrick Flanagan's *Pyramid Power II:*

> Two subjective experiences are worth noting. In the first instance, a female volunteer who was aware of her healing energies (a build-up and discharge of energy from herself to another person during a particular state of consciousness) meditated in the pyramid structure. During the first thirty seconds of meditation, she noticed a definite build-up of her healing energies. This build-up continued for the duration of the 15-minute session and caused her considerable mental anguish as there was no apparent outlet for the energies. At the end of the fifteen minutes, she was visibly very upset from the unexpected build-up of energies and the lack of an outlet channel to discharge it. This experience is similar to many others reported in the literature regarding a build-up and enhancement of psychic energy due to meditation in a pyramid structure in contrast to meditation outside of such a structure. (Note: Should one experience this excessive build up, a quick cold

shower or standing barefoot on the earth—i.e., grounding or 'earthing,'—will effectively discharge the excess.)

THE BENIGN NATURE OF PYRAMID ENERGY

Once the necessary cleansing and detoxifying phases of the work are completed, energy can make its way through the meridians more easily. So at least has been my experience upon a continuing journey through the mysterious realm of 'the fire in the middle'—or pyramid.

LEARNING TO TRUST THE WISDOM OF 'THE FORCE'

There is little remaining doubt as to the ability of certain forms to collect, focus and channel energy. In the end, the choice always remains in our hands; the energy will not violate our will, and we can elect to retain or recreate our locks, blocks and defenses—even while that energy flows into and around them. Conversely, we can allow them to unravel, to open, soften and dissolve—which may leave us feeling temporarily somewhat disoriented, if unburdened—wondering, "Where did my ancient suit of emotional armor just go?" Things may feel a bit strange for a time. A prescient tenderness may suffuse our being; we may suddenly sense 'outer' life in an unexpectedly personal and intimate way; unprepared as we may have been for quite such a close encounter with it. It may even remind us of the perceptual immediacy which was ours when we were fresh very young.

Trust is essential at this point of increased vulnerability and reawakened sensitivities, and disarmed defenses; we need to go with the flow, to abide in the tenderness, the newness, to embrace the disorientation. Positive things are happening—and there is no need to interfere or to second-guess the process. We can have our natural self back again, without all the artifice and angst of the ego, if we're willing to relinquish the synthetic self we somehow allowed ourselves to believe was ourself. We can relax and simply be, just as we once did, so very long ago.

ENERGY FORMS—POWERFUL CATALYSTS

The truth is—we are always living amidst form-energy and experiencing the effects of being in well or ill-shaped shaped structures; but given the insensitively wrought shapes and forms of the contemporary world, much of the time these turn out to be far from healthful or helpful in their effect.

It's not only when we're under a pyramid that we're being impacted by what might be called 'the force of form'; for better or worse—we're being impacted at every moment and place we find ourselves. It is more than likely that most reading this right now are surrounded by various versions of box-like forms—square or rectangular rooms with flat ceilings and walls.

The science of Feng Shui is intimately involved with the energy of form—and of the sub-forms within the overarching or enclosing forms; skilled practitioners have, for centuries, sensed the flow and radiance of more and less conductive forms and spaces. So whether we know it or not we are all the victims or beneficiaries of the forms we inhabit or within which we move.

These forms and their respective energy dynamics can—in very real ways—close us down or open us up, lift us higher or depress us, energize or deplete us. One has only to enter a haphazardly designed house, with disjointed, undersized rooms and oppressively low ceilings to experience how ill-at-ease and uncomfortable one soon begins feeling Such structures constrict and inhibit flow and expansion, and cause a kind of energetic recoil and congestion in the system of the person inside them.

But even without the benign intercession of pyramids and other energy forms there are ways through which we can access universal force—for energy—the Universe's moment-to-moment gift to us—is always flowing, to a greater or lesser extent, through our being. The value—and the opportunity—presented by consciously created energy-forms is that, through them, this sometimes frustratingly slow and gradual process can be greatly accelerated and enhanced.

THE PARAMETERS OF PYRAMID POWER

Pyramids are not magical panaceas or cure-alls, but rather catalysts that enable our systems to clear stress and to more readily absorb and process ambient energy—or chi—that they were previously either too tense or too congested to take advantage of. When energy starts to flow more freely, and the circulation of blood and lymph increase, organs and cells receive greater amounts of nutrients and oxygen, and waste products are more rapidly cleansed from their storage sites. The vital functions are restored, resulting in biochemical balance.

Pyramids will not turn water into wine or raise the dead—but they will enhance and vitalize water, mellow the bouquet of wine—and preserve many substances from decay; they will not by themselves immunize against all damage from unhealthful lifestyles, but they will help to clear stagnation and toxins from the system—which will enable the body do what it is designed to do—repair and balance itself.

Similarly, pyramids will not make a sinner into a saint—although, as the recent Ukranian studies confirm, they stand a good chance of greatly ameliorating the likelihood of anti-social or criminal behavior; they will not suddenly bestow high spiritual experiences upon a person, but they can provide a vibrationally sympathetic space—an atmosphere in which someone can enter into themselves and experience life-changing realizations or an opening of the heart.

WHAT *IS* A PYRAMID?

As noted earlier, what we find when we take apart the word 'pyramid': 'pyr' = fire + 'mid' = middle is the 'fire in the center.'

Why this odd nomenclature? Very possibly because anyone with even a modest degree of sensitivity who experiments with pyramids will soon find themselves experiencing a sensation of internal warmth, flow and fullness.

Paradoxically, this phenomenon is experienced as both stimulating and relaxing, both physical and metaphysical. And yet, despite its mysterious nature, it feels quite natural, not to mention benign.

Theories have abounded ever since the rediscovery of the Egyptian mysteries and the unsolved riddle of the Giza Pyramids—scenarios attempting to decode the meaning and message of these inscrutable structures—enduring through the millennia like sentinels of the race.

Some of these have been intriguing—a few even compelling—suggesting that these structures were created as transducers and generators of atmospheric energies for the upliftment of the race, by beings with highly advanced technological skills and cosmological insights.

Whatever the truth may finally be discovered to be, none of these hypotheses can hope to help us do what can only be done by empirical experience—to determine if, in fact, there is anything behind all the hype about pyramids.

Doubt or rationalize as one might—nothing can begin to explain away results such as those documented by the recent Ukranian and Russian medical and scientific research—all the impressive for having been done in situations which rule out the placebo effect, in which the test subjects—such as babies and uninformed prisoners—were unknowingly exposed to pyramid energies.

On the purely empirical side, there is also the phenomenon of numerous seemingly sane and intelligent people consistently experiencing in the pyramid environment.

Pyramids remain a living paradox—why something as simple as a symmetrical 4-sided structure converging to a single apex should be capable of transfiguring environmental energies as radically as it does remains a 'hat trick' which defies all reason.

VIII

PYRAMIDS FOR WELL-BEING

PYRAMIDS AS ENERGY ANTENNAS

Nick Edwards explains the receiver-like functions of metal frame pyramids:

"An antenna for your TV has a certain length of tube for channel 2, a different length for channel 4, a different length for each of the different channels. We're tuning in (attracting) the life-force channel using Cheops sacred geometry. The base of the pyramid is a hundred percent, the upright tubes are 95%, so there's a difference of 5% from the upright tubes to the base tubes; for example, if you had a 10 inch base, your upright tubes would be 9 and 1/2 inches. That gives you the ratio. So whatever size pyramid you're using that I make, you're going to pick up that wave in the ratio of the two different lengths; you're going to pick up the life-force; it works that way.

"It's really simple: what I did is, I took the ancient technology and sacred geometry of the pyramids and gave them modern antenna technology. I worked with Dr. Gaines Crook at NASA for a while, and he told me, 'If you want to make the most efficient pyramid, make it as an antenna. We have all this broadcasted energy in the atmosphere, much more energy than you'll ever get from the source of the earth's magnetic field.'

PYRAMID—FREQUENCY RESONATORS & FIELD GENERATORS

"They act as antennas because they're tubes. They're called 'tube resonators'. Antennas resonate—that's how they work, they vibrate to the frequency that they're picking up. It's like musical instruments—you tune a guitar string to the right pitch and it vibrates at the proper frequency, which becomes something pleasing to hear. That's basically what the life force is, something we're pulling out of all these waves of broadcasted energy.

"The unique feature of my titanium frame structures is that they actually resonate to frequencies—you get free life force. We're picking up the cosmic stations; life force is everywhere in the universe—as I've mentioned, it's based on the Fibonacci series of spirals. All this is built into nature; it's built into the shells of sea animals, and into land animals. You look up into the heavens—galaxies of billions of stars resonate to the same energy and form the same exact sacred mathematical geometry. That's what we're tapping into.

THE SUBTLE DYNAMICS OF PYRAMIDS

"A recent article on crystals describes how silica is common to both glass and silicon chips which are used in computers. The molecular structure of the silicon chips is symmetrical, and it can therefore store and hold information, whereas the molecular structure of the glass is random, and it cannot store and hold information.

"There is a crystalline structure within the titanium. I convert it into a modified alignment, so there are straighter lines than you see in crystals, and because of that, as in music, they create inner harmonics.

"Some have even experimented with using these for chimes or musical instruments. A good friend of mine—a Ph.D.—not a medical doctor, but someone who invented in vitro fertilization, and who teaches medical doctors—just made chimes that are tuned to the DNA frequency, that—when you listen to them, or apply them to people—strengthens your DNA to replicate perfectly, as opposed to replicating less well as we get older.

RESEARCH & FEEDBACK: PYRAMID ENERGY FOR ANIMALS, SLEEP, NUTRITION & REJUVENATION

There are various sized pyramids available for different uses, ranging from those with bases of 10", 15", 20", 25", 30" and beyond; Many people like to charge their supplements—often costly products which tend to lose their potency after coming into contact with air. Yet, while in the pyramid, these frequently maintain and even gain potency. Astronauts used charged vitamins from pyramids that the Jet Propulsion Lab purchased from pyramid designer Nick Edwards. They were utilized to charge the astronauts' supplements, which in outer space tended to lose potency even more quickly—within a single day as opposed to a week. Edwards reported that if they charge the vitamins and other substances in the pyramid for about a month, they'll stay good for several weeks up in space. The 10-inch and 15-inch are designed for supplements and vitamins, depending on how many you use. I use a lot, so I use a 15-inch. I also have room for essential oils. Anything that has the ability to make the body vibrate better, come into balance—gets more enhanced or potent in the pyramid.

PYRAMID WATER—A POWERFUL ELIXIR

Nick Edwards: "And water bottles can be kept in the pyramid too; the longer they stay the more energy they charge up, so the 15-inch gives you enough room to charge up a few water bottles. And then you can also have a dedicated pyramid like a 20-inch that will hold four one-gallon bottles, and I cycle them in. Each bottle stays in three days—and when one comes out I put another one in. When I take one out I give the charged water to my pets—my cats—with the charged water they stay very healthy. The same thing with dogs, if you give them the charged water they get much healthier, they stay healthy, they stay happy."

OTHER VIEWS OF PYRAMID WATER

Edward Gorouvein, an engineer and inventor, writes:

WHAT IS PYRAMIDAL WATER?

Water, as any other natural formation, has a certain crystalline structure, which largely defines its properties and qualities.

Pyramid Water is water which changes its structure under the influence of pyramid energy. Water is the only substance which found in nature in all three states—solid, liquid and gaseous.

Among all the substances on Earth, water, thanks to its unique physical and chemical properties, plays an exceptionally significant role in human life. Covering three fourths of the planet, water is the cradle of life on Earth.

Advantages of Pyramidal Water
1. pyramidal water has the same properties as ice
2. pyramidal water high surface tension
3. pyramidal water uis high electric potential

WATER IN OUR ORGANISM

Our organism consists mostly of water. At birth we are 95% water; during our lives this share decreases, and by old age it comes down to 60%. During our lives it is necessary to maintain water levels in our organism at around 70% - 75%. Water level in the organism is the indicator of aging. Water balance is the indicator of relative health condition of our body. These two important indicators are determined by the structure of water. There are many natural water sources in the world. Having studied the structure of water from these sources and observing thousands of people with remarkably long lives in various countries, scientists-gerontologists from the USA, Japan and Sweden. Sweden came to a conclusion that the ideal water structure for a healthy organism is water with the structure of ice. Under the influence of the pyramid energy, water acquires that structure, while not freezing even at -40°C.

HOW PYRAMID WATER INFLUENCES OUR ORGANISM

Working on principle of bioresonance on a subtle energy level (similar to homeopathy), when taken either internally or externally, pyramid water harmonizes (regulates) all the processes in our organism. And the effect begins exactly in the location where it is needed the most. Such water is extremely rich with oxygen and negatively charged ions, which makes it easy to assimilate. This in turn increases water concentration levels in cells and the overall water level in the organism.

Various advantages of pyramid water:
increases water concentration in cells
assists in removal of toxins and "cleaning" of organism
rejuvenates skin
increases vitality
speeds up healing processes
strengthens immune system
counteracts stress
heals without external interference (self-healing)
helps heal skin, digestive disorders
recommended for internal and external use.

HOW TO MAKE PYRAMID WATER
Place a bottle of water (1.5 — 2 liters) under pyramid
Time of treatment — at least 3 hours; best time is during the night for 6-8 hours

Resuming Nick Edwards' discussion of the uses of pyramid chargers:

PYRAMID ENERGY FOR PETS

"The 15-inch is a good cat-charger size, the 20-inch is a good small dog-charger that you can put over their sleep areas. If you don't want them in your bed at night, if you put a pyramid over their area, they'll stay there, because they like the energy."

THE PYRAMID INSIGHTS OF NICK EDWARDS

While Nick Edwards passed away only shortly prior to the publication of this book, necessitating the removal of extended portions devoted to his many different energy-enhancing creations, which, alas, are no longer available, many of his pyramid-related insights remain worthy of sharing.

Edwards comments, with reference to a segment about pyramids on the "Mythbusters" television series, which claimed the failure of pyramids to affect various trial substances:

"First of all, they didn't have a good pyramid to work with; it wasn't even based on the Cheops proportions—they intentionally made it look bad just because they wanted to make a big joke out of it. They put a pound of cheese in a little 12-inch pyramid, but of course that's not going to be big enough to affect the cheese; that size pyramid would handle about a sugar-cube sized item, whether it be a piece of meat or cheese, or other type of organic material. If you want to preserve, then you can do tests where you put these sugar-cube size pieces of organic material in other places—without the pyramid—and you'll see that the substances in the other places are rotting, and there's a smell, whereas in a pyramid there isn't; and this can go on for weeks or months.

"A 10-inch—which would be equal to a 100 square inch-base pyramid—would easily mummify a sugar-cube size piece of meat or organic material—that's about a ½-inch cube—so ½-inch to 10 inches would give you a 20 to 1 ratio."

PYRAMID-POWERED SUPPLEMENTS

"For a typical vitamin bottle, a 10-inch or 15-inch pyramid would be the recommended size pyramid charger. In most cases the vitamin bottle will stay in the pyramid more than one day—it will stay in there indefinitely until the vitamins are used up. That's how most people should use them, and the vitamins acquire a longer potency the longer they remain within the pyramid. The minimal time would be to leave the vitamins in the pyramid for a week.

"In fact, besides my own experience, so many people have called or written to me saying, "Nick, I can't believe it—I feel the vitamins for the first time in my life; I feel them, I feel the effects of them—because they're being enhanced, to the point of becoming super vitamins."

PYRAMID-ENHANCED NUTRITION

"To cover a plate full of fruit, the 15-inch pyramid would be a good choice—I do this all the time. I'll put some fruit inside the pyramid and some outside—and when it's outside the pyramid, it has to be at least 10 feet or more from the pyramid to insure it not being affected by the energy. You can really taste the difference—your taste buds will explode with the pyramid energized fruit; it does something to the sugar. If you put a candy bar or some chewing gum inside a pyramid for even just half an hour it will bust your taste buds.

"If you're just doing a local treatment you don't have to worry too much about size—you're just creating a casual effect; you're not trying to mummify it, you're just enhancing the taste, so the size of it may not matter that much. It's only in the outright process of mummification that you would need that 20 to 1 ratio if you're going dehydrate with no putrefaction. But if you want a better taste, or want a detoxing effect, in fact, you can put two or three oranges, tomatoes or apples inside.

"The pyramid-exposed foods that have been dehydrated can be added to a small amount of water to rehydrate them before using, by allowing them to soak for a few hours or overnight. Otherwise they can be used as they are, for camping trips or outings.

"As the Russian-Ukranian research reveals, pyramids can also be used in treating seeds to be planted in gardens, which increased the eventual yield from 20 to 50 percent. Wood frame or metal pyramids can also be positioned over the planting sites to enhance the growth of fruits and vegetables, and to prevent infestation by insects."

PYRAMIDS & RAZOR BLADES—FACT OR FICTION?

Edwards comments upon the much-publicized ability of pyramids to sharpen razor blades:

"With regard to razor blades, it's not so much sharpening old razor blades—old razor blades will stay sharp for years if they're used, say, once a week and kept within the pyramid so that there's plenty of time to regrow the edge. The secret is to put new double-edged blades in the pyramid, and to let them stay for several weeks before you use them. Then you'll have what I call 'an alien shave'. It will be so smooth, so perfect, so without nicks, that you cannot believe that you could ever have such a shave."

A 10-inch generator, for example, could hold a half a dozen razor blades. Again, you're going for a longer term exposure; what it's doing over time is realigning the edges of those blades even more sharply, before they were disturbed by the process of shaving or by the effect of the water.

One experimenter explains the phenomenon as follows: "It has to do with three things—a crystalline build-up on the blade, static electricity and dehydration. The repeated rubbing of the blade on the face hairs induces an ionic crystal formation of the water molecules upon the skin. Ions are electrically charged atomic particles. The positively charged ionic water-based crystals gather on the edge of the blade and consequently the sharp edge of the blade results in being thickened, and so, less sharp.

"Now, a pyramid is basically a cone shape, but with flat sides and corners. Another character of static electricity is that it moves towards the ends of objects, as it did on the blade – the sharp edge. The end of a pyramid side is a corner. Static charges concentrate in the corners. It also gets concentrated directly above the point of a cone, or as in this instance – a pyramid (a square cone, if you like). It seems that pyramid powers come from static electricity.

"Alignment with the magnetic field provides for the naturally present charged particles to be "entrapped" by the pyramid and their resulting focus at the corners. The charged particles are entrained by the magnetic field, just as happens with the aurora. The particular dimensions of the pyramid cause a concentration or focus of a negative static charge at one third of its height at an equal distance from the four corners. The positive ions form just above the apex. This makes the pyramid a static electricity collector and focusing device. It must be electrically non-conductive. Cardboard is useful for containing and focusing pyramid powers.

"The blade is placed at the center of the focal point of the pyramid. The result is that the positive ions of the crystals on the blade are effectively neutralized by the negatively charged ion concentration inside the pyramid. The crystals are stripped of their bonds and water molecules are released. This results in the dehydration (this is the same with mummification) of the crystals, which are destroyed. The blade is now clean and feels sharp once again -- a crystalline build-up on the blade, along with static electricity and dehydration.

PYRAMID-ENHANCED SPIRITS

"People can but their bottles of wine in a 20 or 25-inch pyramid generator. They'll find that the wine gets better and better; it gets so good that, after a week, people can't believe it's the same wine. Anything with alcohol gets more mellow; it becomes aged ten times faster—a hundred time faster. It's as if wine turns into cognac and whiskey turns into the 20-year old charcoal barrel stuff—within weeks. And it's so amazing—like the high you get from this really, really expensive $500-a-bottle liquors that have been aged 20 years.

PYRAMID ALIGNMENT

"The blades should be running north-south—not true north but magnetic north. A lot of writers have gotten it all mixed up—it's the magnetic field, and the magnetic field was aligned with true north at one time, but this was before earth's axis started wobbling around--the compass points to where the energy gathers—it's so simple. So, you want to align even the small pyramid generators that way—unless they're hanging. If they're hanging they'll find their own alignment among the ambient energy fields.

"This would be the case for the larger generators for pets—you would just want to hang it over the bed and let it turn freely. I've seen dogs, smaller dogs like chihuahuas start barking and the pyramid above them start spinning! I've had experiences where the pyramid actually responds to the animal. I can make the structures respond to me—I can make the

Arkatron turn or the Mothership turn by just sending it the intent. I want it to turn, I imagine it turning and it turns—slowly, very slowly. I've never been able to kick it up to a high octane.

PYRAMID NUMEROLOGY

"The most secret number of all time is the number 13, the most powerful number. We're all told it's an unlucky number, but it's not. it's a very lucky number, which was known by the Freemasons and Rosicrucians who helped found our country. They put the secret symbols to the number 13 all over the back of the dollar bill, and that was for us to have in front of us at all times—the most hallowed piece of paper, so that we would never forget this. But we have forgotten it—yet it's still there—so we might as well take a look. The pyramid is there, the original symbol for the New Order of the Ages. Hopefully we'll have a New Order of the Ages where we can live in freedom and peace. There are 13 steps to that pyramid, there are 13 stripes on the shield; there were 13 original colonies, and so forth—13 arrows, 13 laurel leaves, 13 stars, 13 everything on the back of the dollar. If you break down the number of pieces in my pyramid, you get 8 rods and 5 connectors, and that adds up to 13—wow!—a very nice connection there.

PYRAMID PROSPERITY

"Now, the forefathers wanted us to have wealth in our country, and actually our government has stolen our wealth—

they've stolen it by inflation. But, if you fold the dollar where you see nothing but the pyramid on the back side, you can put that inside the pyramid or hang it over one of the tubes if you're hanging the pyramid, and the pyramid will amplify those secret symbols, and that will bring money to you. It works—it really, really works. Everyone who's ever tried it, it's worked for; it's funny, people will get an inheritance; if they have their own business, a big order will come in; people will come up with money for them. It really works. Our forefathers really wanted us to be wealthy, and they gave us that secret information. They gave us the pyramid on the back. So, guess what?—you put those symbols inside a pyramid, and lo and behold, you get money coming to you. It sounds too good to be true, but it's true. Look at the back of the dollar bill—you could spend the rest of your life studying that.

'MAGNIFYING' DOLLARS

"You could put the folded bill on the treatment dish with a crystal on top, or inside the pyramid. I like to fold mine over the bottom tube where the pyramid points to the left. I have so many pyramids hanging with dollar bills that, whenever I run out of money, I just grab a few and go out and eat!

"If you fold the dollar up where you see the pyramid, you'll have two halves—there's a circle around the pyramid—you can put it on the top or bottom bar. I usually put two—one on each side, so it balances the pyramid. Every so often they'll fall off, and when it falls off, I began to realize it was telling me the money was coming. Then after that, I have a big order or something else coming, which translates into money.

"There's nothing wrong with wealth—it's only greed with regard to wealth that makes it bad; you know—when you can afford it all and you don't give to the needy. There's nothing wrong with wealth. Our government seems to love it—they've stolen everything we own from us. If you don't understand that—if you had dollars and your family was alive in the year 1900, dollars were backed by gold and silver. Say you had a hundred thousand dollars—or even ten thousand—it would have been backed by gold or silver. And then flash forward to now, that ten thousand would be worth half a million dollars, but where did all that money go? Well, they took away the gold, they took away the silver, they inflated it—the dollar today is worth about 8 cents of what that dollar was worth back in 1900. That's how our government stole our wealth—they took all that gold. Everybody here would have money if the government let them keep it.

"Why shouldn't we be affluent? There's no reason to allow ourselves to go into poverty. So many people are poor right now. There's so much to learn from the ancient world, and the pyramid is like a key to understanding so many different things. The pyramid's energy brings the body—and everything else that's alive—into balance. It makes everything better and it keeps negative energy away. Even a 10-inch pyramid in a room will keep anything negative away.

PYRAMID TREATMENT DISH FOR CRYSTALS

"Crystals are very special to pyramids; that's why I invented the special pyramid crystal treatment dish that plugs into the top of the pyramid. I have a patent on that. You place a crystal up there and the pyramid becomes the amplifier of the crystal; it captures the life force.

"Cleanse the crystal by running it under cold water. The best place would be a running stream or brook for 5 minutes, and then the pyramid will detoxify it and amplify the frequency of the crystal. All crystals vibrate at a certain frequency, and the pyramid picks that up. It's like a musical instrument, and it just gets louder when you put the crystal in the pyramid. It's like a speaker system for the crystal. Some people can actually hear the crystals talk or sing when they're in the pyramid.

THE SAFETY OF PYRAMID ENERGY

"There's been some mention of negative energy with regard to pyramids, but I have personally never seen a pyramid function in a negative way. I've seen negative people or creatures—like cockroaches and fleas—run off because they don't like being around the pyramid just as maggots run away from meat that's kept under a pyramid—they don't like the energy either!

PYRAMIDS FOR PAIN REDUCTION

"The healing effects of the smaller pyramids are especially appropriate for anti–inflammation and pain reduction. I used to pound my fingers with a hammer all the time because in my earlier life I was active as a cabinet-maker and always building stuff. So I would just sit down in a chair and put my hand in a 10-inch pyramid as I rested my arm on the arm of a chair while I was watching TV. The pain would go away as long as my hand was in there, and when I took it out the pain would resume. Placing it over the head for a headache works wonders; with this super—light alloy of titanium, you don't even feel any weight of it being on you. You can meditate very comfortably.

"We've tested the units with everything from psychics to normal people; to dogs, cats ... birds. We have 10, 15, 20, 25 and 30 inch pyramids for people, all in the exact sacred geometry, for whatever they're used for. For example, birds sing when they're happy; when you have a pyramid by them, they sing all day long.

"I focused on the sleep realm—while you're sleeping you can be slowing your aging process, and be having better dreams and better sex, by having it over your bed while you're sleeping. To be in someone's bedroom, a pyramid needs got to look beautiful, it's got to look like a canopy of art, and that's exactly what it is. The Mothership's been my best seller world–wide since I've been in the business. When it gets down to it, the pyramids were built originally because the Helpers, the people who came from somewhere else to earth, wanted to live longer. They came to this planet and found that too much sunspot activity had detrimental radiation, and pyramids countered that. The whole idea was to live longer, and that's what people did. Plants grew better and stayed alive longer. It's good for you. And I guarantee with every pyramid I sell that if you don't feel better than you've ever felt in your life, you can ask for your money back. I think, since I put it online in 2006, I've had one refund, and that was because the person needed the money.

"It's kind of uncanny—what happens is, when most people buy one, they want more—they want to buy one for their friend, they want to get one for their vitamins, one for their water bottle—to charge them up. People love their pets, and they buy them for their pets; we have dog chargers and cat chargers. The dogs' pyramids run from 20 to 30 inches and the cats' pyramids from 15 to 20 inches.

PYRAMIDS AS SOLAR ENERGY SHIELDS

"When you look at the Mayans, they had a separate calendar that monitored the 11½ year cycles of sunspot activity, and the Egyptians were very much aware of it too. We are being bombarded by energy that's killing us—it's not UV—it's cosmic or whatever—but it's causing us to live a lot shorter lives. The pyramid cancels that out, the same way lead protects you from X-rays; well the pyramid acts like that lead and doesn't let the detrimental rays have an effect on you. It neutralizes them somehow.

"The energy of the pyramids counteracts something that could be solar in nature, but I don't think it is. I think it's a shield, it's a way of preventing yourself from aging fast; it's all about living longer. The Egyptians built them out of stone, and they built them on the surface of the earth to pick up the vibrations of the earth, and that was stepped up with the different chambers, as explained in the books by the engineer

Christopher Dunn, *The Giza Power Plant*—an excellent book, the first I've read in 35 years that contained information I didn't know about. I learned something: through the vibration the pyramid created an energy field that prevented detrimental solar radiation. The crystal capstone, which is now missing, had something to do with it."

CONCENTRATING THE CHARGE: THE POWER OF MULTIPLE PYRAMID—CONFIGURATIONS

While the subject has yet to be researched in any objective manner, some researchers are convinced that creating a juxtaposition of two or more pyramids can substantially heighten the pyramid power effect. In the past, speculation has been made in such venues as Bill Cox's Pyramid Journal, about the possible energy enhancement that might be achieved through the use of nested pyramids—that is, the fitting of one or more smaller or larger pyramids inside or outside the basic pyramid. Aside from this and the previously quoted insights of Jaroslaw Mironski on his counterposed Yantra pyramids, I have never seen reports of any further experiments along this line.

But only just recently, after a brief experiment with a smaller Edwards Nubian sitting atop his large meditation model, I had the idea to affix an 18–inch Nubian to sit atop the meditation model, but offset at a 45 degree angle. My intuitive reasoning was that, in doing this, the combined angles of the respective bases and sides would likely to be capturing or attracting the largest quotient of ambient energy, as opposed to a situation in which the bases and sides were totally congruent with each other—and whose placement were therefore duplicating each other .

Sitting to meditate within this 'eightfold' nest of angles, with my head just below their respective peaks, I almost immediately felt an undeniable increase beyond the field I had consistently felt from sitting under the meditation Nubian alone—which, to be sure, was fairly intensive, but 'quieter' in its effect.

The new cross–angled configuration had a lively, pronounced energy that was hard to ignore, furthering my hunch that they do, in fact, pull in great multi–directional energy due to their multi-directional construction.

Another possible reason for this phenomenon is that, just as we can look at a cone as 'a pyramid with an infinite number of sides', and therefore a potentially even greater generator than a 4- sided structure, because it is conducting flow at every point along its perimeter, we can hypothesize that, to the extent that a pyramid approaches the 'endless' sides of a cone—i.e., to the extent it possesses more numerous conductive surfaces or sides, there is an increase in its net energetic effect.

Whether or not these theories quite do justice to the truth beneath the phenomenon, experimenting with some variation of the experiment described above may produce interesting results. No great investment in time, energy or products are needed— simply two pyramids.

REDISCOVERING THE POWER OF VERTICALITY: THE NUBIAN—PYRAMID

These pyramids in northern Sudan were built from the 4th century BC to 3d century AD. They belonged to Nubian kings.

The number of pyramids in ancient Nubia (also known as Kush, and today Sudan) were a total of 223, (including those of Kerma, Napata, Nuri, Naga, and Meroe), double the pyramids of its neighbor Egypt. The underground graves of the Nubian pyramids were richly decorated. That all pyramids were not monuments of kings is evidenced by their great number. Other grandees of the empire, especially priests of high rank, or such as had obtained the sacerdotal dignity, might have found in them their final resting place. The well–known British writer Basil Davidson described Meroe as one of the largest archeological sites in the world.

Historical note:

Around 1000 BC, following the collapse of the New Kingdom in Egypt, the Nubian kingdom of Kush re–emerged as a great power in the Middle Nile. Between 712–657 BC, Sudanese kings conquered and ruled Egypt, as the XXVth Dynasty. By about 300 BC the center of the kingdom had shifted south to the Meroe region in central Sudan, where the pyramids and tombs were built to house the bodies of their kings and queens.

All the tombs at Meroe have been plundered, most infamously by Italian explorer Giuseppe Ferlini (1800–1870) who smashed the tops off 40 pyramids in a quest for treasure in the 1820s. Ferlini found only one cache of gold. His finds were later sold, and remain at the museums in Munich and Berlin. It was not his intention in any way to study the pyramids.

NICK EDWARDS ON THE NUBIAN PYRAMID DESIGN

"My experience with Nubian pyramids is that, basically, they do have more energy than a Cheops pyramid of the same base size; for meditation I think they're superior. I've found that the Cheops design is better for sleeping and dreams; the Nubian design tends to be a more highly vibrating energy and it's not as easy to sleep in as it is within a pyramid with Cheops dimensions.

"I've tried both of them together, and there lies a new area of research—using a Nubian inside of a Cheops, or vice versa, which is what I'm experimenting with now, and that seems to have the best results—using both designs together. As far as healing, we're finding that a lot of people are having similar results healing-wise with Nubians. We're finding the enhancement of potencies is actually better with the Nubian—it happens faster; putting your vitamins and supplements in a Nubian tends to give them higher potency more quickly. As the Russians found in their research with different types of antibiotics, they were able to triple their capacity to deal with different types of infections. Pets tend to like the Cheops better, I think for the same reason, that it's a softer, more subtle energy; my cat will always go to a Cheops pyramid before a Nubian—if there are both pyramids there she will go to the Cheops.

"The Nubian 9–Pyramid Grid is stronger than the Cheops 9–Pyramid Grid as far as the energy output; I don't know if it's the same energy at a higher frequency or a whole different energy, but it seems to work really well for meditation. Our Nubian Meditation Pyramid is a 40" base structure; I also make a 55" base pyramid for several people meditating at the same time.

"The claim that the part of the pyramid that is two thirds of the way up from the base containing the most concentrated energy comes from the fact that that is where the location of the King's Chamber was found to be in the Great Pyramid; but I find that there's energy all throughout the pyramid, and that the place of highest energy concentration is on top; that's why I invented and patented a treatment disc for the very top of the pyramid, because if you want something to get charged up fast, you set it up there—like your jewelry, your crystals, your favorite vitamins, whatever.

"Again, we're using antenna-designed pyramids, which will work differently than solid granite or limestone or wood or cloth; my research shows that the antenna design is the most efficient, and it's also the most effective at radiating the energy, because antennas do two things at the same time: they attract and they also radiate energy. So the antenna type pyramid makes a good room energizer because not only is it concentrating the life force—it's also radiating it.

The Russians have been using the Nubian design Pyramids for faster healing, increased food nutrition, bigger crop yields and accelerated learning in schools for dozens of years. The Russian researchers found that the Nubian (Fibonacci) Pyramids are as much as 2000 times more powerful than the Cheops design. Not only are our Nubian Pyramids more powerful, but they take up one half the base area as the Cheops type. Our new Nubian Meditation Pyramid has a base of only 40". Our Nubian

Pyramids use Nick Edwards' same gold anodized titanium alloy archery arrows that are charged by his one million volt "Pyramid Tesla Coil Charger". Together, Dr. Flanagan and I have created the finest Pyramids ever made.

XI

PYRAMIDS & PRODIGIES
—THE REFLECTIONS OF DR. PATRICK FLANAGAN

Anyone who has explored the mystique of pyramids has almost certainly encountered the name of Patrick Flanagan. Since the early 1970's intriguing but fleeting appearances of his research and creations have emerged and vanished, leaving the abiding sense that here was a deep and gifted—as well as elusive—explorer at work.

Elusive because, much as the fabled nature spirits—the leprechauns and fairies—of Flanagan's mystic Celtic heritage, the man and his process can be, in equal parts, prescient, playful and unpredictable.

In spirit and essence, nothing comes closer to the mystery behind Patrick Flanagan's elfin exterior than the deva of ancient mystical lore.

The word 'deva' is a Sanskrit word meaning "a being of brilliant light" The consciousness of these mysterious beings functions through instinct and intuition rather than accumulated knowledge, and embraces an intrinsic understanding of cosmic patterns, relationships, and dynamics.

Such creative souls function largely through inner guidance— a process that, in a very literal sense, triggers an expansion of consciousness beyond the physical body, sourcing information from the universe itself—an interior movement that eventually resonates outward.

Deva–spirits are keenly conscious of their cosmic connection and their direct relatedness to the universe—even if unconsciously—until, in time, the brain becomes capable of processing the source data they have been receiving from the universe.

The following is a compilation of reflections by Patrick Flanagan on his life, work and friendship with Nick Edwards; it is the result of many personal dialogues with the author, transcribed to read as a monologue.

PYRAMID POWER—THE BEGINNING

"I had written my book, *Pyramid Power*, and I decided to get it published, but I couldn't find anyone who was willing to publish the book; the publishers said they didn't think it would sell, and so I borrowed $5000 and I published it the first time, 5000 copies of *Pyramid Power* in hardback; they cost me a dollar each and I sold them for, I think, back then—$10. And it took off like wildfire—it was extremely successful, and over the next few years I sold a million and a half copies of *Pyramid Power*.

"This was the first contemporary book on the subject, although there had been mention in P*sychic Discoveries Behind the Iron Curtain* a book by Sheila Ostrander and Lynne Schroeder, which addressed pyramids and spoke about a man in Czechoslovakia who had patented a pyramid razor blade sharpener. I had been doing research on orgone energy; I had built orgone energy accumulators, and had experienced and measured all kinds of energy changes from those. And when I read the Ostrander book, I started building pyramids out of cardboard and pyramid orgone energy accumulators. I found that combining the two was absolutely a compatible synthesis."

"I worked with Dr. Dwight, who was an information specialist, professor of Physics at Harvard and then Tufts University; and he was my partner when we did dolphin research for the Naval Ordinance Testing Center. Wayne Bateau had something he called 'ventilated prose'—and I wrote the book in ventilated prose. In a sentence the spacing was one space and between paragraphs it was three spaces; and between sentences it was two spaces. Each sentence had its own surrounding space, and it was laid out in such a way as to make each sentence so important that it was self–contained, with nothing extraneous in it.

"The result of my doing that was that, over the years, I received many compliments from people on the ventilated prose; that might be one reason why the book took off and sold a million and a half copies—because no book sells a million and a half copies like that—self-published—and making enough money that I was able to stop consulting and stop working for the government. Even though it's true—I'm not a writer—over the years, I've had so many compliments on the layout of the book and the ventilated prose that it would be hard to believe.

"There is something called 'DOR,' which is negative orgone energy, but orgone accumulators do not accumulate DOR. This work should at some point be revealed in my new books on these energies.

"I made my first pyramids from cardboard. But not only that—as a scientist I had developed techniques of measuring the energies of the orgone box and then the pyramids. My technique for measuring this was a differential thermometer; my tests had demonstrated what Albert Einstein had pervasively demonstrated—that the temperature in the orgone accumulator was always a couple of degrees Centigrade higher than the temperature in the environment outside the accumulator—which is theoretically impossible.

"And so I built what is called a wheatstone bridge, using thermal diodes; I built a bridge so that I could neutralize the two diodes in the room temperature so that they were equal, and I put one diode inside the pyramid and one outside, and invariably the diode inside the pyramid and or the orgone accumulator would show a positive temperature differential—it would always be higher inside the accumulator or the pyramid than outside.

"That was my method of measurement, and it was extremely accurate—much more accurate than the method that Wilhelm Reich undertook. It was a 'Eureka!' moment.

... AND A LITTLE CHILD SHALL LEAD THEM ...

"From the age of 8 forward I was a child prodigy and I worked for the government; when I was 12 years old, the government took one of my inventions from me. I'm unique in that I was making discoveries as a child that have never been seen before on this planet.

The first thing, when I was 12 years old, was that I invented an atomic–bomb missile-detector and won a science fair with it; the Houston All–Grade Science Fair, which included levels all the way through college. The following Monday I was in study hall in the 7th grade and the principal's voice came over the loud speaker and said, "Will Patrick Flanagan come to my office immediately—the Pentagon is on the telephone."

"I went to the office and there was a 5-star general on the line, and he wanted to know how I knew about all the nuclear testing and intercontinental ballistic missiles that they had fired and where they had fired them from. I told him about my science fair project and they sent a team of 15 people from Wright Patterson Air Force Base to Houston and took my invention away, and made my father sign one of those agreements that said if I revealed anything to anyone other than the government about my invention that I could be tried for treason, and that if convicted that the penalty was death.

"So that was the beginning, and that science fair project of course hit all the papers—I still have copy of me with my science fair project. You can't explain where this all came from—when I was 8 years old I was designing and building vacuum tube radio receivers and transmitters; I got my general class amateur radio license, I was sending Morse code at 33 words per minute, and I was designing and building all my own equipment and antennas and such.

"Then when I was 13 years old I designed and built the Neurophone, which is a device that transmits information directly into long term memory in the brain, and which balances the left and right hemispheres of the brain creating brain-phase coherence between the two hemispheres and increases IQ—I invented that just coming on to my 13th birthday. Now, these are inventions that no one else in the world has ever seen before— the missile detector and the Neurophone—so I wrote my own patent, I went and studied at the library, and the patent office refused to give a patent because they said there was no prior art. Of course I said, "Isn't that what an invention is—something that no one has ever seen before? But of course 99.9999 percent of the inventions for which people apply for patents are improvements on pre–existing ideas—things that are already known.

SCIENTIFIC EXPLOITS & MILITARY INTERVENTIONS

"It took 40 years before a scientist at the University of Virginia discovered that there is an organ inside the head that responds to a Neurophone ultrasonic energy and that that organ is an organ of balance; but it also turns out that it is a vestigial organ of hearing for all ultrasonic sound, and that it is the hearing organ of whales and dolphins.

"Ultimately, the patent office and closed the file; but by the time I was 19 I was able to afford an attorney and the patent office said that if I came to the patent office with my invention and I was able to help a deaf employee who worked at the patent office hear, the patent office would re–open the file—which has never been done in the history of that office. They would give me my original filing date as well as my patent.

"So, when I was 19 I flew to the patent office with my invention and my lawyer, and we went in—and we put the Neurophone on the head of this employee, who had been stone deaf for 15 years; he happened to love opera music, and back then they only had 78 r.p.m. record players; we put on a 78 r.p.m. of Maria Callas singing, and he heard for the first time—he broke down in tears, sobbing, and everyone in the patent office started crying. They re–opened my file, issued me my original patent filing date and gave me my patent. Later on the patent office gave me an award for that, because it has never happened before or since that they have done such a thing.

"These devices are still available today—we manufacture and sell them. The government and national security reviews all patent applications, and if they think your invention has possible military uses they take the invention. As a result he military then started doing things to prevent me from manufacturing and selling the device.

"I applied for a second patent on the device and they put it under "secrecy" just like the guided missile detector. When I was 17 years old I received an offer to come to San Diego to receive something called the Gold Plate Award of the American Academy of Achievement; for my invention and achievement. So I went to San Diego with my parents, and sitting at the table with me, receiving the same award that I was receiving, for their own achievements, were Dr. Edward Teller, who invented the hydrogen bomb, Admiral Red Raborn, who was director in charge of the CIA, for inventing the polar submarine, and Maury Gellman, Nobel Prize–winner for his discoveries of the genetics of viruses.

"Admiral Raborn said to me, "Son, we would like to put you in any university in the world you want—don't worry about getting in—we'll put you there; we'll give you a $175,000 a year allowance in addition to paying for your schooling—and that was in 1962; and he said, "You can go to school as long as you want, get as many degrees as you want, and when you're done, we want you to work for the CIA for 5 years, at which time we will release you and you can do what you want to do.

"So I talked around to various friends, and they said "They will never let go of you—ever, if you do that." At that time I was making more money than my father because I was working for the Pentagon think tank, and consulting. So I turned down the offer from Raborn and the CIA; and Raborn said, "I'll tell you what, son—let's go into what we call the 'Favors' program." I said, "What is that?" And he said, "If you have any troubles with the government, I'll do you a favor, and no matter what the problem is, I'll fix it." And then he said, "And then you'll have to a favor for me—whatever that favor is, you have to do it," and I said, "Okay, that sounds fine with me."

"In the meantime my second patent application on the Neurophone had been put under secrecy by the government, and so Red Raborn said, "Call the CIA, leave a message for me, and I'll call you back within 24 hours." I was getting frustrated by this, so I called the CIA one night and I said, "I want to leave a message for Admiral Red Raborn," and the guy said, "Never heard of him,"—by then Raborn had gone on to become the director of the National Security Agency. So I said, "He was director of your agency," and the guy said "Still never heard of him." And I said, "Well, he told me I could leave a message for him and he'd call me back within 24 hours," and the guy said, "You can leave a message for anyone you want with me, but I can't guarantee that they'll call you back." I said, "That's fair enough, so I left a message for Raborn, and sure enough, he called me back, and I said, "This patent application is under secrecy, and I want to get it out of secrecy." He said, "Done." And I said, "Okay."

"So they took it out of secrecy and issued my patent. What he didn't tell me was that just because they took it out of secrecy didn't mean that they would allow me to manufacture and sell it. But that said, he then went on to ask me for a little favor, and that 'Favors' program went on for years.

BREAKING FREE

"I was doing and inventing things that no Ph.D. in the world ever dreamed of, when I was a kid. I was beyond that. When I wrote and published *Pyramid Power* they were stalking me, preventing me from manufacturing the Neurophone, blocking me at every stage—and I can prove that—I got a call from a guy in the CIA who said, "Son, the best thing you ever did for yourself is write and publish *Pyramid Power*." I said, "Why is that?", and he said, "They think you went off the deep end, and they let go their reins on you because they don't consider you to be a threat anymore." They didn't consider that subject scientifically viable, and basically considered me a quack.

"And so, my whole life changed—and at that point I was able to put the Neurophone on the market and we've been selling it ever since. The thing about the Neurophone being a hearing aid is that the original model I had was so extremely powerful that it put 3,000 volts across these electrodes that were placed on the head; the electrodes were insulated by mylar tape so that they didn't shock you, but it produced very, very powerful ultrasonic sound. And it turns out the researcher at the University of Virginia duplicated the Neurophone in 1997 and showed that that profoundly deaf people can hear with it, but the power level has to be extremely high. The Neurophones we have on the market don't have that much power; but that said, they still cause phenomena like full brain–phase coherence, an increases in IQ, and transmission of sound information directly into long term memory in the brain, and increasing the growth of neural networks in the temporal lobes of the brain.

"The Neurophone creates a kind of bridge for the deaf to access the world of frequency, and it stimulates opening of the channel between the pineal and pituitary glands. There is a connection between the pituitary and the pineal gland which is shown in Tibetan anatomy. and which is depicted as a musical instrument, with a little, tiny channel between the two glands — a lyre (an ancient harp–like instrument); and when the spinal fluid builds up a certain pressure and starts oscillating back and forth between the pineal and pituitary, it creates a powerful musical sound in the head. It creates a note — a very, very loud tone, and sometimes when it goes off, it cuts off the field of your hearing; that is when the two glands are really communicating and opening up the third eye.

STRANGE & SERENDIPITOUS EXPERIENCES—
THE SAMURAI KID

"When I was a boy, I came in with martial arts skills that were from a past life, because, being a small, short kid who had polio when he was 9 years old, the bullies always would go after me, you know. And whenever a bully would really attack me with the intention of hurting me, something within me would make the right moves and the bully would end up going through the air, landing on his head, on gravel, cut open and bleeding all over the place. Somehow it was always the case that their head would be cut open! Even in school, when someone would attack me, I'd end up bending them over and hitting them in the ass and their head would hit the locker and bleed—it was always the case! In high school, guys from the football team tried that on me and I ended up hurting the biggest football player in school badly, and after that they left me alone—and this was before the advent of the martial arts in the west.

"I have to say though, that when I was 9 years old, my uncle Mickey, who was in World War II, had studied jiu jitsu, and he gave me a book on it, and I learned all the nerve points and pressure points just from reading the book. My father worked for Shell Oil Company, and the vice president from the company was at this company picnic—and I'm 11 years old by this time, and he said to me, "I hear you know judo," and I said, "I know a little bit." He grabbed my hands and said, "Okay, what would you do now?" and I twisted his arms and threw him over my shoulder. And he wound up on the ground flat on his back with the air knocked out of him. And everyone was laughing—but it was all natural to me. I think jiu jitsu is one of the most dangerous arts there is,

"And I seemed to fully remember an art of Tibetan stick fighting, using a stick that's maybe 48" long, and no one taught me—but if I have a stick, I don't know—it's like past life memory or training—and I've never had any martial arts training of any sort.

A GOLDEN OPPORTUNITY

"Years ago, in 1974, when I was in Los Angeles, a Korean qigong master came who was demonstrating some things—he could take a one inch iron bar, which he would hold in both his hands—one hand on each end, and he would put his chi into it and it would turn into rubber, and then he would wind it in a circle. And then no one, of course, could straighten it back out again. He did things like this, so I went to see him, and he told me that he was from a monastery in the mountains of Korea where the master was 300 years old, and he did a thing there called gold needle acupuncture, where you take pure 24 carat gold needles and insert them permanently into the body. They don't migrate because they're 24-carat soft gold, and your body forms scar tissue around them, which holds them in place. If they were hard needles they would migrate and kill you.

"So I underwent a period of 6 weeks in which he put 128 gold needles in my body, up and down my spine and all over my body. He said my chi meridians were the size of your little finger, and that in a few years my meridians would be the equivalent of a meter in diameter. And then he said, "In 15 years you're going to need to have all these gold needles put in your head."

"I said "Where will you be in 15 years?" And he said, "I'll probably be back in the monastery in Korea"; and he was a Korean national martial arts champion. He had told me he was walking in the hills one day when he saw some bandits attacking an old man; he was running to rescue the old man when he saw him put his palm out causing one of the bandits to fall down dead. The old man didn't touch the bandit—but when this man examined the bandit's body, all the bones in his chest were crushed.

"So he said to the master, "Would you please teach me your art?" and the master took him as a student. And in 1974 he put the gold needles in me. In August in 1989, exactly 15 years later—I had then moved to Sedona, Arizona—a 93-year-old Japanese surgeon heard of my products and wanted to come visit me. I said okay, and he came and said he was an acupuncturist and a surgeon.

"I told him of all these gold needles in my body, and he looked at me and said "I studied gold needle acupuncture at a monastery in Korea where the headmaster is 300 years old." He examined me and felt the gold needles in my body and said, "When is your birthday?" I said "October 11th." And he said, "I will go home to Japan, get the gold needles, and on your birthday I will complete the gold needle acupuncture. "

"And so, on my birthday, October 11, 1989, he came back, and he put 120 gold needles in acupuncture points in my head and so now I have 256 gold needle acupuncture points in my body. Who can figure this?

A MYSTERIOUS MESSENGER

"When I was 17 years old, I was a self-trained gymnast, because my school back then in Bellaire, Texas, didn't have any gymnastic program. I had injured myself—dramatically—because I didn't have a teacher, but I still managed to become a world class gymnast. While I was training in the gym in the

YMCA, and I saw this man in white robes, a turban, and a beard, walking across the gym with his eyes on me.

"He glided across the gym and said to me, "Are you Patrick Flanagan?" And I said, "Yes," and he said, "I've come from India to teach you a mantra, and I have to go back to India tomorrow, so will you please come with me to my hotel room—I have to teach you this mantra." So I went with him to his hotel room and taught me the mantra, He had a little kitchenette in his hotel room, and taught me how to cook some Indian dishes with cumin and other Indian spices. Then he said, "Now do this mantra—and then, "I'm leaving for India."

"I said, "Well, how do I get a hold of you?" and he said, "You don't." And I said, "Well, what happens next?" to which he replied, "If you need more instructions someone will come from India and give them to you." I said, "Well, how will they find me?" and he said, "They will find you,"—and he left.

"It wasn't until 3 months later that I heard about someone called Babaji; there was a film of him in 1980 and he only came in for about 3 years and then he died. When I saw the picture of him—he was the person that came in from India in 1962. The mantra was very strange because it was a combination of two mantras—it was a Krishna mantra and a Shiva mantra combined together. When I've told some people who from India—but who were not mystics—they said, "Well—no—that can't be, because, you know, it's not done."

"Then several months ago a person came who was in a Hari Krishna temple for 30 years who had studied Sanskrit; I told him the mantra, and he said that because the Shiva mantra is "Om Nama Shivaya" and the Krishna mantra is 'Hari Om'—okay—

and what he had given me was, "Hari Om Nam Om Shivaya," and not "Nama shivaya" but "Nam Om Shivaya"; and the guy I had talked to said, "Nam Om and Nama" are the same thing; they can be used interchangeably.

"The way he instructed me to do it was that I had to chant it very loudly and resonate it through my sinuses and my whole body.

THE POWER OF VIBRATION

"What happened, is, right after that I entered my first gymnastics competition, which happened to be the AAU Southern United States Gymnastics Championships, and there were people competing who were going to be in the Olympics in Mexico City in a few years from then.

"I went in and they said "Well, you've never competed before so you have to come in as a novice; if you do well there, you could compete as an intermediate," and if you did well there you could go into the senior championships.

"I competed as a novice gymnast, and I won every gold medal that there was in every category; and they said "Well, if you have enough energy tomorrow, you can enter the intermediates." So I went into the intermediates the next day—it was on Saturday—and I won every single gold medal in every category in the intermediates.

"They said, "Well, we know you've competed 2 days running, but if you have enough energy, you can enter the senior competition on Sunday." I was weak, I couldn't even hold a handstand; I did my mantra for 2 hours that night—and did it laying down, because it would resonate my whole body. And I went in on Sunday and entered the senior competition, and I won every single gold medal against Olympic gymnasts and everyone in the senior competition. Then they said, "We'd like you to go to the Olympics in Mexico City."

"In the meantime—my mother, who thought I was gay—for whatever reason—had been talking to the draft board and wanted to have me drafted into Vietnam in order to make a man out of me. But I had met this girl in psychology class who I liked a lot, and we had a date; during that date we told each other about how our families were controlling us, and we decided to get married to get away from them. The following Saturday, one week later we got married, much to the relief of our families. We were married for 11 years, and she's the mother of my two children.

"That marriage got my mother off my back, and I didn't get drafted to Vietnam. My mother was, in many ways, evil, and was doing her best to destroy me, and did things to me that no mother should ever do to a child; it's affected me multiple ways. My partner Stephanie has said to me that she is absolutely amazed that I'm not gay, because they were horrific things—this is all that I can say—but that's another story.

"Gael was my fourth wife—I've had four wives legally; Stephanie is my fifth, and ours is a spiritual marriage. In the lines of my palm, I have four wives, and it says that my fourth marriage would be a long marriage and she would die, and that was Gael; we were married for 14 years and she died. Stephanie and I have been together for 16 years now.

"While not as successful as *Pyramid Power*, my second book on the subject, *Beyond Pyramid Power*, was extremely successful; Pyramid Power, coming first as it did, launched the entire pyramid revolution in the world; people started building and meditating and living in pyramids because of that book—building pyramidal buildings in Las Vegas—especially the people in Russia, who are the principle pyramid people, and who have acknowledged me as being the reason why they started building pyramids there.

PYRAMID POWER IN 2 DIMENSIONS

"I eventually created a flat–disc version of a pyramid–grid that collapses those energies to be functional even on a 2–dimensional surface. Professor Callahan at the University of Florida, Gainesville, had an infrared spectrometer that could detect energies in the range of 1 through 25 millimeter wavelengths; it was then called the XM and is now called the Terraherz Band, I had a pyramid grid that had 20 little 1–inch pyramids, and he tested it. We found out that, when you blow air over the grid, it produces all these wavelengths in that band. Then he took my sensor—the flat pyramid—and put that in his machine, and it was producing the same wavelengths as the pyramid.

"On the Gizeh plateau, where the Great Pyramid is built, there is always a 5 to 10 mile per hour breeze that's blowing—always—and one of the things is that that wind blowing across the pyramid generates these vortices that amplify the pyramid's power. And likewise, if one had a small fan—such as can be found at Radio Shack—blowing and vibrating air across the pyramid structure itself, it would create standing vortices around the structure would amplify its effect.

THE RUSSIAN CONNECTION

"Both the Cheops and the Nubian pyramids are modeled on Golden Ratio (Golden Mean/Fibonacci series) angles; in fact, the Russian pyramid is actually a more perfect Golden Ratio pyramid than the Cheops, although they are both Golden Ratio pyramids, In Russia, they've published hundreds of scientific papers on the Russian pyramids, Just to give one example, they measured the power of antibiotic by how much killing effect it has on bacteria; and they took the same antibiotic and put in a Russian pyramid for one month, and then re-tested it. The found that they could dilute it a million times, and even at a dilution of one millionth it had the same bacteria killing power as the original.

"It was almost like a homeopathic effect, because you could dilute it homeopathically and have the same bacteria killing power as the original. If you took the original untreated antibiotic and diluted it one million times, it had no power. But that's just one Russian scientific paper. In Russia there's a man by the name of Golod who spent $500,000,000 building those Russian pyramids all over the countryside, and in places where he built them, flowers started popping out of the ground that were considered to be extinct a million years ago, growing around all over the pyramid.

"It is interesting to note that results seem to show that increasing the height of the pyramid improves the quality of the results.

"The reports claiming that the vortices coming off these structures are active and visible even at the levels of air flight paths above the earth are absolutely valid. But it's not the air vortices, it's that the air flowing across the pyramid is amplifying what's called the torsion field of the structure. There's a concept in Russia that the torsion field was actually a third force; you have electricity, magnetism and gravitation, but the torsion field is another force that makes everything work. In fact, the torsion field is a 'twist' field—it's what gives DNA its twist, what makes the spiral galaxies spiral; and the mathematics of the spiral are all Golden Ratio—they're all Fibonacci—which is the mathematics of the Great Pyramid, and the mathematics of the Russian pyramids; and it's also the mathematics of the pyramids in Mexico.

NEW REFLECTIONS ON AN OLD FRIEND

"Nick Edwards' and my recent reunion was a whole new chapter in both our lives; it was amazing. I had such respect for Nick and the pyramids he's made, and later, for the pyramids we created together.

"If you didn't know Nick, you could easily mistake him for a retired cowhand, he was so laid-back and laconic—but he was a humble, beautiful spiritual man you who you had to pull these things out of; but once you started pulling, you came to realize how amazing he was. He was very funny as well. My experience is that I can't make it through life without a sense of humor.

"It was Nick who contacted me in the beginning. He was already aware of me and my work. At the time, someone told me about a dentist treating dental implants in pyramids. It was maybe 4 years after I wrote *Pyramid Power*.

"He seemed excited to meet. At first there was a little bit of a challenge, because we were basically in competition with each other—he's selling pyramids and I'm selling pyramids, you know. But the thing is, I was so impressed with what he was doing I had to meet him; and so we met each other and got to know each other, and we hung around together.

"I would have been about 28 years old when I wrote *Pyramid Power*, and in my early 30's when I first met Nick. At first our relationship was collegial, and then it turned into a friendship. We weren't close friends, but we hung around together. I had a Lincoln Mark IV Cadillac Seville—and we'd go somewhere and kind of race each other all over town.

"From Glendale I moved over to these big towers in Marina del Rey, while Nick was living in Burbank at the time. He made his products and I did my research and sold my own products. He never sold my products and I never sold his. I had a partner in my business—his name was Duke Lanfre, and we had a company together called Pyramid Products. Duke and I had a falling out. Duke had intended for his son to take over the business, but his son was kind of like the little rich boy who wasn't tuned into the agenda. Duke ended up giving the business to Nick, unbeknownst to me, something Nick only recently told me.

"He was unable to get those little 1-inch pyramid grids which had 20 pyramids, so the 9-Pyramid Grid is like Nick's version of that. In my book *Pyramid Power* there's a picture of those pyramid grids with energy coming off the top.

PYRAMIDS & THE KIRLIAN PHENOMENON

"A Russian scientist—Karatka, I believe—developed what's called the GDV machine, which is the Kirlian device into which you place your fingers, and which makes a snapshot of the Kirlian discharge of each finger. A computer analyzes it and tells you what organs of your body are out of balance. It's been well recognized and used as a medical diagnostic device all over the world. But does it reflect valid energy emanations from the body? It is not necessarily the case that the brighter or whiter the readout or glow, the higher the energy field; it can mean that you're losing energy.

"My experience now is that I can see auras; I developed that ability when I was 30 years old. Actually, I developed that ability when I was a kid, and it got turned off and turned back on again—and so I always thought the bigger the aura the more powerful the person was. Then I met a Sufi master from Istanbul who had no aura. And I thought, "How can he be a master? He has no aura." But what he was doing wasn't just spinning his energy out all over the place, radiating it out; he collapsed it, so that all of his energy was self-contained. And he would release that energy consciously when he wanted to heal someone or use it in some other way. I'm now of the opinion that a brighter and whiter Kirlian photo doesn't necessarily indicate that the person has more energy.

ENERGY & BRAIN WAVE ENHANCEMENT THROUGH PYRAMID POWER

"When somebody sits under the pyramid, and you use the GDU to scan them, you might find that their energy becomes more balanced, and you may even find that it increases. The consciousness part of it is that, when we learn how to control our energies so we don't spend it. Then you can control your energy and use it consciously; there are two different issues at work.

"One of the first things we noticed, if you use an EEG machine, is that when people sit under the pyramids, they start producing a lot of really strong alpha waves. If you start using my Neurophone, the person starts producing waves like he's meditated in a cave for 30 years. These things are all related.

"In general, I can say that when a person sits under a pyramid, there's definitely an energy enhancement, and that—Kirlian issues aside—there's a consistent, reliable effect from the pyramid.

"In my book, *Beyond Pyramid Power*, I talk about cones. In fact, if you have a pyramid with four sides and you make one with 8 sides, you have an octamid, and if you make one with 5 sides it's a pentamid. A cone is a pyramid with an infinite number of sides, and a cone has the same power as the Great Pyramid, and you don't need to worry about orienting it to the earth's magnetic field. So a cone is a pyramid with an infinite number of sides, and if it's got the right angles, it's extremely powerful. That's why tipis——you know Black Elk who was friends with

Crazy Horse and Sitting Bull—said that when the white man took away their round houses, he took away their power; the earth is round, the sun is round, the moon is round, and that power comes from the round structure, and when the white man put them in square houses, he took away their power.

"I was doing what is now called 'earthing' in 1974—but even if you are 'earthed' or grounded, you could have a square house with a dirt floor and it would still not be the same thing as having a pyramid or a tipi with a dirt floor. So, almost certainly, a conical structure would be exponentially stronger than a pyramid.

"With cones, the angles are critical. I've examined a lot of Indian tipis—and there's just a ratio, aesthetically, that produces the correct angle for a tipi cone/pyramid; they've pretty much approximated the Russian angle instinctively. That is a fairly steep angle, because if they're built too flat and they're low, the poles tend to collapse, the tipi tends to fall down, If the angle is a little steeper, they tend to remain stable.

"It's hard to separate out the actual source of the pyramid's power—whether from it's from the earth or from the atmosphere, but I think that pyramids would work just fine in space. They do act like antennas—but there's still a question of how much more or less effectively they would function if those tubes were made out of aluminum or steel rather than titanium. I believe that titanium has a much higher energy level, crystalline-wise, than other metals. That said, you can make a steel pyramid, you can make an aluminum pyramid, and they still have effects.

PYRAMID–POWERED AQUIFERS

"There's a builder between Chicago and Wisconsin who read my book and started building a pyramid house with a 10,000 square foot base. He built the frame and then he covered it, and then started making gold shingles. He took aluminum and gold-plated it, and they came- out just like shingles, and he started covering it with gold, real 24—carat gold–plate. When he was almost done, a natural spring came out of the ground dead–center under the pyramid and he had to tap it off. It had so much water that he built a moat around the pyramid with a drawbridge. And still he had so much water that he made a lake. Then he started selling the pyramid water—and the whole thing was because that pyramid power pulled that water right out of the ground.

TORSION—THE SPIRAL FLOW OF LIFE-FORCE

"The pyramid actually emits torsion field energy—but basically it's the energy of time—time itself is a torsion field. There's no such thing as a straight line; a curve is a torsion field, and this is what makes the galaxies curve. The planets don't roll around the sun in an ellipse, the planets travel behind the sun as it moves through space in a spiral–torsion manner. It's that energy that makes the whole universe run. It's all Golden Ratio, and it's all the same energy and the same mathematics that pyramids use."

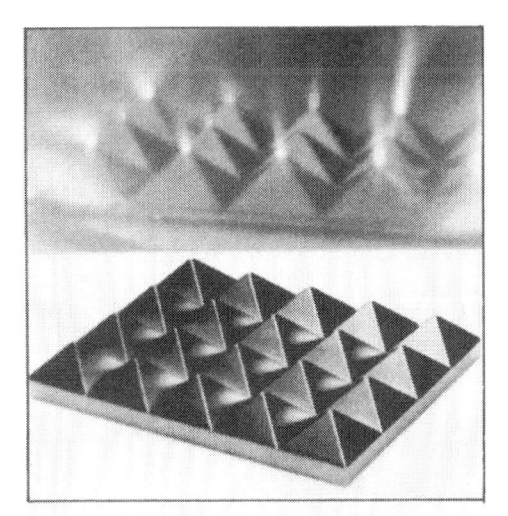

KIRLIAN PHOTO OF PYRAMID
ENERGY IN ACTION

X—APPENDICES

THE GOLDEN MEAN

(Used with permission of livescience.com)

The Golden ratio is a special number found by dividing a line into two parts so that the longer part divided by the smaller part is also equal to the whole length divided by the longer part. It is often symbolized using phi, after the 21st letter of the Greek alphabet. In an equation form, it looks like this:

$a/b = (a+b)/a = 1.6180339887498948420 \ldots$

As with pi (the ratio of the circumference of a circle to its diameter), the digits go on and on, theoretically into infinity. Phi is usually rounded off to 1.618. This number has been discovered and rediscovered many times, which is why it has so many names — the Golden mean, the Golden section, divine proportion, etc. Historically, the number can be seen in the architecture of many ancient creations, like the Great Pyramids and the Parthenon. In the Great Pyramid of Giza, the length of each side of the base is 756 feet with a height of 481 feet. The ratio of the base to the height is roughly 1.5717, which is close to the Golden ratio.

Phidias (500 B.C. - 432 B.C.) was a Greek sculptor and mathematician who is thought to have applied phi to the design of sculptures for the Parthenon. Plato (428 B.C. - 347 B.C.) considered the Golden ratio to be the most universally binding of mathematical relationships. Later, Euclid (365 B.C. - 300 B.C.) linked the Golden ratio to the construction of a pentagram.

Around 1200, mathematician Leonardo Fibonacci discovered the unique properties of the Fibonacci sequence. This sequence ties directly into the Golden ratio because if you take any two successive Fibonacci numbers, their ratio is very close to the Golden ratio. As the numbers get higher, the ratio becomes even closer to 1.618. For example, the ratio of 3 to 5 is 1.666. But the ratio of 13 to 21 is 1.625. Getting even higher, the ratio of 144 to 233 is 1.618. These numbers are all successive numbers in the Fibonacci sequence.

These numbers can be applied to the proportions of a rectangle, called the Golden rectangle. This is known as one of the most visually satisfying of all geometric forms – hence, the appearance of the Golden ratio in art. The Golden rectangle is also related to the Golden spiral, which is created by making adjacent squares of Fibonacci dimensions. Leonardo da Vinci's 'Vitruvian Man' is said to illustrate the golden ratio.

In 1509, Luca Pacioli wrote a book that refers to the number as the "Divine Proportion," which was illustrated by Leonardo da Vinci. Da Vinci later called this *sectio aurea* or the Golden section. The Golden ratio was used to achieve balance and beauty in many Renaissance paintings and sculptures. Da Vinci himself used the Golden ratio to define all of the proportions in his Last Supper, including the dimensions of the table and the proportions of the walls and backgrounds. The Golden ratio also appears in da Vinci's Vitruvian Man and the Mona Lisa. Other artists who employed the Golden ratio include Michelangelo, Raphael, Rembrandt, Seurat, and Salvador Dali.

The term "phi" was coined by American mathematician Mark Barr in the 1900s. Phi has continued to appear in mathematics and physics, including the 1970s Penrose Tiles, which allowed surfaces to be tiled in five-fold symmetry. In the 1980s, phi appeared in quasi crystals, a then-newly discovered form of matter.

Phi is more than an obscure term found in mathematics and physics. It appears around us in our daily lives, even in our aesthetic views. Studies have shown that when test subjects view random faces, the ones they deem most attractive are those with solid parallels to the Golden ratio. Faces judged as the most attractive show Golden ratio proportions between the width of the face and the width of the eyes, nose, and eyebrows. The test subjects weren't mathematicians or physicists familiar with phi — they were just average people, and the Golden ratio elicited an instinctual reaction.

The Golden ratio also appears in all forms of nature and science. Some unexpected places include:

Flower petals: The number of petals on some flowers follows the Fibonacci sequence. It is believed that in the Darwinian processes, each petal is placed to allow for the best possible exposure to sunlight and other factors.

Seed heads: The seeds of a flower are often produced at the center and migrate outward to fill the space. For example, sunflowers follow this pattern.

Pinecones: The spiral pattern of the seed pods spiral upward in opposite directions. The number of steps the spirals take tend to match Fibonacci numbers.

Sunflower seeds grow in Fibonacci spirals.

Tree branches: The way tree branches form or split is an example of the Fibonacci sequence. Root systems and algae exhibit this formation pattern.

Shells: Many shells, including snail shells and nautilus shells, are perfect examples of the Golden spiral.

Spiral galaxies: The Milky Way has a number of spiral arms, each of which has a logarithmic spiral of roughly 12 degrees. The shape of the spiral is identical to the Golden spiral, and the Golden rectangle can be drawn over any spiral galaxy.

Hurricanes: Much like shells, hurricanes often display the Golden spiral.

Fingers: The length of our fingers, each section from the tip of the base to the wrist is larger than the preceding one by roughly the ratio of phi.

Animal bodies: The measurement of the human navel to the floor and the top of the head to the navel is the Golden ratio. But we are not the only examples of the Golden ratio in the animal kingdom; dolphins, starfish, sand dollars, sea urchins, ants and honeybees also exhibit the proportion.

DNA molecules: A DNA molecule measures 34 angstroms by 21 angstroms at each full cycle of the double helix spiral. In the Fibonacci series, 34 and 21 are successive numbers.

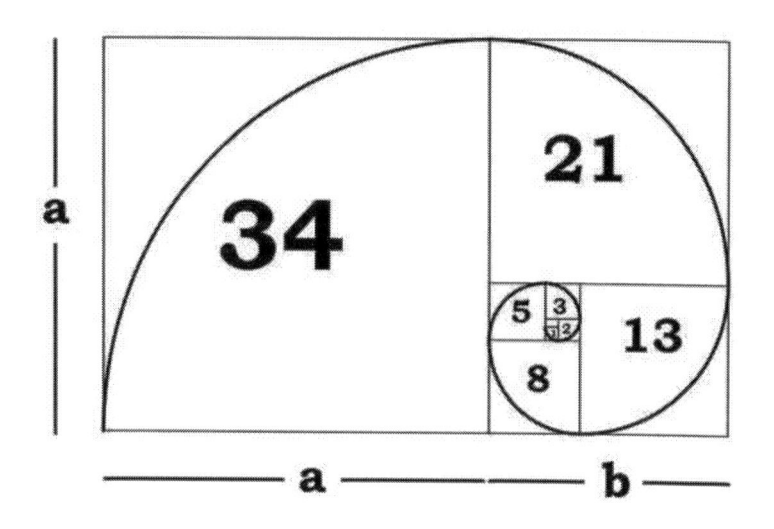

APPENDIX B

THE RUSSIAN/UKRANIAN PYRAMID RESEARCH

Dr. Alexander Golod, PhD. has been doing Russian pyramid research in the former Soviet Union since 1990. This research involved the construction of over twenty large pyramids in 8 different locations in Russia and the Ukraine. The pyramids were built in many places including Moscow, Astrakhan, Sochi, Zoporozhye, Voronezh, Belgorod, the Tver Region, Krasnodar, Tolyatti, Uzbekistan, and France.

All the Russian pyramids are made of fiberglass with the largest is standing an incredible 144 feet high (44 meters) tall, and weighing in at over 55 tons. Built at cost over 1 million dollars, this Russian pyramid is a modern wonder. Many different experiments are being done using these pyramids. They include studies in medicine, ecology, agriculture, physics and health sciences. What is significant about this work is that it is being carried out by top scientists in Russia and the Ukraine and not fringe elements or unknown inventors.

Some of the amazing pyramid power research being done is showing great promise for all mankind. A brief summary of recent research follows:

The Immune system of organisms increased upon exposure in the pyramid (Scientific Research Institute named by Mechnikov, Russian Academy of Medical Sciences.)

Specific properties of medicines increase with decreasing side effects after exposure in the Pyramid (SRI of Virology named by Ivanovskiy, Russian Academy of Medical Sciences.)

Improved regeneration of tissue

The pathogenic strength of different viruses and bacteria becomes less with exposure in the pyramid.

Agricultural seeds placed in the pyramid showed a 30–100% increase in yield.

Soon after construction of the Lake Seliger pyramid a marked improvement of the ozone was noted above the area.

Russian military radar detected an energy column above the pyramids built by Golod which is thought to have repaired the ozone layer in Russia (the same can be done for example in Australia.)

Seismic activity near the pyramid research areas are reduced in severity and size.

Violent weather also appears to decrease in the vicinity of the pyramids.

Pyramids constructed in Southern Russia (Bashkiria) appeared to have a positive effect on oil production with oil becoming less viscous by 30% and the yield of the oil wells increased according to tests carried out by the Moscow Academy of Oil and Gas.

A study was done on 5000 prisoners who ingested salt and pepper that had been exposed to the pyramid energy field. The tests showed that in a few months most crimes almost disappeared and behavior was much improved, with a greatly reduced violence rate and overall behavior much improved. This was attributed to the crystalline structures, which had been placed beforehand in the Pyramid and placed around the territories of jails.

Standard tissue culture tests showed an increase in survival of cellular tissue after infection by viruses and bacteria.

Radioactive substances show a decreased level of radiation inside the pyramid.

There are reports of spontaneous charging of regional capacitors.

Physicists observed significant changes in super-conductivity temperature thresholds and in the properties of semi–conducting and carbon nano materials.

Water inside the pyramid will remain liquid to -40 degrees Celsius but will freeze instantly if disturbed.

APPENDIX C

REPORT OF A MYSTERIOUS ENERGY BEAM ABOVE THE BOSNIAN PYRAMID OF THE SUN

In 2005, a team of physicists detected an energy beam coming through the top of the Bosnian Pyramid of the Sun. The radius of the beam is 4.5 meters, with a frequency of 28 kHz. The beam is continuous and its strength grows as it moves up and away from the pyramid. This phenomenon contradicts the known laws of physics and technology. This is the first proof of non-herzian technology on the planet. It seems that the pyramid-builders created a perpetual motion machine a long time ago and this 'energy machine' is still working.

In 2010, in the underground labyrinth, they discovered three chambers and a small blue lake. Energy screening shows that the ionization level is 43 times higher than the average concentration outside which makes the underground chambers into "healing rooms."

Further electromagnetic detection in 2011 confirmed that levels of negative radiation in the tunnels (as monitored) through the Hartman, Curry and Schneider grids are equal to zero. There was no technical radiation (from power lines or other technology) found in the tunnels and no cosmic radioactivity. Ceramic sculptures are positioned over the underground water flows and the negative energy is transformed into positive.

A similar event occurred in 2009.

On June 24, 2009, a beam of light was captured on photo above the Chichen Itza Pyramid (on the Yucatan peninsula in Mexico).

The witnesses that captured this photo, did not see anything with the naked eye at the time the photograph was taken, suggesting an energy that was evident only with special photo-sensitive technology.

APPENDIX D

RECENT RESEARCH ON THE BOSNIAN PYRAMID OF THE SUN
DR.SCI., SAM SEMIR OSMANAGICH

Dr.sci. Sam Semir Osmanagich (www.samosmanagich.com) Foreign Member of the Russian Academy of Natural Sciences Professor of Anthropology at the American University in Bosnia–Herzegovina. Date: November 2011

PREHISTORIC AND ANCIENT HUMAN SOCIETIES

Almost everything they teach us about ancient history is wrong: the origin of mankind, civilizations and pyramids. Homo sapiens is not a result of evolution, and biologists will never find a 'missing link,' because the intelligent man is a product of genetic engineering. Sumerians are not the beginning of civilized men, but rather the beginning of another cycle of humanity. And finally, original pyramids, the most superior and oldest, were made by advanced builders who knew energy, astronomy and construction better than we do.

In order to understand the ancient monuments, we need to view them through three realms: physical, energy and spiritual. Our scientific instruments are simply not enough to explain the purpose of the oldest pyramids, for example. Mainstream scientists, archaeologists, historians and anthropologists, are often the main obstacle for scientific progress.

The gap between physical and spiritual science needs to be bridged if we want to get fully understanding of the past.

Also, (the issue of the) twelve hundred ton stone block in Baalbeck (Lebanon) needs explanation. Who was able to contour, move and install blocks four times bigger than that which our, 21 century (technical) capabilities can handle? Yonaguni megalithic monuments (in Japan) do belong to the previous cycle of humanity. They are undeniable proof, on the bottom of the Pacific floor, 80 meters below sea level, that advanced cultures lived in the area more than 12.000 years ago, before huge quantities of ice melted and caused the level of the Pacific ocean to rise 80 meters. Machu Picchu (Peru) tells the stories of four distinctive civilizations and (their) different construction styles, the first civilization being the most advanced. At the same time, in recent times all the history books fabricate the story of the Inkas being the builders of 'royal retreat'. New dating of Peruvian, Mexican, Chinese and Egyptian pyramids will take us back much before recognized history and known rulers.

The oldest Chinese and Egyptian pyramids are much superior to those made later, as unsuccessful replicas. The older ones are built from granite and sandstone blocks; more recent ones are much smaller, built from bricks and mud. Traces of more advanced beings are everywhere around us. In the meantime, mainstream scientists try to fit those monuments into their time coordinates, falsifying the truth.

Two hundred Cahokia pyramids show astronomical knowledge of the builders who moved several million tons of construction materials and who knew the difference between cosmic and magnetic north. The Mayan world is an example of the knowledge of the universe. Our Solar system circles the Milky Way and that 26-thousand years cycle ("long count calendar") affects all living life on our planet. Anasazies, ancestors of Pueblo Indians, didn't need an alphabet or physical communication means to recognize danger in different dimensions coming from the depth of Universe.

As long as they stay within the box, mainstream archaeologists will never be able to explain (the) tooling and logistic(s) needed to build stone heads on Easter Island, shape granite blocks of Akapana, the pyramid complex in Bolivia or the chambers of the Giza pyramids.

(The) stone spheres of western Mexico, southern Costa Rica, Easter Island or twenty locations in remote Bosnia–Herzegovina, are obvious proof of (the) understanding and manipulating of shapes and energy in the distant past.

On top of all that, the discovery of the Bosnian Valley of the Pyramids is telling us that we don't know our planet. We might go to the Moon (temporarily, until threatened), but we still need to explore our Mother Earth. More secrets wait to be uncovered and, with the ancient knowledge, help us recover our balance.

THE SIGNIFICANCE OF THE BOSNIAN PYRAMID DISCOVERIES

In April 2005 I first traveled to the town of Visoko, 20 miles northwest from Sarajevo, the capital of Bosnia–Herzegovina. My attention was caught by two regularly shaped hills, which I later named the Bosnian Pyramids of the Sun and Moon. For thousands of years locals have considered those hills to be natural phenomena because they were covered by soil and vegetation. However, when I first saw their triangular faces, obvious corners and orientation toward the cardinal points, I knew that they had to be constructed by a force other than nature. Since I had been investigating pyramids for decades I knew that the pyramids found in China, Mexico, Guatemala and El Salvador had the same type of soil and vegetation coverage.

In 2005 work was begun on this project and construction companies and geologists were paid (out of my pocket) to do core drilling and geo–morphological analysis. We then announced to the world, at the press conference, that the first pyramids in Europe had been discovered.

Shortly thereafter we established the non–profit Archaeological Park: Bosnian Pyramid of the Sun Foundation and since that time the pyramid investigations in Bosnia have become the world's largest inter–disciplinary archaeological project. We have spent over 340.000 man–hours in archaeological excavation, sample testing and radiocarbon dating in the period from 2005 to 2011. We determined that the Bosnian Valley of the Pyramids consists of five pyramids discovered to date which I named: The Bosnian Pyramids of the Sun, Moon, Dragon, Mother Earth and Love. The site also includes a tumulus complex and a huge underground labyrinth.

This discovery is historic and changes the knowledge of the early history of Europe for several reasons:

These are the first pyramids discovered in Europe.

The site includes the largest pyramid structure in the world — The Bosnian Pyramid of the Sun with its height of over 220 meters is much higher than the Great Pyramid of Egypt (147 meters).

The Bosnian Pyramid of the Sun has, according to the Bosnian Institute for Geodesy, the most precise orientation towards cosmic north with the error of 0 degrees, 0 minutes and 12 seconds.

The Bosnian Pyramid of the Sun is completely covered by rectangular concrete blocks. The properties of the concrete, including extreme hardness (up to 133 MPs) and low water absorption (around 1%), are, according to the scientific institutions in Bosnia, Italy and France, far superior to modern concrete materials.

The pyramids are covered by soil which is, according to the State Institute for Agro–pedology, approx. 12,000 years old. Radiocarbon dating from the paved terrace on the Bosnian Pyramid of the Moon, performed by Institute of Physics of Silesian Institute of Technology from Gliwice (Poland) confirmed that terrace was built 10.350 years ago (+/−50 years). These finding confirm that the Bosnian pyramids are also the oldest known pyramids on the planet.

Beneath the Bosnian Valley of the Pyramids there is an extensive underground tunnel and chamber network which runs for a total of more than ten miles.

Ceramic sculptures have been discovered in the underground labyrinth with a mass of up to 20,000 pounds which makes them the largest found so far from the ancient world.

The list of the wonders in Bosnian archaeology does not end here. In the vicinity, we discovered the tallest tumulus in the World: 61 meters high. Its nearest competitor, Sillbury Hill in England is 60 meters high. The Bosnian tumulus consists of two–

layer megalithic terraces, clay layers and artificial concrete layers.

A team of physicists detected an energy beam coming through the top of the Bosnian Pyramid of the Sun. The radius of the beam is 4.5 meters with a frequency of 28 kHz. The beam is continuous and its strength grows as it moves up and away from the pyramid. This phenomenon contradicts the known laws of physic and technology. This is the first proof of non–herzian technology on the planet. It seems that the pyramid–builders created a perpetual motion machine a long time ago and this "energy machine" is still working.

In the underground labyrinth, in 2010, we discovered three chambers and a small blue lake. Energy screening shows that the ionization level is 43 times higher than the average concentration outside which makes the underground chambers into "healing rooms."

Further electromagnetic detection in 2011 confirmed that levels of negative radiation through the Hartman, Curry and Schneider grids are equal to zero in the tunnels. There was no technical radiation (from power lines and/or other technology) found in the tunnels and no cosmic radioactivity. Ceramic sculptures are positioned over the underground water flows and the negative energy is transformed into positive. All of these experiments point to the underground labyrinth as one of the most secure underground constructions in the world and this makes it an ideal place for the body's rejuvenation and regeneration.

Two hundred years of Egyptology has not produced a satisfactory answer to the question of what the real purpose was for the oldest and most superior pyramids.

In only six years, our research in Bosnia has applied inter-disciplinary scientific methods, to look at this complex through the physical, energetic and spiritual dimensions. We have had pioneering results which affects the entire sphere of knowledge and Pyramid Science. Our history is changing with each new discovery.

Perhaps by changing our beginnings or learning to better understand our beginnings we can also change our present and our future for the better.

Bosnian Pyramid of the Sun, Visoko, Bosnia–Herzegovina

The Bosnian Valley of the Pyramids has been visited by 500,000 tourists in the period from 2005 to 2011. An International Summer Camp for Volunteers attracts 500 volunteers from 6 continents every year; the photograph shows an excavated paved terrace on Bosnian Pyramid of the Moon. Ceramic sculpture "K-2" in the underground labyrinth weighs 18,000 pounds. There is an energy beam coming from the Bosnian Pyramid of the Sun.

SUMMARY

(The) unusual influence of the Great Pyramid on animate and inanimate objects of nature may be associated with a special field in the Pyramid. It turns out that the Great Pyramid may have been built as a resonator of that field. In my recent research, the field was called 'inerton' since it arises from a submicroscopic quantum consideration of a moving elementary particle in the structure of actual space in which the motion occurs. In essence, the inerton field is generated by the space treated as a quantum substrate due to friction of a moving particle by the space treated as a quantum substrate, or aether. From the mathematical point of view the substrate may be simulated as a mathematical space that is densely packed by its building blocks—elastic cells. Any particle is also an element of the space. Then when we treat any material object, we should take into account that it is embedded in the spatial substrate that posses its own properties and is able to interact with massive objects. For instance, you may imagine a metallic framework, which is placed in a room filled with air. You know any vibration of the framework will immediately be passed to the air and the latter will vibrate as well; in its turn any vibrations of the air will excite the corresponding vibrations in the framework. The same happens with the moving Earth as long as it fits into the spatial substrate. Atoms of the Earth vibrate and interact with the space generating inerton waves both in the spatial substrate that contained the terrestrial globe and in the surrounding Earth.

We may distinguish two constant flows of inerton waves of the Earth. The flows are caused by the proper rotation of our planet from the West to East and its motion along the orbit around the Sun. Paths passed by the fronts of these two flows are characterized by ratio pi/2. So an object whose dimensions satisfy ratio pi/2 and the orientation coincides with the quarters of the world to be a resonator of inerton waves of the Earth. Using the scanning electron microscope, we studied changes in the surface of metal specimens, which stayed in a small resonator for some time. The fine structure of specimens staying in the resonator were smoothed noticeably. Thus the presence of inerton field in the small resonator was proved experimentally. Besides, the inerton field manifested itself also in other experiments. In particular, it causes the clustering of hydrogen atoms in the KIO3*HIO3 crystal and affords the anomalous photoelectric effect both in rare gases and the surface of the metal. In such a manner, the existence of the inerton field may be taken as proved. And this means that general relativity loses its monopole rights of the all–embracing theory: the static relativity should be replaced for a dynamic theory based on the inerton field that realizes the direct interaction between massive objects.

Summarizing, we may infer that the inerton field, a new physical field, which is as fundamental as the electromagnetic field, may well have been known by the architects of the Great Pyramid. They built the Great Pyramid as the House that was saturated with inerton waves.

PROJECT

We would like to propose a group research project, whose goal is the measuring of different fields inside the Great Pyramid of Giza. We shall not study the Pyramid for new chambers, air shafts or diverse cavities. Our research team does hope to show that the Great Pyramid in fact is a resonator of the inerton field of the Earth. The main purpose of our project is the analysis and detailed classification of fields that imbue the interior of the Great Pyramid. In such a manner, our team would like to record radiations in the three major chambers, the Grand Gallery, the main passages and around the Great Pyramid. Namely, we plan to measure:

i) the total radiation in different points of the inside of the Pyramid and the outside (over a wide range of frequencies, by intensity, by the directions: East, West, North, South and also down and upwards);

ii) the electromagnetic component of the total radiation, i.e. the pure electromagnetic radiation (by frequencies, by intensity, by the geographical directions); 0iii) the inerton component of the total radiation, i.e., the inerton radiation (by frequencies, by intensity, by the geographical directions).

(Let us remind the reader that in terms of the submicroscopic concept of the construction of the natural world, the electromagnetic and inerton fields are treated as only two fundamental fields of Nature. The unification of the fields is reduced to the space net, or a quantum aether, that is simulated by special building blocks—superparticles [or cells, or balls].)

For conducting such a study of the Great Pyramid, we should produce an applicable instrument, with a special detecting piece whose heart is a pyroelectric chip. The threshold of radiation sensitivity of the detector is about 1 picoWatt. Moreover, we will use other techniques which have proven useful in measuring fields in scaled pyramids and composite buildings. Thus, our equipment will be capable of measuring the two said fields separately—the electromagnetic field: optical, thermal and radio–frequency ranges, and, independently of it—the pure inerton field) and their mixture in needed parts of local space. The instruments will show the distinction between continuous and pulse field flows. All our instruments function on a passive operating principle.

As an outcome, we will sketch the broad outlines of the fields' distribution. All the results obtained will be carefully treated and then be presented by way of a scientific report of the expedition on the web page of the Great Pyramid of Giza Research Association.

Some members of the Great Pyramid of Giza Research Association would become part of the research team as well. And we would like to think that the director of the Association, Dr. John De Salvo, could head the given project.

Team Members

Dr. Volodymyr Krasnoholovets, manager of the project, Dr., senior scientist, graduated as a theoretical physicist from the Taras Shevchenko Kyiv National University:

"For about 20 years, I have been working in the Department of Theoretical Physics at the Institute of Physics, National Academy of Sciences of Ukraine (Kyiv, Ukraine). In my scientific work, I am in close contact with experimenters from experimental and applied departments of our Institute and other scientific centers. This is why my research touches conventional and applied physics. The most internationally known results were obtained in the physics of hydrogen–bonded systems. In addition, since the mid-1980s I have taken an interest in the study of foundations of fundamental physics. At present, the results obtained in this area are also coming to light. In particular, at the end of 2000 I was invited: a) to occupy the position of the vice–editor of "Spacetime & Substance," a new international journal dedicated to the rigorous study of all aspects of gravity and fine structure of matter; b) to become an advisory board member of the Great Pyramid of Giza Research Association."

Dr. Olexander Strokach, senior scientist and vice–head of the department, and Dr. Mykola Morozovsky, senior scientist, have been working in the Department of Receivers of Radiation at the Institute of Physics, National Academy of Sciences of Ukraine for approximately 25 years.

Dr. Strokach graduated as a theoretical physicist from the Taras Shevchenko Kyiv National University. At the department, he is working as a theoretical and experimental physicist. He is also a leading technologist in the department. During 1998, he conducted research in the Seul University, South Korea.

Dr. Morozovsky graduated as an experimental physicist from the Taras Shevchenko Kyiv National University as well. He is also a leading specialist in the area of microelectronics. Both doctors have had strong skills and extensive experience in research and development work, and technology associated with the technological elaboration, production and application of pyroelectrical receivers.

This is a unique laboratory involved with other scientists in developing leading edge technologies (It should be noted that, in modern Russia, Germany, France and many other countries no such remarkable specialists exist.) In particular, our receivers have successfully functioned in the spectroradiometric equipment of numerous military and civil spaceships. Specifically: the Russian Mir space station; space satellites, which investigated Venus and comets; artificial satellites and aircrafts, which carried out soil investigations. Being certified in the former USSR, our receivers have worked as standard measuring tools and control devices measuring the energy and power of coherent and electromagnetic radiations. The receivers were introduced in medical facilities, for instance, such as the differential infra-red pyrometer for medical diagnostics that has been functioning in the Ophthalmology Clinic of Odesa (Ukraine) for ten years.

Dr. Valery Byckov is a research scientist at the Department of Physical Electronics, Institute of Physics. He is a remarkable experimenter in the making of sensors based on nanoparticle structures for infrared radiation, temperature, and mechanical strength. He is also an expert in the microanalysis of nanomaterials and nanostructures by use of Transmission Electron Microscopy, Scanning Electron Microscopy and Tunneling Electron Microscopy. He is also a specialist in computer analysis and elaboration of sophisticated experiments.

Dr. Yuri Bogdanov graduated as a PhD in cybernetics and technical sciences. He is a Corresponding Member of the International Academy of Energy-Information Sciences.

For about 20 years, he worked in Moscow in the Research & Development Institute of Air Systems and then in the State Scientific Manufacturing and Design Center for Rocket Production (Korolev, in the Moscow region) at which he constructed cruise missiles. Missiles were tested at Feodosia, Ukraine. Now Dr. Bogdanov is a citizen of Ukraine, lives in Kharkiv and works there in the Joint-stock Company Scientific and Technological Institute of Transcription, Translation and Replication (TTR), where he is the vice-president of the Institute. Today his activity is associated with the development of new instruments for the study of the Earth including its examination from outer space. The device "Tesey" elaborated at his participation allows the detection of peculiar properties of a geological feature of territory, the recording of cues of "breathing" of the Earth, etc. The device has successfully investigated power fields of various buildings including pyramids as well.

Olexander Sokolov is a senior scientist from the same Institute of TTR is a remarkable specialist in the measuring and diagnostics of surface geometry of a territory and the analysis of results with software applyications.

Oleh Kramarenko is a major geologist from the firm Ukrainian Energobuildin in Kharkiv. He was the first to introduce new equipment of the Tesey series for diagnostics deep geological analysis in the Ukraine. In our expedition, he will be responsible for the study of geologic features of the ground of the Great Pyramid.

For the first time in practice with usage of new know–how, i.e. devices of the series "Tesey," the principally new pattern of a constitution of foothills has been constructed by Dr. Bogdanov and his collaborators Mr. Kramarenko and Mr. Sokolov. The territories of Poland, the United Arab Emirates, Pakistan, Oman, and Iraq have been investigated; namely: a) diagnostic of the deep geological structures of the Earth (pinpointing the epicenters of earthquakes); b) system design of safety from natural disasters (optimal systems of the warning of rock bumps in mines); c) engineering–eniological studies of composite engineering buildings.

The partner of Dr. Bogdanov, sheikh Junaid Mohammad Khoory from Dubai, the United Arab Emirates, has also become a member of the team; he is a specialist in the variability of the structural behavior of matter under the influence of the energetic shapes of pyramids. He is a researcher and the director of a joint venture in the UAE. Mr. Khoory is well known in religious and business communities of Egypt. He is a very impressive personality.

Notwithstanding our strong skill and experience, common funds available to our research team are not enough. That is why we would like to appeal to companies, foundations, institutions and all other organizations as well as businesspersons and other individuals.

REFERENCES

Krasnoholovets, V. Byckov. Real Inertons against hypothetical gravitons. Experimental proof of the existence of inertons. Indian Journal of Theoretical Physics, vol. 48, no. 1, pp. 1–23 (2000) [http://arXiv.org/abs/quant–ph/0007027]. V. Krasnoholovets' Home page http://inerton.cjb.net

APPENDIX E

THE HUMAN ENERGY SYSTEM—
THE FIELD UPON WHICH THE PYRAMID ACTS

The following is an excerpt from James Oschman's article, *Science Measures the Human Energy Field*, which can be viewed online at http://www.reiki.org/reikinews/sciencemeasures.htm.

"In the early 1980's, Dr. John Zimmerman began a series of important studies on therapeutic touch, using a SQUID magnetometer at the University of Colorado School of Medicine in Denver. Zimmerman discovered that a huge pulsating biomagnetic field emanated from the hands of a TT practitioner. The frequency of the pulsations is not steady, but "sweeps" up and down, from 0.3 to 30 Hz (cycles per second), with most of the activity in the range of 7-8 Hz (Figure 2). The biomagnetic pulsations from the hands are in the same frequency range as brain waves and scientific studies of the frequencies necessary for healing indicate that they naturally sweep back and forth through the full range of therapeutic frequencies, thus being able to stimulate healing in any part of the body.

"Confirmation of Zimmerman's findings came in 1992, when Seto and colleagues, in Japan, studied practitioners of various martial arts and other healing methods. The "Qi emission" from the hands is so strong that they can be detected with a simple magnetometer consisting of two coils, of 80,000 turns of wire. Since then, a number of studies of Qigong practitioners have extended these investigations to the sound, light, and thermal fields emitted by healers. What is particularly interesting is that the pulsation frequency varies from moment to moment. Moreover, medical researchers developing pulsating magnetic field therapies are finding that these same frequencies are effective for 'jump starting' healing in a variety of soft and hard tissues, even in patients unhealed for as long as 40 years. Specific frequencies stimulate the growth of nerves, bones, skin, capillaries, and ligaments. Of course, Reiki practitioners and their patients have daily experiences of the healing process being "jump started," and academic medicine is now beginning to accept this therapy as logical and beneficial because of these new scientific findings. In Figure 2 we have bracketed portions of the signal that correspond to the frequencies used in medical devices that stimulate the healing of particular tissues. Individual differences in energy projection and detection.

"To study the projection of energy from the hands of therapists, scientists must first recognize that there are huge individual differences between people. Repeated practice of various techniques can enhance the effect.

"There are logical neurophysiological and biophysical explanations for the roles of practice and intention. [Editors note: It would be interesting to use these detection techniques to measure the effect of a Reiki attunement on the strength and frequency of biomagnetic energies coming from the hands and also to measure how therapeutic frequencies may change when treating various conditions in the body.]

"It is not widely understood that "brain waves" are not confined to the brain, but actually spread throughout the body via the perineural system, the connective tissue sheathes surrounding all of the nerves. Dr. Robert O. Becker has described how this system, more than any other, regulates injury repair processes throughout the body. Hence the entire nervous system acts as an "antenna" for projecting the biomagnetic pulsations that begin in the brain, specifically in the thalamus.

"Moreover, waves that begin as relatively weak pulsations in the brain appear to gather strength as they flow along the peripheral nerves and into the hands. The mechanism of this amplification probably involves the perineural system and the other connective tissue systems, such as the fascia that are intimately associated with it."

(James Oschman, Nature's Own Research Association, P.O. Box 5101, Dover, NH 03821, USA, Phone, 603-742-3789, Fax 603-742-2592)

APPENDIX F

PYRAMIDS' EFFECT UPON CHAKRAS, OR ENERGY CENTERS

Joseph Marcello

Every nerve cell generates a magnetic field around itself, and the amassed cell-field presence culminates in what Is known as the aura, or web of pulsating electromagnetic energy. The varying intensity of both emotions and thoughts modulate this electromagnetic energy flow as it circulates through the cerebrospinal centers, which act as transformers.

Thus, the coccygeal or root center or chakra connects directly with the earth or terrestrial energy and governs our relationship with the densest elements of nature, our 3-dimensionality, our 'standing' on the planet, our ability to be present as earth-beings.

The navel or pelvic center—the hara—governs fertility, balance, our relationship with the organic life within us and within the world of nature, and is severely contracted and unnaturally tight in many Westerners, due to the overemphasis on the realms of the emotions and the intellect, and the disconnection from terrestrial rhythms and forces.

The thoracic or solar plexus center, just below the ribcage, is the nexus of instinct, or bodily intuition, and governs pre-rational impulse and perception. It does not so much feel as sense—just as a child immediately senses itself entering a dark and dangerous environment, and it is perhaps the most easily destabilized and stressed of the chakras, requiring consistent cleansing and balancing.

One healer has observed that we do not so much need—as common mythology believes—to 'work on' or 'work out' the opening of our heart center as we do the clearing of our solar plexus chakra, which, even when the best of intentions are present, can act like a warped lens, due to overlays of fear and anger that easily distort our free self-expression.

The heart—or emotional—chakra is measurably the most potent field-generator of all, and can easily therefore overbalance the energies and the functions of the other centers. Its power notwithstanding, it can only properly sing its song when its chakric siblings are doing theirs—that is to say—when the body as a whole is rooted in the earth, the instinctual self or solar plexus is free of stresses and reactions, and the cognitive or third eye center is free of crystallized concepts. As an example, the heart center of a religious extremist may be very intense—and 'brilliantly lit'—but still serving quite dogmatic underlying agendas. due to unexamined or unchallenged belief systems or agendas. In such a case, the intensity of the energy of the heart chakra, while clearly powerful, when coupled with a righteous mindset—could well be experienced by another as extreme, even violent.

Energy, per se, is no guarantee of sanity or balance—and it would be instructive to realize that many of the world's most charismatic demagogues were beings of intense heart-force joined in 'unholy matrimony' with decidedly skewed ideologies.

The throat chakra is the upper creative corollary of the lower procreative center in the pelvis, enabling us to create and express on subtler and higher levels—language and music being perhaps its two most potent emanations, and is considered the center of will.

The third-eye, brow or ajna chakra is the center of vision, imagination and transpersonal or psionic perception and insight; this center, when clear, functions as a lens into other-dimensional seership.

The crown—or sahasrara—chakra provides our connection to the extended cosmos, if often only at a pre-conscious level, enabling us to intuitively feel a sense of oneness with all life. When consciously opened and enhanced, however, it is the most direct and open route to awakening to cosmic consciousness.

The chakras endlessly exercise influence upon each other— 'pushing' and 'pulling', as the case may be, relaying impulses and energies to and through each other and triggering chain reactions that eventually affect them all in turn.

As an example, the visionary brow chakra can powerfully catalyze the transcendent crown chakra, as evidenced in Richard Maurice Bucke's own experience of transcendence, as recorded in his study on the subject in Cosmic Consciousness. Bucke describes how he and several friends had gathered one evening to read poetry by different poets, among them the reigning Czar of the new era, Walt Whitman.

"I had spent the evening in the great city, with two friends, reading and discussing poetry and philosophy. We parted at midnight. I had a long drive in a hansom to my lodging. My mind, deeply under the influence of the ideas, images, and emotions called up by the reading and talk, was calm and peaceful. I was in a state of quiet, almost passive enjoyment, not actually thinking, but letting ideas, images, and emotions flow of themselves, as it were, through my mind.

"All at once, without warning of any kind, I found myself wrapped in a flame coloured cloud. For an instant I thought of fire, an immense conflagration somewhere close by in that great city; the next, I knew that the fire was within myself. Directly afterward there came upon me as sense of exaltation, of immense joyousness accompanied or immediately followed by an intellectual illumination impossible to describe.

"Among other things, I did not really come to believe, but I saw that the universe is not composed of dead matter, but is, on the contrary, a living Presence: I became conscious in myself of eternal life. It was not a conviction that I would have eternal life, but the consciousness that I possessed eternal life then. I saw that all men are immortal, that the cosmic order is such that without any peradventure all things work together for the benefit of each and all, that the foundation principal of the world, of all the worlds, is what we call love, and that the happiness of each and all is in the long run absolutely certain. The vision lasted a few seconds and was gone, but the memory of it and the sense of the reality of what it taught has remained during the quarter of a century which has since elapsed. I knew that what the vision showed me was true. I had attained to a point of view from which I saw that it must be true. That view, that conviction I may say that consciousness has never, even during periods of the deepest depression, been lost."

The chakras or energy vortexes are not, then, mere transformers or relays for our life-force, but mediators of our most intimate activities of consciousness as well—the feelings,

189

thoughts, intuitions, instincts, sensibilities and inspirations of which our lives are made.

Pyramids, being essentially energetic prisms, immediately and intimately begin exerting their influence throughout our chakra-network.

APPENDIX G

INDIAN PYRAMID VASTU

There is also the tradition of Pyramid Vastu, the science of constructional energetic dynamics, perhaps best thought of as a kind of 'Indian Feng Shui'; the following observations are drawn from the work of Kirti Betai, B.Com. LLB., Founder of Modern Vastu (Energy) Science, who has treated over 30,000 patients through the pyramid energy healing Systems which he has developed. A practicing lawyer, he was also in the business of manufacturing plastic raw materials in Mumbai, India.

Perhaps the best incentive to give his claims for pyramid power some credence is Betai's own story:

> Mr. Kirti Betai, age 56, suffered from adverse drug reactions and became comatose due to liver and kidney failure, in the year 1985 in Jaslok Hospital, at Mumbai.
>
> He came out from coma within 7 days, which in itself is a miracle although the doctors had declared him to be virtually dead.
>
> Four years after coming out of coma, he was still extremely weak and his liver and kidney functions were still abnormal which had to be monitored regularly.
>
> Doctors had confined him to bed as they could not prescribe any heavy medication out of fear of repeated liver failure.

In this condition he shifted to Agra from Mumbai where he was provided accommodation in Radhasoami Satsang in view of his services as a legal advisor.

In 1989 he read about the research work and experiments of Dr. Bovis (France), Dr. Baxter (USA), and the Nobel Prize Winner Astrophysicist Dr. Luis Alvarez—relating to cosmic energy, pyramid energy, and pendulum systems.

Within two years thereafter he had created 10,000 pyramids and placed them all over his house and compound with a view to bring about spontaneous healing of his liver and kidney.

At the end of 1990 his liver and kidney function become normal which was confirmed by medical tests and he could now work for 15 hours a day—without any pain or weakness.

Two years ago he could not even sit for more than 30 minutes at a time due to pain and weakness. His diabetes, cervical spondylosis, and his wife's asthma and colitis got healed during the same period. No drugs or any other health care was used.

This was the second miracle in the life of Kirti Betai. Shortly thereafter others who saw his transformation began to take pyramid energy treatment and each one benefited. Diseases cured include frequent and chronic cold to cancer—asthma to allergies and arthritis—migraine to muscular dystrophy—aids and polio and paralysis …. The list is endless.

Over 30,000 patients have been cured and 25,000 premises have been vastu corrected and 500 businesses have turned around from sickness to health including schools, hospitals, hotels, shops, factories, farms, etc.

A summation of Kirti Betai's conclusions relating to the power of pyramids follows:

PYRAMID HEALING ENERGY RESEARCH
THE SOURCE OF INSPIRATION

The Giza Pyramid Complex has been the focus of attention of the mankind for centuries.

It has taken more time, attention, and efforts, of the contemporary scientific community, in trying to understand what was accomplished by the Egyptians, or whoever built the Giza Pyramid Complex, than it took the ancient engineering genius in materializing the Giza pyramid complex into reality.

Hundreds of scientists have invested their in-valuable time, attention, and energy to decode the secret of the pyramids. Equal numbers of scientists have invested their time, attention, and energy, to find flaws in their discoveries.

Those who want to find flaws are bound to succeed, as knowledge of man is imperfect. When knowledge becomes perfect the knower is no longer a man—he becomes God personified in man. He does not find it necessary to collect evidence to satisfy others about the truth of what he has known.

If the others choose to ignore or reject his discovery, he is unconcerned. The Earth was round even before Galileo discovered that it was so.

On a chance reading of an article about the experiments of Dr. Bovis (France) relating to the energy force field of Pyramids, Kirti Betai whose liver and kidney failure due to adverse drug reaction had seen him go through a near death experience in 1984 (hepatic coma), started his Research in Pyramid Energy Systems for healing his own health condition.

In two years 10,000 Pyramids were built by Kirti Betai, of different sizes, shapes, colors, and materials, as indicated by his Pendulum Dowsing to heal his liver, kidney, pancreas, heart, and spine.

Within two years Kirti Betai began to work 15 hours a day without any perception of fatigue, or pain, and without any drugs. Earlier he could not even sit for more than 30 minutes at a time.

Simultaneously Ms. Bhagbhari Betai—Kirti Betai's wife—experienced complete relief of her chronic asthma, colitis, and depression.

In the ten years thereafter over 30,000 patients of every conceivable disease, disorder, and ailment have been cured, with total relief in symptoms and confirmation of internal transformation, through investigative medical tests such as blocked arteries (angiographies), muscular dystrophy and diabetes (blood test), gall stone removal (ultrasound).

Diseases, disorders and ailments treated successfully so far include AIDS, allergies, arthritis, asthma, attention deficiency, blocked arteries, burns, chronic fatigue, cancer, depression, addictions, diabetes, epilepsy, fibromyalgia, gout, hypertension, hypotension, Insomnia, migraine, muscular dystrophy, polio, paralysis, rheumatism, schizophrenia, etc.

The Mother Energy Field of 10,000 Pyramids were fortified by additional 26,000 Pyramids over the next ten years - totaling up to 36,000 Pyramids—their Energy Force Field being unified and integrated in-to one energy wave form.

THE PYRAMID ENERGY SYSTEM

We live in an energy universe. All animate and inanimate energy Forms are life-forms - having an energy nucleus within the core of every atom that constitutes the form.

Inanimate energy forms are visibly inert. Animate energy forms appear to act and interact with their environment, and they appear to survive on a continuous input of energy from their environment, and they produce waste. Inanimate life-forms do the same but their activity is feeble and imperceptible to our sensory system.

All energy systems continuously and spontaneously interact with each other. Distance is no barrier. Every energy system polarizes to become kinetic. Polarizing involves concentration of energy particles at one place (positive pole) and corresponding depletion of energy particles at another (negative pole).

There cannot be any activity unless the energy system becomes bi-polar. Before the beginning of time and Creation, there were two energy systems—one was conscious and kinetic (positive pole)—the other being depleted and dormant (negative pole)—its activity being too feeble to be called conscious—

surviving on continuous input of energy from the positive pole—and not capable of individual action.

So in the beginning, there was one kinetic energy system, and the other dormant or unconscious or potential energy system.

By continuous and prolonged interactions between these two systems the process of Creation ensued. The very first interaction that made the first dormant energy particle active and kinetic marks the beginning of time and Creation.

Now there were two active energy systems, and their interactions continued to bring about more energy particles into a conscious and active state. So one became two—and two became three—and so on—until all energy particles that could be energized and made active by energy interactions were brought to life.

The same is the process of every life-form in this and every other solar system—in the mother's womb two of the parents body cells inter-act to bring about one active cell of the new human body—this new cell divides in-to two—the two divide in-to four—and so on—every process of evolution creates a pyramid pattern.

Without the pyramid pattern there can be no activity or organization or life. Every organization must function in the pyramid pattern for its survival. So a country has one head of state (by whatever name) and each company has one CEO and every home (the smallest organizational unit of society) has to have one head of the family.

The pyramid pattern, therefore, represents the process of evolution—of consciousness—of life.

Every energy system has a unique frequency, size, shape, color, and sound. If two energy systems are absolutely identical in all respects, they cannot remain as two - they will spontaneously merge into one unified energy-wave-form.

For activity and interaction there must be at least two energy systems in existence, one energy that will act upon another Energy, through the medium of energy waves. Through these interactions both will undergo some change. The change will be in one or more or all of the frequencies, sizes, shapes, colors and sounds, the five manifestations of energy.

In this process of evolution, the energy nucleus does not undergo change—the prime energy nucleus, which began the whole process of the ever-changing universe remains unchanged. We often refer to this energy nucleus as God.

At all levels of the Creation the energy nucleus does not undergo any change—only its form changes. e.g., water evaporates to turn into vapor (gaseous state)—vapor turns in-to water (fluid state)—water falling in polar regions turn in-to ice (solid state)—ice turns in-to water—through-out the process the nucleus remains unchanged.

The energy nucleus is in a pyramid pattern—its action is also in a pyramid pattern—e.g. a wave of light grows in a pyramid pattern as it travels away from its Energy Center—the same with magnetic energy wave—and the same with sound energy waves.

So the Pyramid or the energy nucleus remains unchanged in the interaction between the two or more energy systems and what remains unchanged is really the pyramid. 'Pyramid' in Greek is made up of two words—pyr = fire or heat or energy—and amid = middle or center or nucleus. 'Energy nucleus' or 'energy center' is therefore the true meaning of 'pyramid.' Pyramid is that part of a life-form, which does not undergo change, but which brings about change in others in its environment, due to interactions.

In every Energy interaction the form of both interacting energy systems change. In interactions with a pyramid even the energy nucleus of the other energy system changes. That is the key difference between energy nucleus of any energy system and the pyramid energy system.

That is why a dead body cell can remain unchanged (free from decay) when placed within pyramid energy force field.

This is possible only when an energy system has been accelerated (condensed) to a speed of perpetual motion. Perpetual motion means there is no change due to interactions — which can happen only when there is no motion — i.e. the speed of the sub-atomic particles whirling around the energy nucleus is so high that they are present at every place in every dimension i.e. at all levels simultaneously — when this happens, the energy particles are no longer in motion — because they are already present everywhere - so they do not undergo change — this is the state of perpetual motion.

In the state of perpetual motion the energy particles are in continuous interaction with all other energy systems at all levels of the Creation — but they do not change as a result of the interaction. This is the state of pyramid energy system.

This is also the state of the 'prime nucleus' — The God — who is known to be omnipresent and omnipotent. Pyramid energy systems represent and reflect God and His Creation.

Certain facts of life cannot be proved or explained merely in words—they have to be experienced. One can at best explain how drinking water quenches thirst (if water is drunk) but one cannot experience nor understand what it means unless he drinks the water when he is thirsty. Mankind does not understand the phenomena of sleep or how magnetism works—and yet every one sleeps and uses magnetism in daily life. Pyramid Power similarly will have to be experienced, to be understood.

THE CREATION OF A PYRAMID ENERGE FORCE FIELD

Thousands around the world have and are continuing to experiment with Pyramid Power. Most have replicated the Golden Section of the Giza Pyramid, and many have tried different sizes, shapes, colors, and sounds to maximize the Pyramid Power—and most have experienced that Pyramids do not seem to behave consistently from time to time or person to person or place to place. This is seen as one of the mysterious aspects of the Pyramid Power.

Other mysteries that surround the Giza Pyramid Complex are 1) How was it built? 2) Who built it? 3) Why was it built?

Psychokinesis is the only method for transporting heavy objects from one place to another that was practiced not only in the ancient Egypt but in many parts of the world. Evidence of this is available in the ancient Egyptian, Chinese, and Indian literature.

There is enough evidence to suggest that the efforts, technique and technology that was used in creation of the Egyptian pyramids, including the Giza Pyramid Complex, was solely of Egyptian origin.

The result of every activity depends upon its purpose. The purpose of making pyramids for Mr. Kirti Betai was to heal his physical body. So the Mother energy field of the 36,000 Pyramids created at Agra India are predominantly configured for healing.

The purpose for which the Giza Pyramid Complex was created is different and so its energy configuration is also different. The frequency, size, shape, color, and sound of any energy system will reflect the purpose for which the energy system was brought into action—provided the efforts were successful.

So this information is encoded (so to say) within the Giza Pyramid. There are conflicting or contrary views regarding the purpose for which the Giza Pyramid Complex was built. This is not surprising as each researcher has a different perspective and what he sees or experiences will be limited by his perspective. The Giza Pyramid Complex was built for almost each and every purpose, which is being attributed. It is a multi-purpose energy system.

The Pyramids at Agra were built with a single purpose in mind. However, over the period the energy force-field has matured into a multi-purpose energy system. The pyramid energy force-field grows with the efflux of time. It's a living system.

The pyramid shape functions like a giant reflector or antenna, and a powerful energy generator, simultaneously and spontaneously. The function of a particular energy-wave-form will be according to its design and construction. So the function of an energy system is according to its frequency, size, shape, color, and sound, which includes the material of its construction and its location, orientation, and alignment to its environment.

The moment a pyramid shape is created, it begins to inter-act with its environment and generates an energy-wave-form within. So the energy-wave-form (frequency, size, shape, color, and sound) generated by a particular pyramid will be according to its material, shape, size, color, location, orientation, and alignment.

Amongst the seven factors (material, shape, size, color, location, orientation, and alignment) location is the most important factor. This is equally true for any other venture. One well-known management expert has enumerated the three most important factors affecting the success of any business as:- location, location, and location.

For Pyramid Power as well, its location is the first most important factor, due to the fact that the pyramid will generate its power from out of the energy particles available in its environment. The location will determine the end result i.e. the frequency, size, shape, color, and sound of the energy-wave-form of the Pyramid Energy System.

The next most important factor for the end result is the material. The material used will determine the energy configuration i.e. how much will be absorbed from the available energy particles (location), by the pyramid energy system.

The next important factors are the color, size and shape of the pyramid. These will together determine the color, size and shape of the energy-wave-form of the pyramid energy system.

Ultimately the energy-wave-form of the pyramid energy system must conform to the purpose for which it was designed. So the material, shape, size, color, location, orientation, and alignment of the pyramid must be selected according to the purpose for which the pyramid energy system. is to be built.

This is the main reason why most researchers found the behaviour of pyramids built by them to be inconsistent from person to person and place to place and time to time, as they had replicated the shape of the Giza Pyramid but all other factors were different and, in any event, they were perhaps not in conformity with the purpose for which the pyramid was designed, and most of all they were built and used at different locations during the incubation period (so to say) of the pyramid energy system, i.e. the energy-wave-form of the pyramid had not stabilized or was still in its growth phase.

To overcome some of these difficulties, the Pyramid Mother energy field at Agra India was created by using a large number of small Pyramids made from every conceivable material including gold, mercury, silver, copper, brass, steel, aluminum, fiber, plastic, cardboard, paper, canvas, fiberglass, wood, etc.

In the construction of these 36,000 pyramids we used as many as 37 out of the 84 elements found in this solar system (in pre-determined proportions).

The fact is—if one was to build an exact replica of the Giza Pyramid at any other place, it may not have the same energy-wave-form. There are only three locations upon this Earth, where the Giza Pyramid can produce an identical energy-wave-form.

There are at least six more locations upon this Earth where a pyramid energy system can be built for the benefit of the mankind. These locations are not static. They keep changing with the efflux of time.

.There is only one place upon this Earth where the energy-wave-form produced by the 36,000 Pyramids at Agra India can produce the same energy-wave-form—and that is exactly the place where these 36,000 Pyramids have been located.

The pyramid power, i.e. the number of energy waves within each energy band-width - will be according to the size of the energy band width, and the size of the energy band width will be according to the size and shape and number of Pyramids constituting the pyramid energy force-field.

If and only if the power of the pyramid system is adequate for transforming the target energy system back to its original state, then alone the pyramid will be able to bring about permanent change in the target energy system.

The research work done so far by the eminent scientists of our time is remarkable. Special reference must be made of the work done on the pyramid energy system by Dr. Bovis (France), Dr. Lui Alvarez (USA), and Dr. Baxter (USA). Although the work of Dr. Baxter was mainly related to interactions of energy-wave-forms of plants, animals, and humans, his work definitely provided valuable input to Mr. Kirti Betai.

Mr. Kirti Betai expresses his deepest gratitude and conveys his highest regards to all the innumerable researchers who have contributed to his research on pyramid energy healing systems as the source of all Knowledge and all Energy is one - and whoever has invested his time, attention, energy, and other resources on discovery of any information has certainly paved the way for others to tread that path a little more comfortably.

Mr. Kirti Betai is happy to invite every seeker of truth to Agra India to experience the Power of the 36,000 strong Pyramid Energy System in creation of which they all have contributed in some way just as each of the 30,000 patients have contributed — without them the Pyramid Energy System would not have been created.

Mr.Kirti Betai is conscious of the fact that the Pyramid Power at Agra India is not the result of his effort or intellect but it is the Gift of God through thousands of His beloved children, and the same along-with all information pertaining there-to I Is open and available to all the seekers of the Truth.

(Be aware the sometimes awkward English is left unrevised):

"The pyramid has a DC magnetic field. and it flows from peak to middle to base.

"The human aura is also a DC magnetic field, which flows from peak to middle to base!

"The emotions in the chakras are also made of magnetic energy!

"The pyramids' magnetic field strengthens the magnetism of emotions and thoughts in a person's chakras the same way that gasoline strengthens a fire."

"The following beneficial effects have been delineated by Vijnana, Integrative Consultancy and Research Institute for Natural Healing and Health Care.

PHYSICAL EFFECTS

"For instance: place a razor blade inside the pyramid, at about the centre at 2/3 of the height of the pyramid, measured from the bottom. After a while, although using this razor blade daily, you will notice that it always stays perfectly sharp. For this effect, a patent was granted in the US to Karl Derbal already in 1922!

"By placing fruits or vegetables inside pyramids for just a few minutes you might quickly notice that it:
— reduces the consequences of pesticides and chemicals
— treats and energize water, foods & beverages
— balances taste of wine and coffee and any liquid
— Increases potency of vitamins
— restores enzymes of frozen foods
— promotes healthy plant growth

"If you are able to dowse, make use of any pendulum, and/or know how to test with kinesiology, you will see, that any crystal substance (e.g. salt, sugar, clay, MSM, or other such crystalline material) will reach a tremendous energy level, if placed into a pyramid for only a few seconds.

"Water, after it has remained in a Power Pyramid for about 20 minutes, will turn into a highly energized water with body-cleansing properties. The highly accumulated energies inside of the Power Pyramid will reactivate the water and lead it back to its natural active strength.

"So, indeed, any food can be put inside a Power Pyramid, and will be "harmonized" in a very short time.

PHYSICAL EFFECTS & ENERGETIC/ SUB-PHYSICAL EFFECTS

"Did you ever wonder why we feel rested and rejuvenated after a "good night's sleep"?

"Our feelings are controlled by seven levels of consciousness corresponding to the seven major endocrine glands in the body. In order to be in perfect accord with our surroundings, the body's endocrine glands must be functioning perfectly. Consciousness manifests itself through the physical expressions of sex, nourishment, compassion, love, action and discovery respectively. Horizontal sleep brings the glands parallel to the earth's surface, so, like a compass, they become magnetically aligned with each other. This process of magnetic recharging vitalizes the glands.

"The magnetization and recharging effect is greatly enhanced when you sleep under a pyramid due to the large volume of magnetic concentration that exists within the pyramidal boundaries. The astral or emotional body (the first higher inner plane of the human body) cannot relax when it is being disturbed by outer disharmonious frequencies.

SCIENTIFIC TEST RESULTS

"Tests with a Geiger counter have shown, that by the presence of a Power Pyramid, radioactivity is diminished significantly. The natural radioactivity went down from 540 to 403 Impulses/min.

Further test subjects having radioactive test–material in their hands have confirmed, that in the presence of a Power Pyramid no effect at all will be measurable on the person—up to dozens of meters away from the pyramid! Whereas, without the Power Pyramid, the GSR a skin resistance test, immediately displayed very bad values.

"So far, it has not been possible to explain this phenomenon scientifically, one only (justified) if we accept the presence of a very specific and subtle EMF field, which is not yet to be measured with conventional tools of scientific analysis. But modern science is moving straight towards such understandings and soon might be able to make it viable for everybody.

"Another scientific measurement on a disturbed area (deep earth fissure) has shown the following results:

"Without (the) Power Pyramid the Impulses came by 75 per minute, whereas with the Power Pyramid the impulses decreased down to only 5 per minute! This exceeds by far the effect of any other known tool or device of compensation presently on the market.

"Power Pyramids are accumulators of all the different 7 energy levels we are using in our bodies, represented by the 7 main chakras. That means, conscious processes in our bodies are in absolute relation and accordance to the pyramidal energies — our body itself carrying the pyramidal structure within every cell.

"Therefore, if we meditate for example on the workout of a specific problem, be it mental, vital or physical, the power pyramids can help us to recover, charge, enhance, direct and stabilize the energies within us within a very short time.

"Power pyramids are excellent for pranic healing, stress–relief and recovery. Sleeping close to or inside a power pyramid will renew and recover the body functions. as it provides a certain magnetic protection (EMF, X–Ray, Radio—and Micro–Waves, etc.) as well as a prana–concentration / recharging field.

" 3. Pyramidal effects on the human body made visible by the Galvanic Skin Response (GSR)/Skin Resistance Measurement (GSR is also known as "lie–detector" in criminology)

"In the left picture (not included here), we see the neutral scale drawing of an oscilloscope—taken off the skin from a test person.

"In the right picture (not included here) we see the result from the same test person when touching a power pyramid. The skin resistance is decreasing rapidly—(a response) which can be reproduced endlessly.

"Decreasing values of the skin resistance in modern medicine are considered to be significant for stress relief. Average values of 'normal stressed' adults range between 50 and 60 kOhm; the more somebody gets stressed, the closer the skin resistance value can reach about 2000 kOhm.

"By regular energy training (e.g. Kundalini Yoga, Chi Gong, T'ai Chi), it is possible to stabilize this value even at about 15—30 kOhm. <u>By the use of the pyramids, the skin resistance will stabilize after a short time at 10—15 kOhm, when being stressed only rising up to 25 kOhm.</u> Usually, children's values are below that still (5—10 kOhm).

"When sitting close by, or better touching a power pyramid, the skin resistance decreases within minutes in average at about 25—50 %, and after a short while will stabilize at 10—15 kOhm— which otherwise is only to be achieved by long term practice of relaxation techniques.

"Tests have shown that the effects of the power–pyramids on the skin resistance stabilize after about 1 hour to very beneficial values and stay stable like that for a few days. Contact with the pyramid needs to be only a few minutes—having the feet inside or holding the hands above.

"Vastushastra is the science that synchronizes a balance between human life and nature. Nature consists of five elements. These are water, fire, earth, Air (atmosphere) and Sky (space). The five basic elements, the eight directions, the electromagnetic and gravitational forces of the earth, the cosmic energy emanating from the planets as well as the atmosphere and their influence on human life have all been taken into consideration in the Vastushastra, and a harmonious confluence of nature and human life has been brought about.

There are many Vastu defects like a second entrance door opposite the main entrance, the presence of a lift, the staircase, hospital, temple, opposite to an entrance door that are interactive with the living system. Actually we are bearing with at least 15–20 Vastu defects as the integral part of our housing system without which we cannot live a normal life.

"Any kind of structure, which we are using, is called (by the name of) Vastu. It may be home, office, factory, temple, hospital, workshop, farmhouse etc. Vastu Shastra was written or developed to generate and to receive positive energy within your Vastu.

Some pyramid vastu random research results:

1) The seasonal fruit yield, namely mangoes and chikoos, is increasing steadily every year by about 15–20%. There has been a noticeable enhancement in the size as well as taste of the fruits.

2) The rice crop yield has increased by approximately 1/4 the quantity it used to be before placement of Pyramid Energy

Instruments. It is interesting to note that each rice grain size and quality gets even better with each crop of the season.

3) For many years I had tried to grow vegetables for commercial purpose but each time was disappointed I am happy to inform you that since about 6 months I have had very successful results growing varied vegetables like tomatoes, coriander, brinjals (eggplants), spinach, lady's fingers, white and pink pumpkins and chilies. We sell the produce in Valsad, Vapi and Bombay markets. Due to the high quality of these vegetables in appearance (colour and texture), taste and quantity we are being able to make good profits.

4) The most interesting fact is that after several failed attempts prior to Geopathic stress zone corrections, we have now been successful in growing American Corn. The quality and taste is incomparable. Each corn cob is covered completely with corn which is tender and sweet in taste. I am proud to inform you that we are the only ones able to grow such fine American corn in the vicinity."

5) Ever since the Geopathic Stress Zone corrections as mentioned above have been done without any shifting or demolition, the tension and fatigue have virtually gone from my family members' systems. The business has picked up and is more enjoyable than before. Several business problems for which no solution appeared to be possible have been handled beautifully and resolved amicably."

6) I have also experienced the beneficial results of Cosmopathy practiced by Mr. Betai in several health disorders, with excellent results for myself, my family and relations,

7) Standing near the Great Pyramid, I felt this energy in a tangible, tingling way. I had never connected with a place like that before."

APPENDIX H

MELTED PYRAMIDS IN EGYPT?

By Russel G. Chong

Russel Chong is a friend of Nick Edwards, and created the outstanding artwork for the front and back covers of this book; the following is his personal narrative.

My trip to Egypt was approaching, and I was filled with anticipation! I have always been immensely interested in the ancient Egyptian civilization and specifically the Pyramids. This was my first trip to the land of the Nile, and it was a long time coming. I had been reading about it since I was a kid and finally in college as an art major. I went through many art history courses and learned a lot about the different ages stylistically and from a supposed evolution of civilization and intelligence culminating into the modern era. I was finally going to see and experience it first–hand, the majestic remnants of the once mighty ancient Egyptian civilization which to this day is still very mysterious and also highly artistic.

I considered brushing up on orthodox basics, such as the pyramid names, which pharaoh was supposedly buried in them, where they were located in relation to one another, and when they were constructed, but eventually as the departure time drew near I decided it might be better to avoid any preconceived ideas of what was established in the orthodox history books. I wanted to go with an open mind and just get my own point of view on what I was looking at.

I already knew that no pharaoh or mummy had been found buried in a pyramid and a lot of what has been written is still unproven conjecture. Even as a kid I was never satisfied with the 'tomb' theories, nor did it make sense that these ancient peoples constructed these enormous structures for pharaohs with copper chisels and dragged and piled millions of tons of stones into pyramids with such astonishing accuracy in plain view of tomb robbers.

Why the precision? Especially considering how difficult it would be today to build something like the Great Pyramid, or any of the large pyramids for that matter. Truly, if you wanted to bury a great, great, man—a god, would you not want to find a place a little less obvious? If it was filled with golden artifacts wouldn't the structure need to be guarded for millennia and laced with booby traps so it wouldn't be desecrated? If a pharaoh was buried in the pyramid wouldn't the casing stones be festooned with hieroglyphs? There has to be much more to it.

There has been so much controversy and speculation over the purpose of the pyramids, their age, and how they were constructed.

I just had to go see for myself.

Our first stop on my tour was the Red Pyramid of Dashur. The first thing I noticed was its tremendous size. I've been to Chichen Itza, Coba and Tikal, but this was much more massive. I had been to the 'Pyramid of the Sun' at Teotihuacan and it has a large base, of course, similar in area to the 'Great Pyramid' itself, but this one was much taller. Our bus parked in front of the North face, where the entrance to the interior was located. As we climbed up the stairway I noticed there were no casing stones anywhere on the pyramid and dirt was all over the stone blocks. The blocks were not very big, approximately 1' high, 1' deep and 2' long, if that.

I was much too anxious to go inside so I didn't inspect the exterior too much. As I hunched over and climbed down the entrance shaft the first thing that struck me was how low the ceiling was. The next thing I realized was that there were no stairs. Oh, there's ladder-like planking and banisters for us tourists, but they were obviously made somewhat recently and they're made of wood. The shaft ceiling is low, steep, and long (27° and 206' long I found out later). So if you're burying a pharaoh in this thing you somehow slide a beautifully elaborate golden sarcophagus down this shaft? How tall was the average ancient Egyptian person? I'm 5'8" and I have trouble doing it. The recently built plank ladder we were traversing down made it somewhat easier.

Meanwhile the shaft seemed to go down, down, down for a long time. When we finally made it to the bottom there was a very strong ammonia smell. I began to wonder if I was smelling ancient, centuries old urine—maybe even thousands years old! It was not a pleasant thought. I looked everywhere for human-height stains on the walls and there were none. The rooms at the bottom of the shaft had high humidity combined with the noxious smell. The chambers had corbelled ceilings. What purpose do they serve? Is it engineered for load bearing or is there another purpose? Could it be something we don't understand because our industrial and cultural basis is so different?

The second chamber was similar to the first and had a set of wooden stairs that zigzagged up to a passageway that led to the third chamber. The passageway was near the ceiling, about 30' up. This chamber had a 13-stepped corbeled ceiling and floor that had deteriorated badly. The humidity and ammonia smell was the worst here. The stonework, though, was amazing, with no gaps between the huge blocks. In some places it looks like a mortar was used, in others not. Nevertheless, why would such amazing, tightly-engineered stonework be necessary for a tomb?

Another question arises: when this pyramid was first discovered and there wasn't this wooden staircase, no doubt early researchers had to use a tall ladder to reach the final chamber. Did the pharaoh's funeral procession also use a tall ladder to lift the golden sarcophagus into the final chamber 30' up? It seemed like an awfully awkward way to bury someone. Whoever engineered this amazing structure constructed it with millions of tons of granite; couldn't they have included a simple stone stairway for the pharaoh's sarcophagus? Without a stairway or a ladder to reach the final chamber it would seem less than logical—perhaps even impractical. Where were the hieroglyphs? The walls were blank. As artistically, grandiose, and as eloquent as the ancient Egyptians were with their hieroglyphs, why is it that they are absolutely nowhere inside the pyramid? I had seen enough of the interior and it was time to go back outside.

The smell combined with the high humidity was making this visit uncomfortable. As I walked out, the brightness of the sun blinded me briefly but the fresh air was pleasant. I took some time to get used to the light at the entrance and slowly began walking down the steps.

I turned around to look at this massive monument and noticed what poor condition it was in. All the casing stones were gone and the blocks that made up the pyramid looked strange. They should have looked look like steps going to the top but they were round, soft, and sagging. They looked like the tops had expanded over their original block shape and like freshly poured beer, bubbled over its mug. They looked melted! What kind of erosion makes stone bubble, expand, and droop? Acid rain, pollution? Thousands of years of moisture from the Nile? High heat?

I touched the stone half expecting it to crumble beneath my fingers but no, the bubbly, rounded, blocks were (excuse the pun) rock hard. I banged on it with my fist figuring it would crack and crumble but all that succeeded in doing was hurting my hand. As I knelt down to take a closer look, it reminded of the lava rock I had seen on the big island of Hawaii. Although if you hit lava rock with your bare hands your skin will get sliced up. It looked like something heated the rock and it expanded as it melted, created pockets of gas bubbles and expanding over its original block shape. I'm no geologist but that's what it looked like.

I had to take a walk around the pyramid and see if this was consistent with the whole monument. I started on the North side where the entrance was and walked to the west side. I didn't climb it but I could clearly see there were a few drooping stones but overall they remained block–like over the entire face, albeit covered with dirt and sand. The pyramid base is huge and it took longer than I expected but I finally made it around the south side. Like the west, there were a few sagging stones but again, overall they remained consistently firm. It seemed odd that the erosion/melting was not consistent and that blocks here and there were affected while most others were not.

At the southwestern corner apparently some digging was going on presumably to find the foundation as there was a cone shaped pit about 10' deep, but at the bottom there was just more dirt and no floor. How deep did the sand and dirt go down in this huge area? I finally made it to the East side and it also had severe expansion/drooping over the entire face. I was gratified to see some casing stones actually were still intact near the base. Closer inspection revealed something odd: across the few remaining flat casing stones was an area lined with bubbled, slagging stone. This also looked melted to me but in much more specific places. Only certain areas were affected while others were not.

About a mile away is the 'Bent Pyramid.' Approaching this structure is awe inspiring. The size is absolutely massive and it's easy to imagine it when it was new because most of the casing stones are still intact. What can be deceptive is its somewhat simple geometric form and the lack of surface décor or detail, a characteristic which doesn't lend itself any scale. As you walk up to it, you begin to realize how gargantuan it is and how big the blocks are. They're much bigger than the blocks of the 'Red Pyramid.' What also makes the pyramid seem bigger is the initial steep angle from the ground (55°) to the point where the angle changes (43°). You are basically looking at a wall of granite 150' high, and you feel like a tiny bug standing next to this huge, geometric shape.

Standing close you can't actually see the conventionally angled section because it bends away. As you walk farther and farther you start seeing the conventionally angled section. It seems almost inhuman in its monolithic size and lack of surface features and décor, especially compared to the kinds of buildings constructed today. What kind of minds would build such a structure as as this, and for what purpose? It didn't appear to be ancient Egyptian, especially considering all the major sites we visited later on, such as Luxor, Karnak, Dendera, Kom and Ombo. They were very artistically and religiously elaborate, and hieroglyphs were carved everywhere. They were on the inside and outside walls, the pillars, and even the ceilings. The only place that wasn't carved were the floors, which, to me, is highly inconsistent.

This is especially the case, considering the framework of what is known of the ancient Egyptians, which has hieroglyphs nowhere. It seems that this structure is more like a machine rather than a tomb. Would we decorate a factory or a machine? Most likely not. Would we decorate a tomb? Yes. The precision of the stonework was amazing and looked very carefully engineered. I can't imagine the architects and engineers planning this massive edifice, then. halfway through construction, changing their minds and altering an angle because it began to crush itself. I don't buy that. Clearly the people that built this were not stupid. This thing had been engineered deliberately to be built as it is. Perhaps some subsidence occurred later from an earthquake. To me, it is an outdated notion to imagine it was built with copper chisels, and blocks dragged up mud ramps.

Around the base many of the stones were gone, or as orthodox historians say, "… taken to make buildings in Cairo." It's easy to see how perfectly cut the stones were in the undamaged areas. With some blocks you could look up and see the fit was so tight that they looked like they were separate, yet connected. Every undulation, bump, or depression on the surface of a lower block was duplicated on the one on top of it. It was almost as if one block was poured on top of the other, yet they were separate. There were even tight fitting casing stone plugs about the size of a postcard, for reasons I can't even begin to fathom. I continued examining this behemoth and took notice that there was similar damage to the few left on the Red Pyramid, damage much more obviously rampant here, because there are still many remaining.

Much like the few left on the East side of the Red Pyramid, it was obvious that they were all the same kind of limestone. Why would specific areas be bubbly, drooping, and concave and other areas be smooth? Again I reached out and touched the bubbly stone and it was very hard and not crumbling. Yet the color and texture were consistent.

As I backed away I could see missing casing stones on the top. Surely anyone climbing up to the top to harvest stones for construction in Cairo could think of an easier way to do it. It's incredibly steep and dangerous and if you were to slip, you would be dead. With nothing to grab on to if you lose your footing, it would be the giant slide of death.

These stones are both huge and heavy, though they're not as big as the ones on the Great Pyramid, but they do look to be at least a third or half their size — still quite huge and unmanageable for any human being. A crowbar couldn't budge them. It might have been interesting to watch quarrymen in the 1300's breaking off and lifting these 1 ton stones (if one assumes they did) into the back of a wagon and traversing miles of sand and dirt, across the Nile, to make buildings in the city. It doesn't sound very convenient or practical. Or did they just take the stones that had already fallen? There aren't any living eyewitnesses today so we will probably never know.

The east side had even more of the melted casing stones, again in random patterns on the smoothest sections and then nearly 2/3rds of the entire upper left side most of which are missing. Though I couldn't climb to the top I could see with my camera the exposed granite stones at the 43° section on top also had the 'bubbling over the mug' core stones of the Red Pyramid. I walked back to the north side noticed that the exposed granite on top was the same.

It's clear that these pyramids have been through tremendous catastrophic events beyond those of which our orthodox historical records tells us. Much more has happened to them besides erosion and earthquakes, for I see melted stone everywhere.

Later in the trip I noticed similar randomized damage at the top of the Khafre pyramid where the casing stones are still intact. All around the Giza Plateau and especially at the 'Funerary Temple of Khafre' there are stones the size of mini-vans which have been melted/eroded. Interestingly, it appears that a predominate amount of surfaces or facets that were exposed were affected while the blocks still nestled together were unaffected. It's very possible we're looking at eons of time, during which they were constructed, functioning, burned and destroyed, reconstructed, flooded and destroyed again, and finally, abandoned. Who knows how many times that pattern may have been repeated? No written records exist of who or how or why they were built. No hieroglyphs are found in them or on them. While the interior of Unas' pyramid at Saqarra is festooned with glyphs, it's all done on stucco—and it's anyone's guess as to when that was completed. We can't scientifically date the troweling of stucco.

When I arrived back home in Los Angeles after the 1 month whirlwind tour, there were a lot of things to consider, so it was time to do some research. Since stone is undateable with our current technology, what many conservative historians have attempted to answer through the Rosetta stone, Herodotus' writings, and scant physical evidence doesn't make much sense. Until we develop better techniques for dating stone, we're still somewhat in the dark.

What I found is that on the northern and eastern sides of the Red Pyramid there's significant melting of the blocks comprising of the granite core and very little on the western and southern sides. The melting temperature for granite is 1200°. There is also a horizontal pattern of melting on the few remaining casing stones on the eastern side near the base. The melting point for limestone is 825°, but it doesn't become molten, rather it breaks down into dust or lime. This could also be 'tafoni pitting' from salt water tidal erosion, which means at one time the ocean was covering the pyramids and then slowly receded. Thus the height of the inundated pyramid would have been 332' high. The height of the Khafre pyramid, 448' in which we've allowed for the fact that the Giza plateau is 200' above the current sea level. The bizarre random pattern across the faces of the Bent Pyramid puts this into question. So whatever has melted and eroded the Red Pyramid happened at a time when the casing stones were already removed, shaken, or blown off. Very large questions do arise if this is the case.

Despite the Bent Pyramid being the most intact of the pyramids, the North side shows unusual randomized patterns of similarly melted or water-eroded casing stones. The most severely affected sides are the east, south, and west faces, where they are almost entirely destroyed. The absence of a completely compromised northern face possibly indicates lower heat or fewer tidal forces on the surface …Possibly.

Queries:

What has the ability to heat up and melt the exposed granite to 1200°?

Why is the exposed granite melted mostly on the north and east sides of the Red Pyramid?

Why do the Bent Pyramid's casing stones exhibit minor randomized bubbling on the north side and major bubbling on all 3 other sides?

Why are the granite core stones on the top of the Bent Pyramid melted?

Why is the Dashur plateau still mostly buried in dirt and sand? These are structures of immense importance in unlocking keys to man's technological prowess in the distant past. They must be studied by multidisciplinary specialists and not just archaeologists. Chris Dunn is a perfect example.

How long does it take for 'tafoni pitting' to occur? This needs to be analyzed in order to help get a sense of the length of time water has been flowing on the pyramids

Considerations:

If the granite core stones were melted, then something super–heated them after the casing stones were already gone.

Recently, New Zealand Professor Ken MacKenzie chemically analyzed the composition of the chemical signature of the casing stones of the 'Bent Pyramid' and concluded that it is a form of ancient concrete. French chemical engineer Joseph Davidovits discovered that the Great Pyramid's inner and outer blocks are not natural, but were also manufactured. His conclusions showed the engineers knew exactly which kind of stone or aggregate was needed for every aspect of the design—a design we still don't understand to this day!

Further analysis must also be done on the granite used in the construction of the pyramid. The original builders may have had the technology to make and pour granite blocks, besides of course, cutting and lifting them. These may also have a different chemical reaction to environmental stresses.

The ability to create stone is a great technological feat, but engineering them into these enormous structures is an entirely different accomplishment. Considering also that the 'Great Pyramid' is 8 and not 4-sided, earthquake proof, aligned exactly to the cardinal points, its side measurements are equal to a solar year, height and circumference is equal to pi, and the angle of the grand gallery is the same number as the speed of light. This is a structure of pure advanced genius that today's humans still can't figure out and especially reproduce.

There are rumors that a buried 'Dark Pyramid' was found by the U.S. Military in Alaska while doing seismic analysis of China's underground nuclear weapons testing. This is purported to be able to generate and transmit power, and to have the capacity to fulfill electricity needs for all of Canada. If this turns out to be true then pyramids may be generators of some kind.

Recent scientific research on Tutankhamen's ancient Egyptian scarab is carved with what is called Libyan Desert Glass, mostly found in parts of Libya and Egypt, the Gobi and Mojave deserts. The only other green glass on earth was created on the ground at Alamogordo, New Mexico by the nuclear bomb test back in 1945 by 'silica fusion'. This green glass is now called 'Trinitite,' based on the Trinity bomb test. Do we have ancient or modern eyewitness testimony that a meteor or comet coming close to the ground of earth and melting the sand into green glass? No. Do we have eyewitness testimony that this very reaction occurs from our testing nuclear weapons? Yes. So what is the argument? Is it too radical and unthinkable? There's no physical evidence that ancient man had nuclear technology. Yet if he did and it was made of metal, it would've long turned to dust by now.

Fairly advanced artifacts (vase, spark plug, coins, and petrified hammers) are found embedded in rock and coal anywhere from 50,000 to 300,000,000 years old. Recently in Russia a device with a complex series of cogs not unlike the Antikythera (Aegean island) mechanism was found embedded in solid rock. Civilizations appear to come and go.

Hypothesis: The pyramids are generators of some kind, built by an advanced global civilization that built a power grid that circled the earth (as evidenced by the pyramids found all over the earth) and far preceded the Egyptian civilization. A cataclysmic flood occurred, destroying that civilization. The sea level rose and covered the pyramids and caused the erosion on the limestone. The casing stones were either stripped, shaken, or blown off. Exposed granite core stones were melted by tremendous heat, possibly by nuclear weapons (or maybe a meteor?).

Theory: Let's keep up inquires, get specialists onto these questions and find out!

Russell G. Chong

Los Angeles August 14th , 2013

APPENDIX I

IN SEARCH OF UNDERWATER PYRAMIDS

by Nick Edwards

In early June, 1978 I joined George Gele and a research team in an expedition to look for suspected underwater pyramids in the Gulf of Mexico.

George, a fellow researcher from Baton Rouge, Louisiana, alertly discovered pyramid-appearing structures recorded in NASA photos taken from space by satellites in orbit, high above the Mississippi River Delta region.

By coincidence, and from above, the mouth of the Mississippi bears a striking resemblance to the Nile Delta in Egypt. The warming trend since the last Ice Age (over the span of last 12,000 years) has since covered the area with an additional 20 foot depth of water. Some 100 centuries ago in the Delta area, a highly developed civilization came to be. The constant erosion and Sandy deposits created in the lower Mississippi throughout millennia may have completely covered over the last trace of the great ancient civilization. Homes, roadways and other landmarks, possibly with the exception of the tallest and most indestructible structures, were covered by silt from the river bottom. Gele believes these are pyramids.

Further examination of NASA photos revealed several pyramids and structural complexes near the Chandeleur Islands located in the Gulf of Mexico, about 75 miles east southeast of

New Orleans. This group of islands trends north and south and is some 35 miles long.

Ed Tascher, a good friend and also a pyramid researcher, traveled with me to Louisiana to meet George Gele. George was waiting with the "Ashepoo," an all–natural, radar equipped training ship, which was crewed by Sea Scouts, an all-female crew.

Several divers and psychics also came aboard to assist in locating the underwater pyramids. It was my function to outfit the "Ashepoo" with my newest and best pyramid finding equipment and take pictures of the expedition. It was an excellent opportunity to test my newly designed underwater grid system; thus, with boundless excitement and great expectations. I joined the expeditionary force. The first two days at sea were unsuccessful due to violent storms, but on the third day the ocean surface and skies became bright and clear.

Once in the Chandeleur Island locale, the psychics brought us back to an area five consecutive times where we observed some unusual phenomena. In this particular area the Ashpoo's compass spun wildly and the ships generator drew enormous surges of power, enough energy to support three or four seagoing crafts of our size. Our divers also found the underwater pressure against their ears much greater than expected at 20 foot depths. To add to the unexpected, the ocean currents were unusually strong, making it impossible to focus our explorations on one specific site. The apex of one underwater pyramid was apparently exposed about 10 feet above the sandy bottom of the ocean floor. Unfortunately, the recent storm had muddied the water and none of our underwater pictures came out.

Later we learned that various airplanes flying over this region have suddenly dropped several hundred feet in altitude. Shrimp boat crews curiously don't drag their nets over this area because they often snag their gear on things below, things mysteriously protruding above the seabed.

My new underwater grid system proved to be a very good submerged pyramid locater. I believe a pyramid or group of pyramids exist underwater in this area, perhaps similar to one of those found off the coast of Florida in the so–called Bermuda Triangle. George and I plan to mount another expedition to the Chandeleur Island vicinity in the near future. We hope either the Cousteau or National Geographic Society will take interest and research this area.

APPENDIX J

PAUL BRUNTON: A NIGHT INSIDE THE GREAT PYRAMID

From A Search in Secret Egypt by Paul Brunton, published by North Atlantic Books, copyright © 2015 by Paul Brunton Philosophic Foundation, original edition copyright © 1936 by Paul Brunton. Reprinted by permission of publisher.

Paul Brunton (1898-1981) was a 20th century mystic and author; one of the first to make the world aware of some of the greatest—albeit previously unknown—spiritual figures of the modern era, such as the now-renowned Ramana Maharshi. Brunton was a ceaseless explorer of cultures and traditions, authoring such compelling works as In Search of a Secret Indian, In Search of a Secret Egypt and The Secret Path. Brunton was an intriguing figure who, in the minds of many of his students and acquaintances, accounted for numerous catalytic spiritual transformations. His narrative, while almost beyond the borders of belief, is far from fiction, but his actual transcribed memoir of a night spent, alone and without communication lines to the outside world, in the great pyramid.

*

The sleeping cats of Cairo opened their green eyes, yawned prodigiously, and then gracefully stretched their soft paws to the utmost possible limit. Dusk was arriving, and with dusk began the activity which constituted their real existence—friendly chats, f0od-scavenging, mice-chasing, open battle and love-making. And with dusk, too, I was beginning one of the strangest activities of my life, albeit a silent one.

I had proposed to myself to spend an entire night inside the Great Pyramid, to sit, awake and alert, for twelve hours in the King's Chamber, while the slow darkness moved across the African world. And here I was, at last, settling down within the strangest shelter yet built on our planet.

It had been no easy task to arrive at this point, either. I had discovered that, although the public could always approach it, the Great Pyramid was not public property. It belonged to the Government of Egypt. One could no more walk into it and spend an unconventional night inside any of its rooms than one could walk into any strange man's house and spend a night inside his best bedroom.

Each time one visits the interior of the Pyramid one has to buy a ticket for five piastres from the Department of Antiquities. I, therefore, walked into the Department of Antiquities and optimistically asked for permission to spend one night inside the Great Pyramid. Had I asked for permission to fly to the moon, the face of the official who listened to me could not have betrayed more utter stupefaction.

I entered into a brief and apologetic explanation of my request. Surprise gave way to amusement; he smiled. I felt that he regarded me as a fit candidate for a certain institution which few of us would care to enter as inmates. Finally: "I have never had such a request before. I do not think it is within my power to grant it."

He sent me to another and higher official of the same department. The comical scene which had taken place in his room was reenacted once more. My optimism began to drain away out of my shoes.

"Impossible!" declared the second official kindly but firmly, thinking he had before him a tame lunatic. "The thing is unheard of. I regret—" his voice trailed off, the while he shrugged his shoulders.

He rose from his chair to bow me out of the room.

It was then that my journalistic and editorial training, lulled for several years but not dead, rose rebelliously into action. I began to argue with him, persisted in repeating my request in other ways, and refused to budge from the room. He got rid of me, finally, by saying that the matter did not come within the jurisdiction of the Antiquities Department.

Within whose jurisdiction did it come, then, I enquired. He was not quite sure, but thought I had better apply to the police. I realized that my request was eccentric at the least and sufficient to label me as insane at the most. Nevertheless, I could not drop it. The determination to carry it out had become an obsession.

At Police Headquarters I discovered a Permit Section. For the third time I begged to be allowed to spend one night inside the Pyramid. The official did not know what to do with me so he sent me to his chief. The latter wanted a little time to consider the matter. When I returned next day, he referred me to the Department of Antiquities!

I went home in momentary despair of ever achieving my object.

But "difficulties are often made to be overcome" is a saying whose wearying triteness does not diminish its undying truth. My next move was to secure an interview with the genial Commandant of the Cairo City Police, El Lewa Russell Pacha. I walked out of his office with a written authority, which requested the police chief of the area in which the Pyramid was situated to give me all the assistance necessary to achieve my purpose.

And so, early one evening, I reported at the Mena Police Station to the local chief, Major Mackersey. I signed a book which was handed to me and which made the police responsible for my safety till the following day. A station constable was detailed to accompany me as far as the Pyramid, and to give instructions to the armed policeman who is placed outside the building to guard it at night.

"We are taking a risk in leaving you alone inside all night. You won't blow up the Pyramid, will you?" said Major Mackersey, humorously, as we shook hands in parting.

"I promise you not only that, but I shall not even run away with it!"

"I am afraid we shall have to lock you in," he added. "We always shut the entrance to the Pyramid at dusk with a locked iron grille. So you will be a prisoner for twelve hours."

"Excellent! Today, no residence could be more desirable to me than such a prison."

The approach to the Pyramids runs along a road shaded by lebbek trees. Houses appear on its sides at rare intervals. Finally the road winds gradually up the side of the plateau on which the Pyramids themselves are built, ending in a steep incline. As I drove up the avenue I reflected that of all the travelers who had taken the same direction for several centuries past, few if any had come on so curious a mission as mine.

I mounted the small hill across the western shore of the Nile to where the Great Pyramid and its good companion, the Sphinx, maintain silent watch over Northern Africa.

The giant monument loomed up ahead of me, as I walked across the mingled sand and stones. Once more I gazed at the triangular sloping hanks which enclose the oldest architecture that the world knows today, at the enormous blocks which stretch away from base to apex in diminishing perspective. The perfect simplicity of this building, its utter freedom from any trace of ornament, the absence of any curves amid all these straight lines—these things did not in any way detract from the massive grandeur of this creation.

I entered the silent pyramid through the gaping hole which Caliph Al Mamoun had made in its side, and began my exploration of the titanic structure, not for the first time, it was true, but for the first time upon such a strange quest as had brought me again to Egypt. After making my way some distance, I reached the end of this horizontal hole and my path changed into the Pyramid's original entrance passage.

Then, torch in hand, with head bent down almost to my knees, I descended the long, low, steep, narrow and slippery continuation of the corridor. This awkward posture was exceedingly uncomfortable, while the declivity of the stone floor compulsorily hastened the speed of my descent.

I wanted to preface my sojourn in the King's Chamber with an examination of the underground region of the Pyramid, access to which in modern years has been barred by an iron portcullis which prevents the general public from entering this dismal region and being half suffocated. The old Latin tag, "Facilis descensus Averni," ("the descent of Avernus (is) easy" ["Aeneid," VI.126], in reference to Avernus, a deep lake near Puteoli and a reputed entrance to the underworld; hence, "it is easy to slip into moral ruin.") recurred unexpectedly to memory, but this time there was a grim sardonic humour in the words. I saw nothing in the yellowish beam of torchlight but the hewn rock through which this floor had been cut. When, at long last, I reached a small recess on the right, I seized the opportunity to slip into it and straighten out my body for a couple of minutes. I discovered that the recess was nothing else than the terminus of the nearly perpendicular shaft, the so-called Well, which descends from the junction of the ascending passage and the Grand Gallery. The old name still sticks to this shaft because for nearly two thousand years it was thought to have water at the bottom. Not 'til it was cleared out by Caviglia of the mass of debris which had accumulated in it was the bottom discovered to be perfectly dry.

It was narrower than the passage which I had just left, this unattractive, roughly excavated opening that yawned up into the solid rock. I discovered little niches cut into the sides, parallel with each other, which afforded foothold and handhold for the somewhat perilous climb.

It led upwards irregularly and tortuously for a considerable distance until it reached a large roughly cut chamber shaped like a bowl, the one now called the Grotto, which marked the level of the rocky plateau upon which the Pyramid had been built. The

Grotto had been partly constructed in an enlarged natural fissure in the rock. Beyond this, the Well had evidently been cut through the masonry and not built up with blocks, as all the other overground passages were formed. This section of the Well widened out in diameter and was thus more difficult to climb than its narrower sub–Grotto section.

At last I emerged from the torn and ragged opening which formed the mouth of the shaft, and found myself in the north-western corner of the Grand Gallery.

Why and when had it been cut through the body of the Pyramid? The question automatically registered itself and as I meditated on it, the answer flashed up. Those ancient Egyptians who had closed down an epoch of the Pyramid's history by closing the entrance to the upper chambers and Grand Gallery with three monstrous granite plugs, had to create a way of escape for themselves or they could never have got out of the Pyramid.

I knew from my own researches that the shaft and the Grotto had been cut at the same time as the building of the Pyramid, but that the Well did not descend any farther than the Grotto itself at the time. For thousands of years there was no direct link between the upper passages and the subterranean one.

When the Great Pyramid had fulfilled its mysterious purpose, those who were responsible sealed it. The sealing had been foreseen by the original builders, who had left the necessary material in place and had even made a contraction in the lower end of the ascending passage to hold the three granite plugs.

Working at their task, the last tenants cut the lower section of the Well through solid rock as a way of escape for themselves.

When the work was finished and they had made their retreat, it was only necessary to block up the exit of the newly cut section securely, at the point where it joins the descending passage, and then ascend the 300–foot slope to the original entrance. Thus the Well, although originally created as a means of reaching the Grotto, finally became a means of leaving the blocked-up Pyramid.

Under caliph, Al Mamoun, the Arabs broke into the great pyramid (since they could not find the hidden entrance) by boring into the limestone with crude instruments. After months they did manage to break in and find the descending passage.

I returned again by the easier route to the long slanting tunnel which connects the interior with the outer world, to resume my downward journey into the rocky plateau of Gizeh. Once, at a corner, an enlarged shadow was suddenly thrust across my path so that I drew back, startled, until I realized it was my own. In this weird place one expected everything; nothing was too strange to happen. Slipping and crawling the comparatively short remaining distance, I was relieved to find myself at the end of the descent and upon a level floor, but inside a still smaller tunnel. I crawled forward about ten more yards and then arrived at the open entrance to the strangest room I had ever seen—the so-called Pit. It was a little less than fifty feet from wall to wall on its longest side.

This gloomy vault, which lies beneath the exact centre of the Pyramid, gave to the eye an impression of a task hurriedly abandoned; it seemed to be a chamber whose excavation out of the solid rock was suddenly stopped. The ceiling had been well cut but the floor rolled up and down like a trench that had been bombarded.

The old Egyptian masons usually worked downwards in cutting rock vaults and therefore finished the floors last; why this particular floor should never have been finished when more than a lifetime of labour at least was later devoted to building the superstructure that rose above the rock level, is an archeological nut which no one has yet been able to crack. But then, the whole Pyramid itself is really such a nut.

I flashed my torch into the turgid gloom of the vault and focused a beam of light upon the centre of the floor. I moved closer and peered over the edge of a deep yawning hole, mute testimony to the one-time presence of treasure-seekers, who had fruitlessly and laboriously excavated a pit within the Pit. I felt the unpleasant touch of the wings of a bat as it flew past my head and squawked around the airless room. Down in the hole I noticed the light disturb the sleep of three other bats, which hung upside dawn on the roughly cut sides. I moved away, awakening two more bats which hung suspended from the ceiling. Alarmed and bewildered as I thrust the light mercilessly upon them, they scurried to and fro, also squawking, and then disappeared into the gloom of the entrance passage.

I climbed over the hilly floor and reached the farther end of the chamber, where a tiny level tunnel presented itself in the wall. It was just wide enough to enable one to squirm inside but too low to permit anything else except crawling dead flat upon the stomach. The floor was thickly covered with the dust of several thousand years and the journey was anything but pleasant. I endured it for the sake of examining the tunnel's terminus. After penetrating nearly twenty yards into the rock I found it ended abruptly; apparently this tunnel, too, had never been finished.

Nearly suffocated, I groped my way back and returned to the airless Pit, took a final glance around the room, and began my return journey to the upper regions of the Pyramid. When I reached the beginning of the low passage, which sloped upwards in a perfectly straight line for three hundred and fifty feet of solid rock before it continued as a built-up corridor, traversing the masonry, I stretched myself out on the floor and gazed up through the open exit into the darkened sky, as through a giant lens–less telescope. There, an easily seen twinkling silver point in indigo-blue space, was the Pole Star. I checked the direction by a wrist-compass, which indicated dead north. Those early builders had not only done a massive job but an accurate one.

I crawled back through the steep passage and reached, at length, the level corridor which conducts into the Queen's Chamber.

A score or more paces and I stood under its inclined arch roof which meets in a ridge in the middle. I examined the two ventilating shafts which slant upwards from the northern and southern wall. Here was clear proof that the room had never been a tomb, but was intended to be used. Many have been puzzled by the circumstance of the discovery of these shafts, in 1872, when it was found that they stopped five inches short of the Chamber itself and apparently were not originally cut right through the walls. In their discovered state, therefore, they could not admit air; so it is thought that they had some other and unknown use. But the best explanation is that the time came when they had served their purpose and, like the rest of the upper passages of the Pyramid, were completely sealed at their orifices by new stone blocks.

Waynman Dixon, a civil engineer then employed on some works near the Pyramid, chanced to discover these air tubes while examining the walls of the Queen's Chamber out of curiosity. He noticed that one wall, which sounded hollow at a particular spot, also seemed slightly cracked. He had the spot broken into and five inches from the surface found a small shaft; then, by the same process, he discovered its mate on the opposite wall of the Chamber. Both shafts extend right through the body of the Pyramid: this has lately been proved by means of probing-rods, which have been run up them for about two hundred feet.

I turned back to the level corridor and walked to the point where it meets the Grand Gallery. And then, for a hundred and fifty feet, I slowly progressed to the top of this steep, corbel-sided ascent. A slight weakness, engendered by a three days' fast, began to trouble me as I climbed that incline. Finally, I rested for a few seconds on the three-feet-high step which marked the end and which was so placed as to be exactly in line with the vertical axis of the Pyramid. A few paces forward through the Antechamber, a forced stoop under the granite block which hangs down from grooved side-walls, and which bars the exit of this horizontal corridor, and I had reached the most important room in the Pyramid, the famous King's Chamber.

*

Here, too, the presence of a couple of air tubes, each about nine inches square, killed the tomb-chamber theory. Their openings into the room had never been sealed, as were those in the Queen's Chamber, but they had been completely filled with loose stones, which Colonel Vyse had to clear out when he wanted to determine the nature of these shafts. That this filling operation had been carried out at the same time as all other attempts to conceal the internal arrangements of the overground portion of the Pyramid, was extremely probable.

I flashed the lamp over the bare walls and flat ceiling, noting anew the admirably accurate fitting of the immense polished granite blocks at their joints, and then began a slow circuit of the walls, carefully examining each individual stone. The rose–tinted rocks of far Syene had been split in twain to provide these blocks. Here and there treasure-seekers had scarred both floor and wall in their vain quests. On the eastern side of the floor, part of the stone flags had disappeared and beaten earth had taken its place, while on the north–western side a deep rectangular hole remained unfilled. A long rough stone block which had once formed part of the floor and covered this hole stood against the wall on one side, left there by early Arab hands, perchance. Parallel with it, and but a few inches away was the fiat–sided, coffin-like sarcophagus: a lidless, lonely object, which was the only other thing to be found in this bare room. It was placed exactly north and south.

The dislodged flooring-block offered a possible seat, so I sat down on it, tailor-like, with folded feet, and settled there for the remainder of the night. On my right I had placed my hat, jacket and shoes; on my left reposed the still-burning torch, a thermos flask with hot tea, a couple of bottles of iced water, a notebook and my Parker pen. A last look around the chamber, a final glimpse of the marble coffer beside me, and then I extinguished the light.

I kept beside me a powerful electric torch ready to be switched on.

The sudden plunge into total darkness brought with it the wondering question of what the night would bring forth. The only thing one could do in this strange position was to wait ... and wait ... and wait.

The minutes slowly dragged themselves along, the while I slowly 'sensed' that the King's Chamber possessed a very strong atmosphere of its own, an atmosphere which I can only call 'psychic.' For I had deliberately made myself receptive in mind, passive in feeling and negative in attitude, so that I might become a perfect register of whatever super–physical event might transpire. I wanted no personal prejudice or preconception to interfere with the reception of anything that might come to me from some source inaccessible to the five physical senses of man. I gradually diminished the flow of thoughts until the mind entered a half–blank state.

And the stillness which descended on my brain rendered me acutely cognizant of the stillness which had descended on my life. The world, with its noise and bustle, was now as utterly remote as though it did not exist. No sound, no whisper, came to me out of the darkness. Silence is the real sovereign of the kingdom of the Pyramid, a silence that began in prehistoric antiquity and which no babble of visiting tourists can really break, for every night it returns anew with awe-inspiring completeness.

I became aware of the powerful atmosphere of the room. It is a perfectly normal and common experience for sensitive persons to become aware of the atmosphere of ancient houses, and my own experience began with something of this sort. The passage of time deepened it, enhanced the sense of immeasurable antiquity which environed me, and made me feel that the twentieth century was slipping away from under my feet. Yet, following my self–imposed resolve, I did not resist the feeling, instead I let it grow stronger.

A strange feeling that I was not alone began to creep insidiously over me. Under the cover of complete blackness, I felt that something animate and living was throbbing into existence. It was a vague feeling but a real one, and it was this, coupled with the increasing sense of the returning Past, that constituted my consciousness of something 'psychic.'

Yet nothing clear–cut, definite, emerged from this vague and general sense of an eerie life that pulsated through the darkness. The hours slipped on and, contrary to my expectation, the advancing night brought increasing coldness with it. The effects of the three–day fast which I had undertaken in order to increase my sensitivity, now showed themselves in growing chilliness. Cold air was creeping into the King's Chamber through the narrow ventilation shafts, and then creeping past the thin barrier of my light garment. My chilled flesh began to shiver under its thin shirt. I got up and dressed myself in the jacket which I had put off only a few hours before on account of the intense heat.

Such is Eastern life at certain times of the year—tropical heat by day and a heavy fall of temperature by night.

To this day no one has discovered the mouths of these air channels on the outside of the Pyramid, although the approximate area of their positions is known. Some Egyptologists have even doubted whether the channels were ever carried right through to the outside, but the complete chilling of the air during my experience finally settles the point.

I sat down for the second time upon my stone seat and surrendered myself anew to the oppressive death–like silence, and to the all—prevailing sombre darkness of the chamber. With pliant soul I waited and wondered. For no reason at all I remembered irrelevantly that somewhere to the east the Suez Canal pursued its straight course through sand and marsh, and the stately Nile provided a backbone to this land.

The queer sepulchral stillness in the room, the empty stone coffin beside me, were not reassuring to one's nerves, while the break in my vigil seemed to have broken something else too, for very quickly I found that the sensing of invisible life around me rapidly rose into complete certainty. There was something throbbing and alive in my vicinity, although I could still see absolutely nothing. With this discovery, the realization of my isolated and uncanny situation suddenly overwhelmed me. Here I was sitting alone in a queer room that was perched more than two hundred feet above the ground, high up above all the million people of Cairo, surrounded by total darkness, locked up and imprisoned in a strange building on the edge of a desert that stretched away for hundreds of miles, while outside this building—itself probably the oldest in the world—lay the grim tomb–cluttered necropolis of an ancient capital.

The great space of the King's Chamber became for me—who had investigated deeply into the psychic, into the mysteries of the occult, into the sorceries and wizardries of the Orient—peopled with unseen beings, with spirits who guarded this age-old building. One momentarily expected some ghostly voice to arise out of the all–embracing silence. I now thanked the early builders for those narrow vent–shafts which brought a steady but tiny supply of cool air into this hoary old room. That air traveled through nearly three hundred feet of the Pyramid before it arrived; no matter, it was still welcome. I am a man accustomed to solitude—indeed glad to enjoy it—·but there was something uncanny and frightening in the solitude of this chamber.

The all–encompassing darkness began to press on my head like an iron weight. The shadow of uncalled-for fear flickered into me. I brushed it away immediately. To sit in the heart of this desert monument required no physical courage, but it did require some moral fortitude. No snakes were likely to emerge from holes or crevices, and no lawless wanderers were likely to climb its stepped sides and enter it at dead of night.

Actually, the only signs of animal life I had seen came from a scared mouse which had met me early in the evening in the horizontal passage, and which had darted hither and thither between the creviceless granite walls in a frantic effort to escape out of reach of the dreaded beam of torchlight; from two incredibly aged yellowish-green lizards I had discovered clinging to the roof of the narrow cutting which extends inwards from the niche in the Queen's Chamber; and, lastly, from the bats in the subterranean vault. It was also true that a few crickets had chirped a good deal upon my entry into the Grand Gallery, but they had soon ceased. All that was over now, unbroken silence held the whole Pyramid as in a thrall. There was naught of a physical nature which could possibly injure one here, and yet—a vague uneasiness, a feeling that invisible eyes were watching me, recurred for the second time. The place possessed a dream–like mysteriousness, a ghostly unreality.

There are vibrations of force, sound and light which are beyond our normal range of detection. Laughing song and serious speech flash across the world to waiting wireless listeners, but they could never detect them were not their receiving sets properly tuned. I had now brought myself out of the state of mere receptive waiting into a forcefully concentrated condition of mind which focalized the whole of its attention upon an effort to pierce the black silence which surrounded it. If, in the result, my faculty of awareness was temporarily heightened to an abnormal extent by the intense inward concentration, who shall say that it is impossible I began to detect the presence of invisible forces?

I know only that as I 'tuned-in' by a method of interiorized attention which I had learnt long before this second visit to Egypt, I became aware that hostile forces had invaded the chamber. There was something abroad which I sensed as evil, dangerous. A nameless dread flickered into my heart and returned again and again soon after it was driven away. I, still following my method of intense, single–pointed, inward–turned concentration, feeling followed its usual trend and changed into vision. Shadows began to flit to and fro in the shadowless room; gradually these took more definite shape, and malevolent countenances appeared suddenly quite close to my own face. Sinister images rose plainly before my mind's eye. Then a dark apparition advanced, looked at me with fixed sinister regard and raised its hands in a gesture of menace, as though seeking to inspire me with awe. Age–old spirits seemed to have crept out of the neighbouring necropolis, a necropolis so old that mummies had crumbled away inside their stone sarcophagi; the shades that clung to them made their unwelcome ascent to the place of my vigil. All the legends of evil ghosts who haunt the areas around the Pyramids came back to memory with the same unpleasant detail with which they had been related by Arabs in the village not far off. When I had told a young Arab friend there of my intention to spend a night in the old building, he had tried to dissuade me.

"Every inch of ground is haunted," had been his warning. "There is an army of ghosts and genii in that territory." And now I could see that his warning was not a vain one. Spectral figures had begun to creep into and around the dark room wherein I sat, and the undefinable feeling of uneasiness which earlier had seized me was now receiving fit and full justification. Somewhere in the centre of that still thing which was my body, I knew that my heart beat like a hammer under the strain of it all. The dread of the supernatural, which lurks at the bottom of every human heart, touched me again. Fear, dread, horror persistently presented their evil visages to me in turn.

Involuntarily my hands clenched themselves as tightly as a vice. But I was determined to go on, and although these phantom forms that moved across the room began by stirring in me a sense of alarm, they ended by provoking me to summon whatever reserves of courage and combativeness I could muster.

My eyes were closed and yet these grey, gliding, vaporous forms obtruded themselves across my vision. And always there came with them an implacable hostility, an ugly determination to deter me from my purpose.

A circle of antagonistic beings surrounded me. It would have been easy to end it all by switching on the light or by leaping up and dashing out of the chamber and running back a few hundred feet to the locked grille–entrance, where the armed guard would have provided gregarious comfort. It was an ordeal which imposed a subtle form of torture, that harried the soul and left the body untouched. Yet something inside me intimated just as implacably that I must see this thing through.

At last the climax came. Monstrous elemental creations, evil horrors of the underworld, forms of grotesque, insane, uncouth and fiendish aspect gathered around me and afflicted me with unimaginable repulsion. In a few minutes I lived through something which will leave a remembered record behind for all time. That incredible scene remains vividly photographed upon my memory. Never again would I repeat such an experiment; never again would I take up a nocturnal abode within the Great Pyramid.

The end came with startling suddenness. The malevolent ghostly invaders disappeared into the obscurity whence they had emerged, into the shadowy realms of the departed, taking with them their trail of noxious horrors. My half-shattered nerves experienced overwhelming relief such as a soldier feels when a fierce bombardment ends abruptly.

I do not know how long a period elapsed before I became conscious of a new presence in the chamber, of someone friendly and benevolent who stood at the entrance and looked down upon me with kindly eyes. With his arrival the atmosphere changed completely—and changed for the better. Something clean and sane had come with him. A new element began to play upon my overwrought sensitive being, soothing and calming it. He approached my stony seat, and I saw that he was followed by another figure. Both halted at my side and regarded me with grave looks, pregnant with prophetic meaning. I felt that some momentous hour of my life was at hand.

In my vision the apparition of these two beings presented an unforgettable picture. Their white robes, their sandalled feet, their wise aspect, their tall figures—all these return at once to the mind's eye. Withal they wore the unmistakable regalia of their office, High Priests of an ancient Egyptian cult. There was light a-glimmer all around them, which in a most uncanny manner lit up the part of the room. Indeed, they looked more than men, bearing the bright mien of demi-gods; for their faces were set in unique cloistral calm.

They stood motionless as statues, regarding me, their hands crossed upon their breasts, remaining absolutely silent.

Was I functioning in some fourth dimension, aware and awake in some far-off epoch of the past? Had my sense of time regressed to the early days of Egypt? No; that could not be, for I perceived quickly that these two could see me and even now were about to address me.

Their tall figures bent forward; the lips of one spirit seemed to move, his face close to mine, his eyes flashing spiritual fire, and his voice sounding in my ear.

"Why dost thou come to this place, seeking to evoke the secret powers? Are not mortal ways enough for thee? " he asked.

I did not hear these words with any physical ear; certainly no sound-vibration disturbed the silence of the chamber. Yet I seemed to hear them much in the manner in which a deaf man, using an electric earphone, might hear the words sounding against his artificial ear–drum; but with this difference––that they were heard on the inside of the drum. Really, the voice which came to me might be termed a mental voice, because it was surely heard within my head, but that might give the wrong impression that it was a mere thought. Nothing could be farther from the truth. It was a voice.

And I answered: "They are not!"

And he said :

"The stir of many crowds in the cities comforts the trembling heart of man. Go back, mingle with thy fellows, and thou wilt soon forget the light fancy that brings thee here."

But I answered again : " No, that cannot be."

Still he strove once more.

"The way of Dream will draw thee far from the fold of reason. Some have gone upon it—and come back mad. Turn now, whilst there is yet time, and follow the path appointed for mortal feet."

But I shook my head and muttered: " I must follow this way. There is none other for me now."

Then the priestly figure stepped forward closer and bent down again to where I sat.

I saw his aged face outlined by the surrounding darkness.

He whispered against my ear:

"He who gains touch with us loses kin with the world. Art thou able to walk alone?"

I replied: "I do not know."

He whispered again:

"Come with me and then, when thou hast seen, answer again."

And I saw, as in a far-off vision, a great city with a maze of streets. The picture approached rapidly until I noticed, close by, an old house that stood near a railed-in square. I saw a gloomy staircase that led up to a small garret on the top floor. My ghostly interlocutor appeared suddenly within the room, sitting by the bedside of an old man, whose matted hair and unkempt grey beard formed a fit frame for his rugged face. He must have long passed the evening of his life, for his ashen skin hung loosely upon the bones. His skinny, exhausted face drew my pity, but as I looked at him a chill came over me, for I saw his spirit struggling to leave its body, and in this ghostly battle there could be but one victor.

My guide gazed with pitying eyes at the figure in the bed. He held up his hand and said:

"A few more minutes, brother, and then thou shalt have peace. Behold, I have brought one who seeks the secret powers. Let thy last legacy be a few words to him."

I suddenly became actor as well as witness in this strange scene.

With a croaking gasp that was terrible to hear, the dying man turned his head and looked me in the face. And though I wander to far Cathay, I shall never forget the brooding terror I saw in those eyes.

"You are younger than I," he muttered. "But I have wandered the world once, twice, three times. I, too, sought them—Oh I how I searched." He halted for a minute, the while his head lay back on the pillow and he searched the pages of memory. Then he raised himself on his elbows, and stretched out a long thin arm. With its bony fingers and unyielding grip, his hand seemed like a skeleton's. He took my own and held my wrist as in a vice; he peered into my eyes and I felt he was searching my soul.

"Fool! Fool!" he croaked, "The only powers I found were the powers of the flesh and the devil. There are no other. They lie! Do you hear me?" he almost shouted, "They lie!" The effort was too much for him. He fell back upon his pillow—dead.

My guide made no comment, waiting for a full minute by the bedside. Then the vision was blotted out, I was back in the Pyramid once more. He looked at me in silence, and I returned his glance with equal silence. He read my thought.

Out of the darkness came his last words: "So be it. Thou hast chosen. Abide by thy choice for there is now no recall. Farewell," and he was gone.

I was left alone with the other spirit, who so far had only played the part of a silent witness.

*

He moved closer so that he stood now in front of the marble coffer. His face revealed itself as the face of a man, very, very old. I dared place no guess of years upon him.

"My son, the mighty lords of the secret powers have taken thee into their hands. Thou art to be led into the Hall of Learning tonight," he explained dispassionately. "Stretch thyself out upon this stone. In olden days it would have been within that yonder, upon a bed of papyrus—reeds," and he pointed to the coffin–like sarcophagus.

It did not occur to me to do other than obey my mysterious visitant. I laid myself prone upon my back.

What happened immediately afterwards is still not very clear to me. It was as though he had unexpectedly given me a dose of some peculiar, slow–working, anesthetic, for all my muscles became taut, after which a paralyzing lethargy began to creep over my limbs. My entire body became heavy and numb. First, my feet became colder and colder. The feeling developed into a kind of iciness which moved by imperceptible degrees up my legs, reached the knees, whence it continued its mounting journey. It was as though I had sunk up to the waist in a pile of snow while on some mountain climb. All sensation in the lower limbs was numbed.

I appeared next to pass into a semi-somnolent condition and a mysterious intimation of approaching death crept into my mind. It did not trouble me, however, for I had long ago liberated myself from the ancient fear of death and arrived at a philosophic acceptance of its inevitability.

As this strange chilling sensation continued to grip me, to pass up my shivering spine, to overpower my entire body, I felt myself sinking inwards in consciousness to some central point within my brain, while my breathing became weaker and weaker.

When the chill reached my chest and the rest of my body was completely paralyzed, something like a heart attack supervened, but it passed quickly and I knew that the supreme crisis was not far off.

Had I been able to move my stiff jaws, I might have laughed at the next thought which came to me. It was this:

"Tomorrow, they will find my dead body inside the Great Pyramid and that will be the end of me."

I was quite sure that all my sensations were due to the passage of my own spirit from physical life to the regions beyond death.

Although I knew perfectly well that I was passing through all the sensations of dying, all opposition had now vanished.

At last, my concentrated consciousness lay in the head alone, and there was a final mad whirl within my brain. I had the sensation of being caught up in a tropical whirlwind and seemed to pass upwards through a narrow hole; then there was a momentary dread of being launched in infinite space, I leapt into the unknown—and I was Free!

No other word will express the delightful sense of liberation which then became mine. I had changed into a mental being, a creature of thought and feeling, yet without the clogging handicap of the heavy flesh body in which I had been shut up. I had gone ghost-like clean out of my earthly body, like a dead man rising out of his tomb, but had certainly gone into no sort of unconsciousness. My sense of existence in fact, was intensely more vivid than before. Above all, with this exodus to a higher dimension, I felt free, blissfully, languorously free, in this fourth dimension to which I had penetrated.

At first I found myself lying on my back, as horizontal as the body I had just vacated, floating above the stone floor–block. Then came a sensation of some invisible hand turning me upright on my heels, after pushing me forward a little, and placing me properly on my feet. Ultimately, I had a curiously combined feeling of both standing and floating simultaneously.

I gazed down upon the deserted body of flesh and bone, which was lying prone and motionless on the stone block. The inexpressive face was upturned, the eyes were scarcely open, yet the pupils gleamed sufficiently to indicate that the lids were not really closed. The arms were folded across the breast—certainly not an attitude which I could remember having assumed. Had someone crossed those hands without my being aware of the movement? The legs and feet were stretched out side by side, touching each other. There lay the seemingly dead form of myself, the form from which I had withdrawn.

I noted a trail of faint silvery light projecting itself down from me, the new me, to the cataleptic creature who lay upon the block. This was surprising, but more surprising still was my discovery that this mysterious psychic umbilical cord was contributing towards the illumination of the corner of the King's Chamber where I hovered; showing up the wall-stones in a soft moonbeam–like light.

I was but a phantom, a bodiless creature sojourning in space. I knew, at last, why those wise Egyptians of old had given, in their hieroglyphs, the pictured symbol of the bird to man's soul–form. I had experienced a sense of increased height and breadth, a spreading out just as though I had a pair of wings. Had I not risen into the air and remained floating above my discarded body, even as a bird rises into the sky and remains circling around a point? Did I not have the sensation of being environed by a great void? Yes, the bird symbol was a true one.

Yes; I had risen into space, disentangled my soul from its mortal skein, separated myself into two twin parts, left the world which I had known so long. I experienced a sense of being etherealized, of intense lightness, in this duplicate body which I now inhabited. As I gazed down at the cold stone block upon which my body lay, a single idea obtained recognition in my mind, a single realization overwhelmed me. It expressed itself to me in a few brief, silent words:

"This is the state of death. Now I know that I am a soul, that I can exist apart from the body. I shall always believe that, for I have proved it."

This notion clutched hold of me with an iron grip, the while I was poised lightly above my empty fleshly tenement. I had proved survival in what I thought the most satisfactory way—by actually dying and then surviving! I kept on looking at the recumbent relic which I had left behind. Somehow, it fascinated me. Was that discarded form the thing which, for so many years, I had considered as myself? I perceived then, with complete clarity, that it was nothing more than a mass of unintelligent, unconscious, fleshly matter. As I regarded those unseeing unresponsive eyes, the irony of the whole situation struck me forcibly. My earthly body had really imprisoned me, the real 'me,' but now I was free. I had been borne hither and thither upon this planet by an organism which I had long confused with my real central self.

The sense of gravity seemed to have gone, and I was literally floating on air, with that strange half–suspended, half–standing feeling.

Suddenly, by my side, appeared the old priest, grave and imperturbable. With upturned eyes, his face more ennobled still, with reverent mood, he prayed: "O Amen, O Amen, who art in Heaven, turn thy face upon the dead body of thy son, and make him well in the spirit–world. It is finished." And then he addressed me:

"Thou hast now learned the great lesson. Man, whose soul was born out of the Undying, can never really die. Set down this truth in words known to men. Behold!"

And out of space there came the half–remembered face of a woman whose funeral I had attended more than twenty years before; then the familiar countenance of a man who had been more than a friend and whom I had last seen laid to rest in his coffin twelve years previously; and, finally, the sweet smiling picture of a child I knew who had died in an accidental fall.

These three peered at me with tranquil faces, and their friendly voices sounded once again around me. I had the shortest of conversations with the so-called dead, who soon melted away and vanished.

"They too live, even as thou livest, even as this Pyramid, which has seen the death of half a world, lives 0n," said the High Priest.

"Know, my son, that in this ancient fane (temple) lies the lost record of the early races of man and of the Covenant which they made with their Creator through the first of His great prophets. Know, too, that chosen men were brought here of old to be shown this Covenant that they might return to their fellows and keep the great secret alive. Take back with thee the warning that when men forsake their Creator and look on their fellows with hate, as with the princes of Atlantis in whose time this Pyramid was built, they are destroyed by the weight of their own iniquity, even as the people of Atlantis were destroyed.

"It was not the Creator who sank Atlantis, but the selfishness, the cruelty, the spiritual blindness of the people who dwelt on those doomed islands. The Creator loves all; but the lives of men are governed by invisible laws which He has set over them. Take back this warning, then."

There surged up in me a great desire to see this mysterious Covenant and the spirit must have read my thought, for he quickly said:

"To all things there is an hour. Not yet, my son, not yet." I was disappointed.

He looked at me for a few seconds.

"No man of thy people hath yet been permitted to behold such a thing, but because thou art a man versed in these things, and hast come among us bearing goodwill and understanding in thy heart, some satisfaction thou shalt have. Come with me!"

And then a strange thing happened. I seemed to fall into a kind of semi–coma, my consciousness was momentarily blotted out, and the next thing I knew was that I had been transported to another place. I found myself in a long passage which was softly lit, although no lamp or window was visible: I fancied that the illuminant was none other than the halo–like emanation around my companion combined with the radiation from the luminous vibrant cord of ether which extended behind me, yet I realized that these would not sufficiently explain it. The walls were built up with a glowing pinkish terra–cotta coloured stone, slabbed with the thinnest of joints. The floor sloped downwards at precisely the same angle as the Pyramid entrance itself descends. The masonry was well finished. The passage was square and fairly low, but not uncomfortably so. I could not find the source of its mysterious illuminant, yet the interior was bright as though a lamp were playing on it.

The High Priest bade me follow him a little way down the passage. "Look not backwards," he warned me, "nor turn thy head." We passed some distance down the incline and I saw a large temple-like chamber opening out of the farther end. I knew perfectly well that I was inside or below the Pyramid, but I had never seen such a passage or chamber before. Evidently they were secret and had defied discovery until this day. I could not help feeling tremendously excited about this startling End, and an equally tremendous curiosity seized me as to where and what the entrance was. Finally, I had to turn my head and take a swift look backwards at what I hoped was the secret door. I had entered the place by no visible entrance, but at the farther end I saw that what should have been an opening was closed with square blocks and apparently cemented. I found myself gazing at a blank wall; then, as swiftly whirled away by some irresistible force until the whole scene was blotted out and I had floated off into space again. I heard the words: "Not yet, not yet," repeated as in an echo and a few moments later saw my inert unconscious body lying on the stone.

"My son," came a murmur from the High Priest, "It matters not whether thou discoverest the door or not. Find but the secret passage within the mind that will lead thee to the hidden chamber within thine own soul, and thou shalt have found something worthy indeed. The mystery of the Great Pyramid is the mystery of thine own self.

The secret chambers and ancient records are all contained in thine own nature. The lesson of the Pyramid is that man must turn inward, must venture to the unknown centre of his being to find his soul, even as he must venture to the unknown depths of this fane to find its profoundest secret. Farewell!"

My mind whirled into some vortex that caught me; I slipped helplessly, sucked downwards, ever downwards; heavy torpor overcame me, and I seemed to melt back into my physical body; I strained my will, pushing and trying to move its rigid muscles, but failed, and finally I swooned ....

I opened my eyes with a shock, in inky blackness. When the numbness passed, my hands groped for the torch and switched the light on. I was back in the King's Chamber, still tremendously excited, so excited in fact, that I jumped up and shouted, my voice echoing back in muffled tones. But, instead of feeling the floor beneath my feet, I found myself falling through space. Only by throwing both hands on the edge of the stone block and clinging to the sides did I save myself. I then realized what had happened. In rising I had unwittingly moved to the far end of the block and my feet were now dangling over the excavated hole in the north-west corner of the floor.

I picked myself up and got back to safety, secured the lamp and threw a beam of light upon my watch. The glass was cracked in two places, where I had struck my hand and wrist against the wall in jumping up, but the works still ticked merrily away; and then, as I noted the time I almost laughed outright despite the solemnity of my surroundings.

For it was precisely the melodramatic hour of midnight, both hands pointing to twelve, neither more nor less!

When the armed police guard unlocked the iron grille soon after dawn, a dusty, weary, tired-eyed figure stumbled out of the Great Pyramid's dark entrance. He made his way down the large square blocks of stone into the early morning sunlight and gazed, with eyes that blinked, at the flat, familiar landscape. His first act was to take several deep breaths, one after the other. Then he instinctively turned his face upwards towards Ra, the sun, and silently thanked him for this blessed gift of light to mankind.

*

Dr. Abbate Pacha, Vice–President of the Institut Egyptien, spent a night in the desert near the Pyramids, together with Mr. William Groii', a member of the Institut. In the official report of their experiences, the latter said: "Towards eight o'clock, in the evening, I noticed a light which appeared to turn slowly around the Third Pyramid almost up to the apex; it was like a small dame. The light made three circuits round the Pyramid and then disappeared. For a good part of the night I attentively watched this Pyramid; towards eleven o'clock I again noticed the same light, but this time it was of a bluish colour; it mounted slowly almost in a straight line and arrived at a certain height above the Pyramid's summit and then disappeared. By pursuing enquiries among the Bedouins, Mr. Groff discovered that this mysterious light had been seen more or less frequently in the past, the traditions of its existence stretching back centuries. The Arabs put it down to guardian· spirits of the Pyramid, but Groff tried to find a natural explanation for it, though without success.

APPENDIX K

DAVID WILCOCK
SUMMARY OF RUSSIAN & UKRANIAN PYRAMID RESEARCH

Used courtesy of David Wilcock ©

Grebennikov's discoveries with the 'cavity structural effect' show that long, tubelike structures, especially if gathered in bundles, will harness torsion waves in a way that can be confusing and damaging to most forms of life.

However, he also found that if such structures are placed above a person, such as in a specially-built chair that he designed, the added torsion energy that they draw up from the earth has beneficial health properties.

Such devices can be built rather simply by gluing several large egg crates above each other at their mutually shared points and mounting them above a chair where a person will sit.

The beneficial health effects of a person being placed under a CSE generator can be duplicated and enhanced with the pyramid shape.

Grebennikov did a certain degree of interesting research in this area, but until Dr. John DeSalvo of the Giza Pyramid Research Association published the Russian and Ukranian pyramid research of A. Golod, V. Krasnoholovets and associates, the complete picture of how much progress had been made in these areas was not available online.

This research comes from the Institute of Physics in Kiev, Ukraine, a basic institution of the National Academy of Sciences of Ukraine, which was one of the leading scientific centers in the former USSR and the premier military research association.

Two steep pyramids with 70–degree slope angles were constructed in Russia near Moscow, one at a height of 22 meters and another at a height of 44 meters [144 feet,] costing over a million dollars to build.

Over the last 10 years, a total of 17 different pyramids have been built altogether. In order for the pyramid effects to emerge, it was found that no metal could be used in the construction of these structures, thus modular fiberglass plastics were used instead.

The pyramids were aligned to the North Star and built away from populated areas in the natural countryside. At the base of the 22–meter pyramid, the fiberglass wall was 36 centimeters thick, and at the base of the 44–meter pyramid the fiberglass wall was 70 centimeters thick. The 22–meter pyramid weighed a total of 25 tons and the 44–meter pyramid weighed a total of 55 tons.

Several different teams from the Russian Academy of Sciences carried out all sorts of experiments in these pyramids, with surprising results. [These results are discussed in greater scientific detail in the article, referenced at the end of this chapter.]

1 . STRENGTHENING OF ANTI–VIRAL MEDICINE

The first study cited in Dr. Krasnoholovets' summary paper is by Prof. S.M. Klimenko and D.N. Nosik, MD from the Ivanovskii

Research & Development Institute of Virology within the Russian Academy of Medical Science.

This study involved the drug venoglobulin, which is a naturally-occurring antiviral compound in human beings. When the drug was diluted into a concentration of 50 micrograms per milliliter and stored in the pyramid for a time, it then became approximately three times more effective at fighting viruses than it normally would.

2. STRENGTHENING OF HEALING BENEFITS OF GLUCOSE AND WATER

The team of Prof. A.G. Antonov from the Russian Research & Development Institute of Pediatrics, Obstetrics and Gynecology tested the effects of a solution of 40% glucose in distilled water after it had been stored in the pyramid.

By administering only 1 milliliter of the glucose to 20 different prematurely born infant patients with compromised immune systems, their levels of health were seen to rapidly increase up to **practically normal values**.

The researchers furthermore discovered that the glucose was not necessary, as **the same effect could be produced by simply using 1 milliliter of ordinary water that had been stored in the pyramid.**

3. INCREASED HEALING RESPONSE FOR ORGANISMS WITHIN PYRAMID

Another study was performed by Dr. N.B. Egorova at the Mechnikov Research & Development Institute within the

Russian Academy of Medical Science. In this study, the torsion–wave harnessing capability of the pyramid was tested directly on living organisms placed inside.

An experimental and a control group of white underbred mice weighing 12 to 14 grams were both tainted with strain 415 of the virus S.typhimurium in equal amounts over the course of one day.

In smaller doses of contamination, the mice stored in the pyramid survived at a rate of 60%, whereas only 7% survived in the control group.

In larger doses of contamination, 30% of the mice in the pyramid survived as opposed to only 3% in the control group. In other experiments, mice were exposed to various carcinogens, and an experimental group drank water from the pyramid whereas the control group drank ordinary water.

The mice drinking the pyramid water had significantly fewer tumors develop than the mice drinking the ordinary water.

4. CHANGES OF ELECTRICAL RESISTANCE OF MATERIALS IN PYRAMID

Prof. V.I. Kostikov and Dr. A.C. Katasonov from the Research & Development Institute "Graphite" within the Russian Academy of Sciences performed various studies on the changes in electrical resistance that can be induced by a pyramid structure.

In one example, a pyrocarbon material was tested that normally had a resistance of 5 to 7 micro–ohms. After a one–day stay in the pyramid, the material became **200% more resistant to electric current**, which is an abnormal effect for pyrocarbon.

Irradiating the same material with ~10^19 neutrons per square meter would only change the resistance of the pyrocarbon by about 5% in comparison.

Similarly, **silicon semiconductors would have an exponential** *lowering* **of their electrical resistance,** moving from 10^5 to 10^4 ohms per centimeter, and high–temperature superconducting materials would lose their superconductive properties after a one–day stay in the pyramid.

5. ROCKS FROM PYRAMID DISTRIBUTE ELECTRICAL CHARGES MORE EVENLY

A group of researchers from the All–Russian Electrotechnical Institute in Moscow conducted an experiment to demonstrate how pyramid–charged rocks could dissipate strong electric charges, rendering them less harmful.

The setup involved a flat metallic plate that was zapped by positively–charged electric blasts at up to 1400 kilovolts in intervals between 250 and 2500 microseconds. The electric blasts were generated by a rod that was suspended 5 meters above the metallic plate.

Each of these blasts will typically "discharge" and burn up a portion of the metallic plate, which is known as a "defeat," and these defeats are logged and plotted.

Two identical systems of this type, and experimental and a control, were created. In the experimental system, seven 100–gram chunks of granite that had been stored inside the pyramid were then placed on the flat plate in a one–meter wide ring.

The researchers discovered that there were five times more burn marks on the control plate as opposed to the experimental plate.

Obviously, normal granite rocks would not produce such an effect—only those that have stayed in the pyramid. It seems that the rocks exposed to the torsion fields in the pyramid were much more capable of distributing the electrical charges.

This appears to be due to the fact that the electron clouds of the atoms in the rocks became more uniformly spin–polarized in the pyramid, thus helping to absorb and spread out electrical charges more evenly.

6.1 WATER DOES NOT FREEZE IN THE PYRAMID UNLESS DISTURBED

In the first experiment, plastic bottles of distilled water were kept in the pyramid over the course of three winter months. During this time, the air temperature in the pyramid sank as low as $-38°$ C, or $-6°$F.

Thermometers inside the bottles revealed that the temperature of the water was the same as the below–freezing air temperatures surrounding them, yet the water remained in a liquid form and would not turn into ice!

However, if the water in any of the bottles was shaken or bumped in any way, it would immediately start crystallizing and quickly turn into a block of ice. Golod and his associates have videotaped these results.

This first experiment obviously suggests that the presence of the torsion–wave energy was able to keep the water molecules from crystallizing into ice, yet a simple disruption in the harmonic stillness of the water would cause this equilibrium to disappear and ice would quickly form.

One slight bump on the edge of the bottle would disrupt the even flow of the torsion radiation and allow the molecules to begin crystallizing.

This same experiment also showed that <u>water would retain its purity indefinitely while within the pyramid.</u>

7. VISIBLE RINGS FORM IN ROCKS SCATTERED INSIDE THE PYRAMID

In the second of Golod's experiments, chunks of granite and crystal were scattered along the floor of the pyramid for longer periods of time.

A visible ring would appear evenly throughout the chunks, showing a clear change in the appearance of the stones when under the torsion–wave influence.

Between the end of 1997 and the beginning of 1999, this result was able to be duplicated 40 different times in the same pyramid, with different rocks each time.

Each ring would cover between 50 and 300 rocks, with a total weight from 20 to 200 kilograms. Golod et al. have gathered evidence to suggest that when the rings form most visibly, the amount of epidemics in the surrounding area will decrease.

8. A COLUMN OF "UNKNOWN ENERGY" APPEARS ABOVE THE PYRAMID

In the third of Golod's experiments, the Joint–stock company "Research & Development Institute TTR" conducted studies of the air above the pyramid with a Russian instrument similar to radar known as a "military locator." A column of 'unknown energy' was detected at a width of 500 meters and a height of 2000 meters.

Further studies confirmed that a larger circle of this energy surrounded the area above the pyramid in a 300–kilometer–wide range, with the highest concentration being directly above the vertical fulcrum of the pyramid.

Golod's team calculated that if such an energy column were to be produced electromagnetically, it would require *all the energy of the various power plants in Russia combined.*

Furthermore, less rigorous was the observation that, after the pyramid's presence was established, an ozone hole that had existed over that area of Russia was seen to repair itself in only two months' time.

This column of unseen energy did have other immediate uses and effects as well. Electrical energy from the pyramid could be harnessed by a capacitor that was placed at the apex of the pyramid; the capacitor would spontaneously take on a charge.

Furthermore, pieces of the capacitor assembly were seen to break away and rise into the air on the energetic column that the pyramid was producing.

It was also discovered that people working near the top of the pyramid might start to experience dizziness and nausea, and need to be taken some distance away from the pyramid for these effects to subside.

In Golod's fourth experiment, a series of pyramids were built over one of a number of oil wells. It was discovered that the viscosity of the oil under the pyramids decreased by 30%, while the **production rate accordingly increased by 30%** compared to the surrounding wells.

There was a decrease in the amount of unwanted materials in the oil, such as gums, pyrobitumen and paraffin. These results were confirmed by the Gubkin Moscow Academy of Oil and Gas.

10. AGRICULTURAL SEEDS INCREASE THEIR YIELD

In Golod's fifth experiment, agricultural seeds were kept in a pyramid for 1 to 5 days before being planted. More than 20 different seed varieties were planted across tens of thousands of hectares.

In all cases, the seeds from the pyramid had a **20 to 100-percent increase in their yield**; the plants did not get sick and they were not affected by droughts.

11. ADDITIONAL PYRAMID EFFECTS RELATED TO BIOLOGY AND HEALTH

Under less strenuous laboratory conditions, Golov's team determined the following:

Poisons and other toxins become less destructive to living systems after even a short term of exposure in the pyramid.

Radioactive materials held inside a pyramid would decay more rapidly than expected.

Pathogenic viruses and bacteria become significantly less damaging to life after being held in the pyramid.

Psychotropic drugs have less of an effect on people either staying inside a pyramid or within close range of a pyramid.

Standard solutions such as glucose and iso–osmotic solution become effective for treating alcoholism and drug addiction after being placed in the pyramid. They can be administered either intravenously or outwardly.

12. PYRAMID STUDIES OF DR. YURI BOGDANOV

Dr. Yuri Bogdanov conducted pyramid studies on behalf of the Joint–stock Company, "Scientific and Technological Institute of Transcription, Translation and Replication" (TTR), in Kharkiv, Ukraine.

In one experiment, a 12–meter pyramid was used to increase the productivity of wheat by 400% in the Ramenskoe settlement of Moscow. The following effects were also discovered:

The half–life of radioactive carbon was altered.

The crystallization patterns of salts would change.

Concrete would change in its strength.

Crystals would exhibit different optical behaviors.

In the biological arena, rabbits and white rats exposed to the pyramid gained 200% more endurance and their blood gained a higher concentration of leukocytes, or white blood cells.

13. WATER PURIFICATION BY PYRAMID POWER

Dr. Bogdanov also built a complex of pyramids in a town near the Arkhangelsk region of Russia by order of the domestic administration there.

In this case, strontium and heavy metals that had contaminated a well were able to be cleared by the effects of the pyramids, similar to how unwanted materials were filtered out of oil in the above example.

In the town of Krasnogorskoe, near Moscow, a pyramid was constructed that would reduce the amount of salt in water, again making it more drinkable.

In addition, Dr. Bogdanov performed many laboratory studies on medicinal preparations, fungi and so forth. In the city of Kiev, Dr. Bogdanov studied how matter interacts with different torsion–field patterns created by various pyramid shapes, and these investigations also studied how the consciousness of the person would affect these energy fields.

These studies were performed by a torsion–wave detecting device that he named the "Tesey," which allows its user to detect peculiar properties in a particular geological feature, energetic 'breathing' activity in the Earth as well as the torsion effects of various buildings including pyramids.

These results were discussed at the Conference on Problems of Harmonization of Mankind, held in Kiev, and were subsequently published.

14. INCREASED HARDNESS AND PURITY OF SYNTHESIZED CRYSTALS

The torsion–wave–focusing properties of the pyramid structure were seen to have a direct effect on how crystallization takes place. Diamonds that were synthesized within the pyramid turned out harder and purer than they would otherwise.

Again, this suggests that the torsion–wave component is of central importance in the forming of chemical bonds to create a crystal.

15. DIMINISHED SEISMIC AND WEATHER ACTIVITY

Teams from the Russian National Academy of Sciences also studied the earthquake data from the areas surrounding the pyramids and compared it to earlier data before the pyramids were built.

They discovered that the pyramids have the ability to dissipate the energetic buildup that would normally create sudden, violent earthquakes.

Instead of seeing one large and powerful quake, several hundred tiny earthquakes are registered. Furthermore, the atmosphere surrounding the pyramid seemed to be shielded from severe weather as well, causing an overall decrease in the amount of violent weather patterns.

This gives a clear illustration of the usefulness of pyramids for balancing the aetheric energies streaming into a planet.

16. FOODS STORED IN PYRAMID INCREASE HUMAN COMPASSION

Another experiment was conducted where a quantity of salt and pepper was stored inside the pyramid. This salt and pepper was later removed and fed continually to about 5000 people in different jails in Russia.

Amazingly, within a few months there was a dramatic improvement in their overall behavior, and **criminal behavior almost completely disappeared.**

This is one of the more important points, as it validates the idea that aetheric energy is 'spiritual energy' and that as a person is exposed to higher intensities of it, there is a propensity for greater feelings of love and compassion for others.

17. LIGHT–PRODUCING EFFECTS AND RAZOR–BLADE SHARPENING

Dr. Krasnoholovets built a small and simple resonator to study these pyramid effects, which appears to have been a piece of cardboard or glass folded in half to form a small 'roof' structure. Within this small resonator, a KIO3*HIO3 **crystal experienced a greater clustering of hydrogen atoms** inside the crystal.

Rare gases and the surface of metals were also seen to have a photoelectric effect while in the resonator, meaning that they were producing light. This seems to explain why the large outdoor pyramids could not involve metal in their construction.

Furthermore, Dr. Krasnoholovets replicated Patrick Flanagan's historic 'pyramid power' experiments by studying the effects on a razor blade within this resonator. The blade was aligned east to west, perpendicular to the Earth's magnetic field, while a piece of the edge was removed and stored away from the resonator.

Under scanning by electron microscope, the edge of the razor blade from the resonator was seen to take on a smoother, less angular form over time.

A radar shows a huge ionic column reaching a few kilometres into the sky above The 44-meter Golden Section Pyramid (see details below)

With the help of a series of radars working in the centimetre range and placed at 60 km, 32 km and 30 km from the Pyramid, scientists conducted radiolocation of the area of vertical axis of the Pyramid. During this research, the existence of an ionic column with a height of 2000 meters and width of 500 meters along the vertical axis of the pyramid was established. This allegedly ionic column was constantly changing its height from 800 meters to 2000 meters. The reflecting ability of this formation is comparable to the reflecting ability of a plane.

Moreover, a circle with a diameter of 300 km, with a higher degree of ionization and a center within the zone of the Pyramid was discovered with a significant degree of authenticity. It is possible to hypothesize about existence of a vortical radiation in the zone of the Pyramid with a diameter of hundreds of kilometres. Registered ionization is the effect of this radiation. Discovered ionic column above the Pyramid outlines the neck of the funnel of this vortex.

Regular water does not freeze inside the Pyramid, even at −40° C (see below)

Several plastic bottles with regular water were placed inside the Pyramid and their state was observed within a period of 3 winter months. The water did not freeze and had all the properties of a liquid during this whole period. The lowest air temperature inside the Pyramid was −40°C. Measuring water temperature inside the bottles showed that it was the same as the temperature of the air (i.e. the water did not freeze even when its temperature was 40°C).

However, it was noted during this research that if a bottle of this water was shaken or hit a crystallization process began inside and the water would turn into ice within 3–20 seconds (depending on the degree of water super-cooling).

Pyramids have powerful protective characteristics against lightning strikes.

The Electrotechnical institute conducted research on effects of the Pyramid field on the electrical field in a long air space axis-plane under impulse voltage of positive polarity from 250/2500 mcs.

As a base system the researchers used air space axis-plane with distance between electrodes of S=5.0 m. As a test system they used the same thing, but the plane had 7 pieces of granite 100 grams each, which were previously placed inside the pyramid. Granite pieces were placed on the plane in a circle with a diameter of 1 meter and with a center placed 0.5 meters away from the center of the plane.

Each system was subjected to 100 impulses. Researchers were registering trajectory of discharges and points of hits of the plane. Based on the results fields of hit points were generated. Discharge voltage during the research was approximately 1400 kV. Test results showed that the number of hit points in the base system was 5 times higher than that in the test system. Therefore, a contour of granite stones exposed to the pyramid energy has powerful protective characteristics against lightning bolt hits within the area of the contour.

A Golden Section Pyramid harmonizes space within its radius of influence

New streams appeared in the area of the 22–meter pyramid on the Seliger Lake, a stork set up a nest, and nearby fields became covered with previously extinct kinds of flowers.

Many substances and materials change their physical and chemical properties

The Graphite institute researched the influence of the pyramid field on the electrical resistance of carbon–based materials. The research object was pyrolitic carbon. Measurements were conducted by the 4–probe method with direct current. Sizes of carbon plates were ~ 25x10x1 mm, distance between potential contacts ~ 3 mm. Density of the measuring current was ~ 1500 mA/cm2. Before the plates were placed inside the pyramids, electrical resistance was ~5–7 mcOhm/m2. After 1 day inside the pyramid, electrical resistance had doubled. Such measurements are anomalous for pyrolitic carbon. Even the neutron radiation does not yield a resistance change of more than 5%.

Qualitative structure of all changes

A complex of pyramids was installed on an oil field. Within the next few days the viscosity of oil decreased by 30%, which correspondingly led to the increased oil production. Gradually, the structure of oil began to change, i.e. amounts of tars, paraffin, etc in oil decreased. Fractional structure of oil has shifted towards the light fractions (Moscow Academy of Oil and Gas).

Increase in crop productivity

Before planting the crops, their seeds were placed inside the Pyramid for 1–5 days. Tens of thousands of hectares were seeded with more than 20 crops. In each case crop productivity was from 20% to 100%, the crops were not sick, were not bothered by droughts. Quantity of toxic substances in plants decreased. Similar results were obtained when closed contours of stones, previously exposed to the Pyramid energy, were placed around the crop fields. 500 small stones with total weight of 20 kg were placed around a 10 hectare field.

APPENDIX L

TORSION FIELDS

" ... from my point of view, Torsion Fields truly are the Unifying Field that Einstein said would unite all of the other fields and interactions in physics. In the science of mechanics, Torsion Fields prove through fields of inertia that the phenomenon of intertia is more fundamental than even the gravitational phenomena. In quantum mechanics, inertial fields define the wave functions that describe physical phenomena in a truly universal way. Thus, in the Theory of Physical Vacuum, we can reduce all physical motion to rotation—and thus we can realize (a) vision of Descaresian Mechanics.

APPENDIX M

TORSION: A "FIFTH FORCE" SYNONYMOUS WITH CONSCIOUSNESS?

With permission, & © Brendan D. Murphy

The first research generally credited with the discovery of this "fifth force"—torsion—was that done in the late 1800s by Russian professor N.P. Myshkin. Einstein's colleague Dr. Eli Cartan first coined the term torsion in 1913 in reference to this force's twisting movement through the fabric of space-time—but his important work was virtually buried by the rampant success and notoriety of Einstein's theories. In the 1950s—the same decade Watson and Crick discovered the helical structure of DNA—pioneering Russian astrophysicist Dr. N.A. Kozyrev (1908–1983) conclusively proved the existence of this energy, demonstrating that, like time (and not dissimilarly to DNA), it flows in a sacred geometric (phi) spiral, as I detail in my recently released science–meets–metaphysics epic The Grand Illusion: A Synthesis of Science & Spirituality—Book 1 (TGI 1). Russian scientists are reported to have written thousands of papers on the subject in the 1990s alone, and more recently, award-winning physicist Nassim Haramein has, along with his colleague E.A. Rauscher, re-worked Einstein's field equations with the inclusion of torque and coriolis effects.

Torsion fields are generated by spin or angular momentum; any object or particle that spins produces torsion waves and possesses its own unique torsion field. According to some, torsion waves are the missing link in the search for a final 'theory of everything (TOE),' a unified field theory, or GUT (grand unified theory). Unfortunately, with the current mainstream mindset they cannot be reconciled with the established concept of a quantum wave as it stands in physical theory.

Since torsion fields influence spin states, one object's torsion field can be changed by the influence or application of an external torsion field. "As a result of such an influence, the new configuration of the torsion field will be fixed as a metastable state (as a polarized state) and will remain intact even after the source of the external torsion field is moved to another area of space. Thus torsion fields of certain spatial configuration can be 'recorded' on any...object." This realization of the unique properties of torsion fields immediately suggests compelling links to various psi or parapsychological phenomena (such as the 'charging' of an object with intent in voodoo, or the informational recording of events in 'inert matter' so that the record can later be 'read' by a psychometrist).

Kozyrev, Time and Torsion

Dr. Kozyrev discovered experimentally that human thoughts and feelings generate torsion waves. Such a discovery opens the door for a 'physical' understanding of consciousness, and a much more complete model of reality. Kozyrev was able to measure physical effects that were caused by sudden psychological changes (including his own), proving that consciousness is related to vibrations within a fluid–like 'aetheric' medium. In his ingenious experiments he detected minute changes in systems, that mimicked psychokinesis using an unknown form of hard–to–detect energy. Time itself, he believed, united all existence into a unified field, connecting all things in real–time (thus facilitating nonlocality or "action at a distance".) Changes in mechanical systems produced subtle alterations in the density of time/the aetheric medium, as did gravity, thunderstorms, changes in season, and changes in matter density. Likewise, Kozyrev found that consciousness also affected time density. Emotional thoughts produced larger effects on his equipment than did intellectual thoughts.

"The measurement systems are especially strongly affected by a person in emotional excitement," Kozyrev's colleague V.V. Nasonovtold an audience at Moscow University in 1985. "For instance, [Kozyrev] was able to deflect a torsion balance pointer by 40° or more when reading his favourite 'Faust.' Meanwhile, as a rule, mathematical calculations did not cause pointer deflections." [v] Thus, Kozyrev believed that our thoughts could change the density of time. He believed that in mastering the ability to make time dense at will we would be able to make telepathy occur at will. Under his conception, all psi phenomena would be stripped of their paranormal trappings and accepted into the world of natural phenomena. These are just a few of the reasons why authors S. Ostrander and L. Schroeder identified Kozyrev as possibly the most important scientist they spoke with in their research for their classic 1970 book: Psychic Discoveries Behind the Iron Curtain.

Storing Intention and Information in Water

Virtually all anomalous warping effects or other 'law–defying' effects caused in matter by various technologies can be replicated by the human mind, as I make a point of illustrating at some length in TGI 1. The imprint of human intention into the ice crystals of Dr. Masaru Emoto is just one example that might be explained by torsion waves radiated by human thoughts and emotions. Dankachov showed in 1984 that water is "a good medium for storing static torsion fields." [vii] The torsion fields created by human intention are simply memorized in water, especially water containing ionized salts.[viii] At a sub-microscopic level the internal structure of water has changed causing the resultant differences in the ice crystals.

At Sound Energy Research scientists created torsion field imprints in distilled water using scalar wave technologies. The result is structured water called 'scalar wave–structured water'™. They sent samples to Emoto who froze them and studied the crystals, which formed hexagonal structures like those created by human consciousness. [ix] The scalar/torsion technology creates the same effects as mental intent. The inference to be drawn is compelling: perhaps torsion waves—which are bereft of any intrinsic electromagnetic (EM) properties or mass—are 'carrier waves' of consciousness that produce real, measurable physical effects.

According to Dr. W.E. Davis, the psionic device patented and used for years by the De LaWarr laboratories in England was a variation of the Heironymus machine that is capable of registering photographs of the L(ife) field surrounding an object.

In 1958 Dr. De La Warr took a picture of a drop of ordinary tap water. The results were 'normal': there was a central point with seven bright, thin lines radiating from it. Then he asked a priest to bless the water before he took another picture. This time, the 'brilliant lines of force' formed the shape of a cross! [x] This phenomenon is somewhat akin to the use of kind words to metamorphose the shape of water molecules as documented in Emoto's research. The spin states of the water's atoms were presumably altered by the priest's own torsion field as he imprinted his intention by blessing the water.

Nonlocal Interactions and Torsion in Nature

The fact that plants are able to respond to human intention in measurable ways could perhaps be related to the torsion waves created by human consciousness and broadcast to the plant, which senses them and responds accordingly, on instinct. After all, if we can observe the Phi ratio (signifying the presence of this spiraling torsion energy) throughout nature and realize that plants, humans, and animals are all created out of this mathematically embedded matrix or "implicate order," it is not so surprising that plants can detect human thoughts (which generate torsion waves)—as Cleve Backster has shown with his breakthrough studies (starting in the 1960s) on human–plant telepathic interactions. Backster documents, among other fascinating things, that when he was away from his office, the plants in his office space actually produced immediate measurable electrical reactions to his intent to return—even when he was nowhere near the building. By connecting a plant's leaves to a polygraph machine, Backster found that his office plants not only responded stressfully to silent mental threats by a human to harm them, but also to the deaths of nearby organisms, such as brine shrimp and even bacterial colonies.[xi]

Russian scientist Dr. Victor Grebennikov is an entomologist who discovered what he called the /cavity structural effect' (CSE) created by bee nests. The particular shape of the nests caused them to harness and throw off large amounts of torsion waves that were detectable to human hands even when the nest was shielded with thick metal. These torsion waves act as a guide to trees, who detect them and guide their roots around the bees' structures rather than growing into them, as well as offering a form of nonlocal 'communication' between the bees themselves. The torsion harnessed by the CSE can also alter the passing of time, as Grebennikov showed, replicating Kozyrev's findings.

Dr. Frank Brown, a pioneer in the study of interactions between magnetism and living organisms, found that when bean seeds were placed near one another there was an interaction between them that could not be explained in orthodox terms: it seemed to be due to the presence of a biofield or spin force. That the biofield was involved is supported by Brown's observation of a connection between rotation and bean seed interaction. He found that the beans interacted more strongly when they were rotated counter–clockwise than when they were rotated clockwise. Brown also draws attention to the research of R.I. Jones, who reported in 1960 that plant growth could be altered by uniform daily rotation. Clockwise rotation depressed growth, suggesting the presence of a spin force around all plants might be a factor.

The human biofield is usually observed as a clockwise force as seen from above, though it reportedly flows in one direction for men and the opposite for women. Few people can perceive the two interlocking vortices/torsion fields that comprise a human spin field, though I was recently contacted by a woman who can see them and claims that the spin direction is indeed opposite for men and women. Her observations support already available information from other researchers, including near-death researcher P.M.H. Atwater, and sacred geometry teacher Drunvalo Melchizedek, who claims that two interlocking tetrahedra of opposite spins are a fundamental aspect of the human energy field. The geometry results from the fundamental vortical movement's effect on the fluid-like properties of the 'fabric' of space itself.

Pyramids as Torsion Conductors and Generators

Russian and Ukranian research into pyramids has yielded some truly astonishing results regarding torsion waves. The Russians found that the pyramid shape naturally harnesses torsion waves, as if amplifying them. It has been experimentally established that objects that feature the Golden Section (which expresses Phi) can be described as passive torsion generators. [xv] In point of fact, objects featuring the phi [1] ratio of 0 to 0.618 made the best passive torsion generators in the research carried out at the Physics Institute of the Ukraine Academy of Sciences and at Chernovitsky University by the Akimov group. The logical inference to make, then, is that torsion waves are phi spirals.[xvi] This spiraling force can enhance not only biological functions, but psychospiritual operations as well.

The team of Prof. A.G. Antonov from the Russian Research &Development Institute of Pediatrics, Obstetrics and Gynecology tested the effects of a solution of 40% glucose in distilled water after it had been stored in a pyramid. By administering only 1ml of the glucose to 20 different prematurely born infant patients with compromised immune systems, their levels of health were seen to increase rapidly up to practically normal values. The researchers furthermore discovered that the glucose was not necessary, as the same effect could be produced by simply using 1 ml of ordinary water that had been stored in the pyramid.

Another study in Russia showed that mice drinking torsion–affected pyramid water had significantly fewer tumors develop than the mice drinking the ordinary water. Elsewhere, Russian scientists have reported that mice subjected to static torsion fields showed significantly enhanced immune function. (Given the ridiculously ineffective and expensive mainstream 'cut,' 'slash" and 'burn' cancer treatment techniques, these findings deserve serious attention.)

Blunted razor blades also spontaneously sharpen again when placed in a pyramid as the crystalline structure is regenerated by the harnessed energy. Dr. Karel Drbal, who first discovered this effect (apparently in the late 1950s), was awarded a Czech patent for his Cheops Pyramid Razor Blade Sharpener—and in 2001, Dr. V. Krasnoholovets showed with scanning–electron microscope photography that the molecular structure of the edge of the blade was indeed being altered.

In Russian jails, 'pyramid power' reduced criminal behaviour in a total population of about 5,000 prison inmates. By storing crystalline substances in one of the fibreglass pyramids built under the direction of Dr. Alexander Golod, and later distributing those objects through the jails, the incidence of criminal behaviour within the jails virtually disappeared within a few months. [xxii] We see similar results with the Maharishi's Transcendental Meditation (TM®) groups, whereby a certain minimum number of meditaters gather together simply to meditate in an attempt to effect positive social change. Researchers found that the square root of 1% of a given population participating in the meditation was all it took to measurably affect the mental ecology of that population for the better. Crime rates measurably and significantly drop for the duration of the exercise, and rise once more when it is terminated. This has been dubbed the Maharishi Effect.

These are just a few of the many incredible effects observed and verified by large numbers of qualified scientists researching torsion physics and consciousness. Another pyramid 44 meters in height was constructed by Golod with Edward Gorouvein's company Pyramid of Life in Russia in 1999 for research purposes. Its proportions were again based on the Golden Section (phi). Incredibly, radar measurements revealed an enormous anomalous column of ionised energy (plasma) had formed around this small pyramid over a radius of 300 km(!) and with a varying height of 800 m to 2 km. Gorouvein speculates that the center of the column of ionised radiation represents the "funnel" of a massive vortex. (A toroidal vortex is a naturally stable and self-sustaining energy field—the primal cosmic form.)

Not only that, but even at −40° C, regular water inside normal plastic bottles would not freeze in this pyramid, defying the apparent 'laws' of physics once more. Just as startling, when the water bottles were hit or shaken, a rapid crystallization process was immediately initiated, with the water turning to ice within 3 to 20 seconds. Meanwhile, a smaller, 22 m tall Golden Section pyramid near Lake Seliger in Northern Russia provided perhaps the most unbelievable result: the reappearance of apparently extinct flower species in the surrounding countryside! New water streams even appeared in the area, drawing in animals, such as a stork, which set up a nest.[xxiv] The land was being healed and rejuvenated, perhaps being returned to a prior healthy condition (as indicated by the return of once–extinct flowers)! This apparent time–reversed effect signals the enhanced presence of aetheric torsion waves—time itself was being engineered! The many pyramid experiments carried out in Russia and elsewhere offer us a new vision of possibility: the means to heal ourselves and our planet by utilizing truly ancient non–electronic pyramid technology, which harnesses the earth's torsion waves.

As noted previously, 'pyramid power' doesn't just influence chemical and biological processes: it influences the operations of consciousness as well. This has been shown experimentally (as above), as well as anecdotally. For instance, some time around 1980, out–of–body explorer Robert Monroe was driving past his old home in Westchester County, New York—the site of his first out–of–body experiences. As Monroe recalled, a psychologist friend who was with him in the car took one look at the house, turned, and smiled, as he noted that the roof of the house formed a "perfect pyramid." "You were living in a pyramid. That did it!"

The ancient pyramids, in particular the Great Pyramid at Giza, served multiple esoteric functions such as facilitating OBEs and cosmic consciousness in initiatory rituals. Pyramid placement at certain node points on the geometric planetary energy grid strongly suggests that they act to harness the planet's life–enhancing energies, and perhaps stabilize the grid itself. The Great Pyramid, not coincidentally, "is built over the single most powerful vortex on the planet, where the lines of the tetrahedron, cube, octahedron, dodecahedron, and icosahedron all cross."

As 'solid–state' energy conductors, Egypt's ancient pyramids are obviously not merely gigantic tombs for dead pharaohs, that much is certain. While they may have been co-opted for those purposes later on, that is a topic beyond the scope of this article. Any cone–shaped or cylindrical object will harness and focus the torsion fields spiraling out of the Earth; since this energy is fundamentally intelligent, harnessing it not only enhances one's physical health, but one's 'spiritual consciousness' also. Hence the Great Pyramid's likely use in initiation rituals.

Torsion waves have the potential to initiate a fundamental paradigm shift. They are bridging the gap between mind and matter in a way that was never thought possible, and in the process they are validating the perspectives of mystics and occultists. Various researchers consider torsion as being synonymous or identical with consciousness itself. Since torsion waves are a fundamental and ubiquitous feature of the cosmos we can see how consciousness is also; consciousness has a real and detectable force which can act on the environment both locally and remotely. Suddenly the notion of something like psychokinesis is not so 'paranormal.' For author Sol Luckman (creator of the Regenetics Method), terms like prana, chi, and orgone are just different names for 'the light–based aspect of…torsion energy.'

Torsion/spin fields are fundamental to the universe's existence: they mediated the creation of our universe from out of the undifferentiated information in the aether/implicate order/time–space/zero point field/vacuum. As spin fields or vortexes within gravity, torsion forces can even be used to mitigate and nullify gravity, an idea I explore in TGI 1.

Phi with a capital "P" is 1.618, whereas phi with lower case "p" is .618. Phi/phi = Golden Section/Mean/Ratio.

Torsion, Psi, and the Brain

Every electromagnetic or electrostatic field is accompanied by or contains a torsion component, meaning that all organic and inorganic objects have their own signature torsion fields. While most organic substances will not shield torsion fields, Kozyrev found that strongly right–handed molecules such as sugar can, while strongly left–handed molecules such as turpentine will strengthen them. Subsequent Russian investigations also determined that polyethylene film served as an effective shield for torsion waves. Aluminum was also effective: Kozyrev stated that it was an excellent reflector of time. If the principle of complementarity operates at all scales, then, as torsion physics researcher and patent–holder D.G. Yurth points out, that means that wherever we find local/linear effects, we must also find non-linear/nonlocal (torsion/scalar) effects.

Relatedly, Kozyrev discovered that torsion waves can move through space at tremendous speeds—billions of times the speed of light—meaning they propagate in the future and past as well as the present,[xxxvi] so tapping into them could facilitate retro—or precognition, psi experiences involving glimpses of the past or future in other words. (Recall the pyramid experiment that led to the spontaneous regeneration of previously extinct flowers.) If you think of torsion waves as connections not through space, but in the realm of time (or time-space/aether/implicate order), then real–time (instantaneous) telepathic communication between people separated by thousands of miles may become slightly more comprehensible—and less 'unusual.' Such phenomena ordinarily looks to us as 'acausal' (since there is no discernible exchange of EM energy or force between the two parties in space–time, and therefore no time lag), but torsion waves may facilitate nonlocal correlations through 'causal nonlocality.' Torsion/scalar forces actually epitomize quantum nonlocality.

According to A. Akimov, torsion fields coupled with the standard electric, magnetic, and gravitational fields should offer a unified field theory that will extend the realm of science to include the effects of consciousness. It's interesting to note that certain effects on the spin structure of matter caused by torsion waves in experiments could only be reproduced by psychics. Furthermore, according to Russian physicist G.I. Shipov, torsion fields transmit information without transmitting EM energy. "From the late 80s till the late 90s…It was established that torsion generators allow us not only to replicate all 'phenomena' [such as PK and ESP] demonstrated by so called 'psychics,' but they also are able to demonstrate effects that were never demonstrated by any 'psychic.' "

The Akimov group have represented the brain as a non-magnetic spin torsion system where it is simultaneously a torsion transmitter and receiver. Iona Miller wrote in an online article that "...standing scalar [torsion] waves can be coupled at exactly 180° out of phase in a resonant cavity to create zero sums through scalar resonance. There is just such a resonant cavity in the brain, between the pituitary and pineal glands. These waves of potential co-modulate each other and 'lock or zip together' as a zero-vector system [scalar] wave. This allows for cross talk or translation between dimensions."

Interestingly, the pineal gland is believed to produce the hallucinogen DMT, known informally as the 'spirit molecule.' This molecule is known to facilitate intuitive functioning and mystical experiences. Perhaps it acts as an antenna for and amplifier of hyperdimensional scalar/torsion waves? If a resonance can be set up within the cavity between the pineal and pituitary glands, does this stimulate higher levels of DMT production, allowing us to access different levels of reality? Rick Strassman's fascinating experiments with DMT on volunteers showed that intravenously administered DMT produces extremely real other-dimensional experiences, replete with interactions with non-human intelligences—some resembling 'aliens' referenced in the UFO and abduction literature.

According to veteran independent scientist Lt. Col. Tom Bearden, "all mind operations are time-like, i.e., they are comprised as scalar EM photon functions and scalar EM wave functions. Thus the mind is a very special kind of electromagnetic system, existing in the time domain [aether]." [xlii] In other words, the mind does not have its origins in the material world, but in the non–local 'implicate' realm, the holographic template for our reality (also referred to as the field of scalar potential).

"A sizable list of attributes has been experimentally identified which demonstrates that the torsion field operates holographically, without regard to time and distance." So too then does consciousness. Pertinently, it has long been a metaphysical tenet that in terms of human experience 'like attracts like,' and this is the case with torsion field dynamics. If torsion 'energy' is consciousness operating in time—space/aether/ZPF/implicate order, then this is a profound point. It appears to be the missing link that facilitates Jung's sychronistic phenomena, and our ability to draw certain people and events to us at a distance. This could prove to be the ultimate scientific support for the 'law of attraction.'

In terms of psi phenomena such as remote viewing and other functions of consciousness that allow us to access information from anywhere in the cosmos, the significance of torsion fields should now be obvious. Indirect support comes from the employment of gravimetric devices by various scientists who have used torsion fields to measure and record distant astrophysical events and processes in real time. Their results support the notion that information at any single place in the cosmos can be instantaneously obtained at any other location.

Likewise, by generating a torsion field (which can be done by counter–rotating two magnets or even other objects in close proximity), information can be 'pumped' into it to instantly manifest elsewhere in the universe—no matter how large the distance between the sender and receiver. "The information 'packets' we insert into the non–linear field [implicate order/aether] at our local address becomes accessible anywhere in the hologram at any other address simply by matching the field effects that created the torsion field in the original locale."[xlvi] In 2001, Dr. Hartmut Müller used the spin/torsion fields within gravity to make a real–time telephone call from the Toezler Medientage building in Germany to Saint Petersburg in Russia—no EM (electromagnetic) fields were used. The communication was therefore instantaneous, without the time lag normal EM communication systems present.[xlvii] With such a communication system it would be impossible for Big Brother/government to 'tap' your phone calls because there would be no EM signal propagating through space–time to hack into.

Conclusions

Psi and consciousness researchers have typically discussed only electromagnetism in relation to the operations of the mind, when all along the much harder to detect 'fifth force' (known as torsion since 1913) may have been the most important aspect of bio–energy in accounting for the anomalous "quantum" functions of consciousness. Physicist Michael Talbot wrote in his early 1990s classic The Holographic Universe that some legitimate psychics had sensed the presence of another non–EM force or energy that composed part of the human aura or bio–field, but could not quite pinpoint what it was. Thanks to pioneers like Myshkin, Cartan, Kozyrev, Golod, and many more whose work we lack the space to cover here, we may surmise that the other 'mysterious' non–EM component of the human bio–field spoken of by those psychics was torsion—the fundamental carrier wave of consciousness itself.

Shipov quote above from R. Hoagland, "A Most Hyperdimensional Eclipse…and Final Venus Transit",

www.enterprisemission.com/Hyperdimensional–Eclipse.htm. (Accessed November 2012.)

About the author:

Brendan D. Murphy is the author of the critically acclaimed epic "The Grand Illusion: A Synthesis of Science and Spirituality, Vol. 1," and a contributing writer for several popular magazines and websites (including New Dawn, Nexus, Mindscape, DNA Monthly, and others).

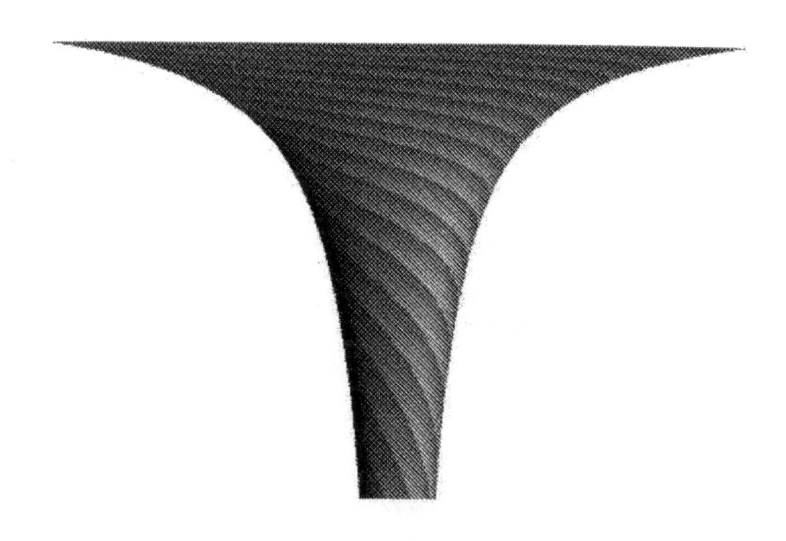

APPENDIX N

THE COMPLETE RUSSIAN/UKRANIAN STUDIES

(with occasional linguistically awkward translations left intact.)

UNUSUAL EFFECTS INDUCED BY MODELS OF THE PYRAMID

During the last decade, some scientists have used the pyramid form to study the fluctuations in energetic and informational fields. In particular, in Russia, near Moscow two pyramids were constructed to a height of 22 meters and 44 meters made from modular glass fiber plastics.

For the last years, different teams from the Russian Academy of Sciences have carried out many experiments in the pyramids. Some of the experiments are enumerated below.

1. Prof. S. M. Klimenko and M. Dr. D. N. Nosik from Ivanovskii R&D Institute of Virology, Russian Acad. Med. Sci., have studied the pyramid field's effects on the antiviral activity of immunoglobulin. The object of investigation was venoglobulin—a human polyvalence immunoglobulin for the intravenous introducing, lyophilized. The study was conducted on a culture of diploid cells of fibroblasts of the person. They utilized the virus of encephalomyocarditis (EMC) of mice for the determination of antiviral activity of immunoglobulin. Antiviral activity of the drug was determined by its capacity to protect cells of the person from cytopatic impact of the virus. Venoglobulin was diluted pursuant to the operating instruction

in distilled water up to the concentration 50 mg/ml. In this study, the drug was tested in two concentrations: 50 and 0.5 microg/ml. Then aliquots of venoglobulin in both concentrations were housed in the pyramid. Venoglobulin was deposited to cell–like cultures 24 hours prior to their contamination by the virus.

Conclusions: It was found that venoglobulin in concentration 50 microg/ml considerably inhibited the breeding the virus, approximately 300%. The antiviral effect was still maintained at further dilution of venoglobulin up to the concentrations 0.005 and 0.00005 microg/ml with consequent exposures in the pyramid. Antiviral activity of venoglobulin practically ceased to develop by these concentrations.

2. Prof. A. G. Antonov's team from Russian R&D Institute of Pediatrics, Obstetrics and Gynecology (the department of reanimation of pathology newborns) investigated the influence of 40%–s solution of glucose intravenously and distilled water outwardly after exposing them in the pyramid. The patients were newborns with extremely grave pathologies. Then they compared the indices of instantaneous state (IIS), which mirror the state of sympatho–adrenal system of the patient. The data on 20 patients was analyzed.

Conclusions: In all cases of applying of 40%–s solution of glucose in amount 1 ml the IIS essentially increased practically up to normal values even for the patients with very low initial values of IIS, close to zero point. It was the same after applying 1 ml of water, which stayed in the pyramid.

3. In the laboratory of Dr. N. B. Egorova at the Mechnikov R&D Institute, Russian Acad. Med. Sci., the impact of a field of the pyramid on living organisms was studied in respect to the

reactivity of an organism to a taint (a stressful or infectious biological agent). The study was conducted on a model taint of mice called by the exciter S.typhimurium, the strain 415. White underbred mice weighing 12 to 14 g were kept in the pyramid in differing numbers and for differing times. Mice were infected in four increasing doses, each 10 times stronger, of S.tiphimurium, starting from 10 up to 104 microbial cells. The control was served with mice from the same batch not held in the pyramid.

Conclusions: It is authentically established that the survival rate of mice, after their exposure in the pyramid, considerably exceeds those in the control group of animals. At contamination by smaller doses, 60% of mice held in the pyramid have survived, in the control group only 7%. At contamination by large doses accordingly 30% of mice held in the pyramid have survived and 3% in the control group. Conclusions: Exposure of mice to the pyramid essentially promotes the heightening of their resistance to consequent contamination of S.tiphimurium. Therefore, it is possible to speak about a powerful immuno-modulating influence of the pyramid on nonspecific reactivity of the organism of animal. An analogous pattern was observed with the mice introduced to different carcinogens. An experimental group of mice drank water that was kept in the pyramid. Control animals drank customary water. Result: The odds of appearance of swellings for control animals has appeared more times, than for animals drinking water that stayed in the pyramid.

4. Prof. V. I. Kostikov and Dr. A. C. Katasonov from the Graphite Research & Development Institute, Russian Ac. Sci., studied the effect of a field of a pyramid on the resistance of

carbon materials. The subject of their study was pyrolytic carbon subject to precipitation of products of a pyrolysis of methane on a graphitic substrate with temperature 2100 C. The measuring was conducted by the four–sounded method on direct current at normal conditions. The size of laminas was 25 mm x10 mm x 1mm, spacing interval between potential contacts was 3 mm. The ganging current was by density 1500 mA /cm^2. Before putting it in the pyramid the resistance came out to 5 to 7 microOhm*m.

Conclusions: After a stay in the pyramid for 1 day, the resistance increased twofold. These variations are abnormal for pyrocarbon. Even the neutron irradiation with the fluence ~10^{19} neutrons/m$^-$ did not give a variation of more than 5%. In addition, they detected the decrease of the resistance of silicon of semiconducting purity from 10^5 to 10^4 Ohms*cm and loss of the high–temperature superconductivity by samples after the mentioned exposure in the pyramid.

5. A group of researchers from the All–Russian Electrotechnical Institute, Moscow examined the rate of action of a pyramid field on an electrical field in a lengthy aerial gap between a rod and plain when the gap was affected by an electric pulse of positive polarity with a duration of 250 and 2500 microseconds. A kernel system for the aerial gap rod-plain with an interelectrode spacing interval of 5 m was utilized. The system tested was the same; however, it included seven chunks of granite put on the plain. The weight of each chunk was 100 g and they formed a circle with diameter of 1 m on the plain; the center of the circle distanced 0.5 m from the center of the plain. Before the experiment, the chunks were placed in the pyramid. 100 voltage pulses were given to the control system and the test

subject. The discharge voltage ranged up to 1400 kV. The pathways of the discharges and the dots of defeat of the plain were logged.

Conclusions: As a result of the result of the trials, dots of defeat were plotted. It was authentically recorded that the amount of defeats in the kernel system exceeded five times their amount in the test system. The deduction: rocks that kept in the pyramid had powerful defensive properties.

6. Researchers from the Scientifically Manufacturing Union "Gidrometpribor" (Russia), the director A. A. Golod, conducted a series of experiments associated with the pyramids.

a) Several plastic vessels with distilled water were placed Inside the pyramid and observed over the course of three winter months. The water did not congeal, and preserved all condition of fluids during this period of time. The minimum temperature of the air inside the pyramid was −38 C. The gauging of temperature of water inside a vessel showed that it corresponded to the temperature inside the pyramid (i.e. water did not congeal even when its temperature reached −38 C). Customary mineral water in plastic bottles also behaved similarly. When the vessel with water was shaken up or struck, crystallization inside the vessel started and the water quickly turned to ice.

b) Ring–type outlines from chunks of granite and crystal kept within the pyramid were circulated around Moscow and the Moscow region since the end of 1997. By the beginning of 1999, 40 such rings had been made. Each ring contained from 50 up to 300 rocks with a total weight ranging from 20 to 200 kg.

Conclusions: It is anticipated that the odds of an appearance of any epidemics will drop with each year. This fact is already well evidenced in the cases of influenza over the last two winters. The younger the age, the more intense is the effect.

c) With the help of radiolocation setups working in the meter range and distanced 30, 32 and 60 km from the pyramid, the Joint–stock company, The TTR Research & Development Institute conducted detections of space in the neighborhood of a vertical fulcrum of the pyramid. The study researched the presumed availability of an ionic formation of an altitude up to 2000 meters and a width of 500 meters. This ionic pile permanently changed its altitude from 800 m up to 2000 m. The breaking off of pieces of an ionized pile over the pyramid and its migration with an upward flow of the air also were noted. The pieces saved the configuration on large spacing intervals from within the pyramid.

d) A small pyramid was installed at a number of oil wells. In a few days the viscosity of the oil in the seams decreased by 30% and the production rate of the wells accordingly increased. The petroleum composition (amount of gums, pyrobitumen and paraffin) began to change. The fractional composition of oil was offset the side of mild fractions. Experiments made with the participation of the Gubkin Moscow Academy of Oil and Gas have affirmed these results.

e) Before sowing, seeds of agricultural cultures were kept in a pyramid from 1 to 5 days. Tens of thousands of hectares were sewn affect the crop.

Conclusions: The amount of toxiferous matters in plants was decreased sharply. When an outline of small rocks that had stayed previously in a pyramid were placed around the crop, similar results were obtained.

Among other studies with less conclusive, results the following was noted. (a) The level of toxicity of any substances, including toxic and poison substances, which had been under the exposure in a pyramid even short time decreased. (b) The level of radioactivity of matters held in a pyramid diminished. (c) The level of pathogens of different albuminous formations (viruses, bacteria), that were placed in a pyramid was slashed. (d) The effect of any psychotropic influence placed in a pyramid upon people diminishes. (e) There was somewhat promising data gained in applying standard solutions (glucose, isoosmotic solution, etc.) intravenously and outwardly in cases of alcoholism and drug addiction.

7. Of special note is the study of pyramids conducted by Dr. Yuri Bogdanov, the Joint-stock Company "Scientific and Thechnological Institute of Transcription, Translation and Replication" (TTR), (Kharkiv, Ukraine). The Bogdanov's investigations were based on a special device called "Tesey" constructed by Dr. Bogdanov and his colleagues. Dr. Bogdanov participated in the choice of a place under the building of several big model pyramids in Russia. Then he conducted consequent examinations of the properties of each of the pyramids and the effects which originated in and around them. One of the pyramids was built in the Ramenskoe settlement of the Moscow region. There a 12 meter pyramid was constructed.

Conclusions: With the help of 'the Pyramid Effect,' it was possible to augment productivity of wheat fourfold in the Ramenskoe domestic state farm.

Studies of changes of properties of matter were conducted as well. It was revealed that the half-life of carbon was altered; the structure of salt patterns changed; the strength properties of concrete varied; the optical behavior of crystals under consideration changed.

Conclusions: The studies of influence of the pyramid on animals showed the following: the physical endurance of rabbits and white rats was twice increased; the leukocytic composition of blood was altered.

A complex of pyramids was constructed by the order of the domestic administration In Blizhnii Bereznik, a town that is situated in the Arkhangelsk region of Russia, These helped clear water in a blow well from raised levels of strontium and heavy metals. This was successfully carried out In Krasnogorskoe, a town situated near Moscow, where a pyramid for reducing elevated salinity of water was constructed as well. Many laboratory studies have been performed on medicinal preparations, fungi, etc. In Kyiv, the properties of the interaction of matter with the pyramid field were studied; the investigation included also the interplay of the patterns of the field with the consciousness of the person. The basic results of these interactions have been discussed in the Conference on Problems of Harmonization of Mankind, held in Kyiv, and have been published.

I am thankful to Dr. Y. Bogdanov who placed at my disposal materials used in the writing this section

Many substances and materials change their physical and chemical properties (when exposed to the Pyramid.)

The Graphite institute determined the influence of the pyramid field on the electrical resistance of carbon–based materials. The research substance was pyrolitic carbon.

Measurements were conducted by the 4–probe method with direct current. Sizes of carbon plates were ~ 25x10x1 mm, and the distance between the potential contacts ~ 3 mm. Density of the measuring current was ~ 1500 mA/cm2.

Conclusions: Before the plates were placed inside the pyramids, electrical resistance was ~ 5–7 mcOhm/m2. After 1 day inside the pyramid, electrical resistance had doubled. Such measurements are anomalous for pyrolitic carbon. Even the neutron radiation does not yield a resistance change of more than 5%.

APPENDIX O

PYRAMIDS—SOME FREQUENTLY ASKED QUESTIONS

Bill Cox

Bill Cox, life-long explorer of subtle energies, and mentor to Nick Edwards.

Note: Bill Cox, whose friend and mentor was the late Verne L. Cameron, and has been an instructor, professional dowsing consultant and avid researcher of the marginal sciences for over forty years. A major field of experience and investigation has been in the area of Dowsing (Radiesthesia). Bill is the author of a number of books and articles on Dowsing and the ancient, rediscovered science of *Form Energy*. Of Bill, Nick Edwards recalls:

"The pyramid researcher Bill Cox was a dear friend of mine; he wrote about me in his Pyramid Guide; he wrote an article about me in his Pyramid Guide when I went off looking for the underwater pyramids in the Gulf of Mexico, and was instrumental in my getting into pyramids with Pat Flanagan—those were the first two people. He used to carry my products, I used to carry his—the Aurameter, which is the most sensitive aura meter in the world. He used a heavy copper–pipe pyramid structure with a very expensive set of connectors. He sold my stuff for years—we were very close; he lived in the same area, and I was with him almost every day. He was my mentor, and was teaching me dowsing."

Compatible with this work, Bill has made a thirty-year study of the two-thousand year old, oriental landform, earth-sky, energy-placement science of Feng Shui and the various prephysical forces operating in the invisible side of life.

Bill has participated in more than 20 exploratory team expeditions to Egypt, Mexico, South America, India and Islands of the world in search of information to validate the existence of intuitive (subjective) physics. Together with team members, he has made extensive tests involving measurements, orientation, electrical, magnetic, ionic and sound tests obtaining surprising scientific results. Certain knowledge and wisdom, apparently known to ancient seers, is not easily explained away in terms of modern science

For nine years Bill edited and published 55 editions of the international, bi-monthly newsletter called the Pyramid Guide. The Guide emphasized research and experiments dealing with Form (Pyramid) Energy, among those of other geometric cavity resonators. In addition, he has appeared on numerous television and radio programs as a leading expert and writer of investigations concerning marginal sciences research.

Q. What is pyramid energy? (So–called Pyramid Power?)

A. Abundant evidence exists to show that the 'energy of form' is attracted by, stored in, and emanated from model representations of the Great Pyramid. Years of investigation reveal that we are dealing with a multitude of energies, even though various researches tend to give the phenomenon a single name.

Q. What does it do?

A. It is a fact that properly constructed Pyramid replicas (based upon the measurements of the Great Pyramid) enhance meditation inside the form. Models repeatedly produce preservation in organic matter and induce accelerated growth in plants. Replicas also improve the flavor of charged foods and liquids and sharpen or polish dull metals.

Q. Is it scientific?

A. If we are to conclude that test results are always 99% effective—which seems to be a strict requirement by orthodox scientists—the answer is no. Pyramid energies fluctuate due to solar and lunar cycles. Still, successes and quality of results are remarkably high beyond the laws of chance and mundane explanations often given by science.

For example, some scientists claim that outside mechanical forces are solely responsible for the phenomenon. Others declare that pyramid replicas cause freshness in the manner of an ordinary cookie jar. But how can they make this theory stand when organic substances are naturally preserved within " open-frame" wire and metal tubing pyramids, rather than enclosed ones?

Q. Will a pyramid replica mummify organic substances?

A. Numerous tests spanning several decades have established the fact that a dehydration process takes place when living substances are cut off from their life source (such as a plant severed from its root system, or fruit removed from a tree).

Preservation, or mummification, generally takes place when the specimen is exposed to the Pyramid's interior environment for a sufficient time.

Q. How long does this take?

A. Depending on the quick or slow decay rate of the specimen, its size, thickness, composition and other considerations, the results may be evident within a few hours up to several days.

Q. Does this always happen?

A. No, there are exceptions. The expected outcome may vary. Years of experimentation have shown that accuracy of measurements, rigidity and orientation of the Pyramid, its location, time and environment; weather conditions and even the operator, all contribute to the success or failure of any pyramid experiment.

Q. Will pyramid exposure mummify my brain?

A. No. First of all, humans are self–contained, living organic systems. If a severed part of an animal, for example, were placed under a pyramid, it would tend to mummify, but the whole creature is immune to mummification. A living plant, for example, is usually energized when placed inside a pyramid. But once the plant, or any portion of it (such as a leaf), is cut off from the root system, dehydration and subsequent mummification usually occurs.

Preservation is the by–product of the expected mummification process. Bacteria (microorganisms) that normally cause breakdown, decay and putrefication in organic matter are somehow retarded from carrying out their normal function.

Q. What happens when I meditate under, or inside of a pyramid?

A. Preliminary research shows that one's brain waves may be altered in favorable ways. Early experiments with test subjects connected to an electroencephalograph (EEG) show ED signs of increased Alpha and Theta brainwave production, higher frequencies and greater amplitudes. Alpha and Theta brain waves appear to increase with higher amplitudes, when one is in a meditative, intuitional creative state of mind.

Q. How large should a meditation pyramid be?

A. The standard meditation size pyramid, suitable for one or two sitting subjects, has a six–foot base length on each of its four sides. This produces a model approximately three feet, ten inches high.

When the base lengths are increased to ten feet on each side, the pyramid should be approximately six feet, four inches high. A model of this size should accommodate six or more persons sitting in lotus positions.

Overhead: Pyramid replicas suspended above reading, work area or sleeping zones are effective when base sides each measure three feet in length. The rays projecting downward from the base are thought to be more gentle than emanations near the apex. Tubular frame replicas, with six foot base lengths, are also popular for sleeping areas.

Table Model Pyramids: of 12" on each base side are standard. Wire frame pyramids are ideal for razor blade sharpening tests or on aiding plant growth when small test specimens are used.

Q. Is a larger pyramid more effective than a smaller one?

A. Not necessarily so. This is a mistaken belief described in various books on the subject which were written during the 1970's. The specimen's location within the pyramid, whether on the floor, mounted on a platform, or just under the apex, affect the time and ultimate results.

Q. What will sleeping under a pyramid do for me?

A. In hundreds of tests over the years, results have been mixed. Sometimes, in the early stages (the first few weeks for example) sensations and psychological aspects can be quite dramatic, and nearly always positive. Later on, changes are sometimes less noticeable. Over the years, we have received numerous reports that over-the-bed pyramid exposure can be quite stimulating, sometimes making it difficult for one to sleep many hours during the night. Personal comments and letters suggest that small pyramids aligned under one's bed may produce a more tranquilizing effect.

Q. Is the King's Chamber level, one-third up from the base center, the best location for tests?

A. Pyramid energies seem to increase as the specimen is raised up toward the interior apex. The most efficacious spots are, in most cases, just below (inside), or just above (outside) of the peak. There are some exceptions, however. Over exposure may occur with certain plants being placed too close to the apex, as if they had been over-fertilized with strong chemicals.

Q. Will an ordinary experimental pyramid sharpen metal? If so, how long does it take?

A. Yes, a cardboard replica may even sharpen knives, scissors, razor blades and surprisingly, even electric shavers. Correct exposure time depends upon many factors. But, if the test is set up properly, noticeable results have been reported after over-night pyramid exposure. Electric razors and heavy duty cutlery may require two days or more. Interesting to note that WWI Russian soldiers discovered that a full moon dulled a razor's edge.

APPENDIX P

MAKING HOME PYRAMID MODELS

The simplest and easiest way for most people to make their own pyramids is to purchase firm matboard from any local art supply store. A simple roll of strong masking tape, or better yet, duct tape, will serve as the bonding agent. A metal yardstick and an exacto knife complete the list of needed tools. A T-square is optional but very helpful in achieving clean right angles.

Measure the base-widths. At the center of the baseline, draw a vertical line the height of the pyramid you wish to build. Draw diagonals from the apex to both base corners. Cut along these two diagonals and use this side as a template for the other three. Lay the four sides against each other on the floor, each apex aligned with the others. Tape the segments together on both sides. Enjoy!

A fringe benefit of pyramids constructed out of mat board or a similar substance is that, while they retain their firmness when erected, they can easily be collapsed into completely flat form should one ever wish to store them when not in use, or even to lay them inside a suitcase or portfolio for travel. Three foot-long pyramids will usually cover the vital regions of head, torso and pelvis of most people.

A further plus is that one will receive their effects when positioned either below or above the body. For example, where space allows, pyramids can be positioned below a chair or bed, with the energies coming into the body from the apex. Alternately, they can be suspended from above or simply lain upon the body while laying supine, a position in which the energies spiral up from below on their way through the apex. For longer periods of time where one wishes to have fresh air within the head area, one can cut triangular vent openings in all four sides without compromising the energetic effect.

CHEOPS PYRAMID DIMENSIONS

Height	Base	Sides
6"	9$_{1/8}$"	8$_{7/8}$"
8"	12$_{1/2}$"	12"
10"	15$_{1/4}$"	15
12"	18$_{3/4}$"	17$_{1/4}$"
8'	12'6"	12'
6'	9'5"	8'11"

SUGGESTED READING:

A Search in Secret Egypt — Paul Brunton (Larson Publications)
The Complete Pyramid Sourcebook — John de Salvo (AuthorHouse)
Pyramid Power; Science of the Cosmos I — Dr. G. Patrick Flanagan (CreateSpace 2015)
Beyond Pyramid Power; Science of the Cosmos II — Dr. G. Patrick Flanagan (CreateSpace 2016)
Pyramid Power II — The Scientific Evidence (CreateSpace 2017) — Dr. G. Patrick Flanagan
Elixir of the Ages You Are What You Drink (CreateSpace 2016) — Dr. G. Patrick Flanagan
Pyramid Energy Handbook — Serge King (Warner Books)
The Secret Power of Pyramids (Fawcett Gold Medal)
— Bill Schul & Ed Petit
The Psychic Power of Pyramids (Fawcett Gold Medal)
— Bill Schul & Ed Petit
Pyramids and the Second Reality (Fawcett Gold Medal)
— Bill Schul & Ed Petit
Pyramid Power (Destiny Books) — Max Toth
Pyramid and Temple Vastu (Diamond Pocket Books) Dr. Bhojiraj Dwived
The Pyramid (Acres USA 1994) Les Brown

ABOUT THE AUTHORS

Joseph Andrew Marcello is an American author and composer, the winner of the Delius Award for Composers and the writer and editor of some 8 books on life energies and well-being. He has pursued the study and practice of the energy arts for over half a century, and was certified as a teacher of yoga in 1968 by Sachindra Kumar Majumdar, founder of the Yoga Institute of New York City. He has studied Tai Chi Chuan under its most renowned exponent, Cheng Man Ching; Aikido with Jacques Castermanne, director of the Centre Durckheim in France, Taoist Yoga with Mantak Chia, and Zhineg Qigong with Luke Chan and Xiaoguang Jin.

He has been a student of comparative religions for most of his life and has traveled widely in exploring paths to inner awakening, studying *Hara* body/mind integration with Karlfried Graf von Durckheim, author of *Hara, the Vital Center of Man*, at his center in the Black Forest region of Germany, with Roy

Eugene Davis and Donald Walters (Swami Kriyananda) , disciples of Paramhansa Yogananda and ministers of the Kriya Yoga tradition, with Indian teacher Vimala Thark, Krishnamurti's only then living spiritual heir, and with English sage Douglas Harding, author of *On Having No Head—Zen and the Rediscovery of the Obvious* and *The Hierarchy of Heaven and Earth.*

Among his writings are newly edited editions of Dr. G. Patrick Flanagan's groundbreaking bestsellers *Pyramid Power, Beyond Pyramid Power, Pyramid Power II* and *The Elixir of the Ageless: You Are What You Drink.* In addition he has published a rare book of personal notebooks and teachings by Barbados mystic, Neville Goddard entitled *Living Vision: The Secret Teachings of Neville Lancelot Goddard,* and a new edition of of the little-known book out of print since 1940—*The Hindu Secrets of Vitality & Rejuvenation: the Art of Restoring Sexual Vitality,* from which the popular classic *The Ancient Secret of the Fountain of Youth* was illicitly cloned and repackaged.

He makes his home near the borders of Vermont and New Hampshire, in the pine-clad hills of Northfield, Massachusetts. When he is not immersed in a manuscript or seeking the lost chord, he may be found, in season, swimming in all and any available natural bodies of water, cycling, rebounding or embracing his favorite tree.

He may be contacted at JosephMarcello@verizon.net.

As a boy, Dr. Patrick Flanagan invented a missile-detection system that effectively tracked the times and positions of launches in the United States, winning first prize in a local all-grades science fair with it; within a matter of days it had garnered the attention of the Pentagon, who confiscated the technology with threats of dire consequences should he fail to comply with their requests.

Flanagan created the Neurophone in 1958. It is an electronic nervous system excitation device that transmits sound through the skin directly to the brain, for which he received U.S. Patent no.3,393,279 in 1968.

The invention earned him a profile in Life magazine, which called him a "unique, mature and inquisitive scientist". Flanagan has continued to develop the neurophone and it is currently being sold as an aid to speed learning.

Flanagan at age eleven developed and sold a guided missile detector to the U.S. Military, aged seventeen gained his air pilot's license and was employed by a Think Tank at The Pentagon and later as a consultant to the NSA, CIA, NASA, Tufts University, the Office of Naval Research, and the Aberdeen Proving Grounds for the Department of Unconventional Weapons and Warfare.

Since 1981 Flanagan has invented a series of useful devices and products based on water and specific mineral structures, in the area of health. Several of these have been very successful in the marketplace. His identification of the special properties of the negative hydride ion while once ridiculed got serious attention when the Nobelist Chandrasekhar proposed it as a major component in far space. Several scientific papers by Flanagan, about Silica Hydride have been published in peer reviewed jo

Flanagan actively continues his activities as scientist and inventor and philanthropist, promoting the really new science and new approaches to human healing, especially those based on the great traditions of India and Egypt.

For decades, Dr. Flanagan has openly invited stringent scrutiny of his research and discoveries by the medical and scientific communities. The seeds of this effort are blossoming at an exponential rate as the scientific community is validating and embracing his extraordinary contributions. Academics and researchers at universities from Oxford to Stanford are beginning to study Dr. Flanagan's breakthrough discoveries and teach them to Scientists of the future.

He is the author of *Pyramid Power, Beyond Pyramid Power, Pyramid Power II* and *The Elixir of the Ageless: You Are What You Drink* and his researches may be accessed at *www.phisciences.com*.

Made in the USA
Columbia, SC
30 March 2021